CRITICAL ESSAYS
on Resistance in Education

Studies in the Postmodern Theory of Education

Shirley R. Steinberg
General Editor

Vol. 376

The Counterpoints series is part of the Peter Lang Education list.
Every volume is peer reviewed and meets
the highest quality standards for content and production.

PETER LANG
New York • Washington, D.C./Baltimore • Bern
Frankfurt • Berlin • Brussels • Vienna • Oxford

CRITICAL ESSAYS
on Resistance in Education

EDITED BY
David M. Moss & Terry A. Osborn

PETER LANG
New York • Washington, D.C./Baltimore • Bern
Frankfurt • Berlin • Brussels • Vienna • Oxford

Library of Congress Cataloging-in-Publication Data
Critical essays on resistance in education /
edited by David M. Moss, Terry A. Osborn.
p. cm. — (Counterpoints, studies in the
postmodern theory of education; v. 376)
Includes bibliographical references and index.
1. Socialism and education—Philosophy. 2. Social justice.
3. Educational change. I. Moss, David M. II. Osborn, Terry A.
HX526.C75   370.11'5—dc22   2010021233
ISBN 978-1-4331-0788-7
ISSN 1058-1634

Bibliographic information published by **Die Deutsche Nationalbibliothek**.
Die Deutsche Nationalbibliothek lists this publication in the "Deutsche
Nationalbibliografie"; detailed bibliographic data is available
on the Internet at http://dnb.d-nb.de/.

© 2010 Peter Lang Publishing, Inc., New York
29 Broadway, 18th floor, New York, NY 10006
www.peterlang.com

All rights reserved.
Reprint or reproduction, even partially, in all forms such as microfilm,
xerography, microfiche, microcard, and offset strictly prohibited.

From David
For Tim Weinland, Christine Barry, and David Patterson

From Terry
For Nancy Lauckner, Steve Kercel, and Terry Cicchelli

Contents

Acknowledgments　ix

Introduction: Considering Resistance
David M. Moss & Terry A. Osborn　1

1. Planting the Seeds of Resistance: The Times they have a-Changed
   Terry A. Osborn　7

2. Resisting Traditional Notions of Teacher Certification:
   Reflecting on "Teach For America"
   Molly K. Ness　17

3. Resisting the State: Christian Fundamentalism and A Beka
   Dina C. Osborn　35

4. Critical Pedagogy in the Foreign Language Education Context:
   Teaching Esperanto as a Subversive Activity
   Timothy Reagan　47

5. Teaching (and Learning from) the White Rose
   David I. Smith　67

6. Dialogic Resistance in Education: Tsunesaburo Makiguchi, Daisaku Ikeda and Transformative Language Learning
 Jason Goulah   83

7. Resisting Mandated Literacy Curricula in Urban Middle Schools
 Marshall A. George   105

8. Fighting the Fear of Failure: Resisting the Effects of THE TEST in a Thinking-based Writing Class
 Kristen Hawley Turner   125

9. "A Small Group of Thoughtful, Committed Citizens": Social Studies Classrooms as Communities of Practice That Enable Social Action
 Thomas H. Levine   143

10. The Challenge of Bullying in U.S. Schools: Resistance and Reaction
 Jo Ann Freiberg   159

11. "We Want to Be Heard": Using Instructional Technology to Resist Student Silence
 Kathleen P. King   179

12. Resisting an Unbecoming Science
 John Craven & Tracy Hogan   201

13. Being at Crossroads: Resisting the Typical Conference Format to Rekindle Passions and Priorities in Science Education
 Julie M. Kittleson & Robert J. Ceglie   223

14. Should We Teach Resistance?
 David M. Moss   239

Contributors   249

Index   255

Acknowledgments

We are grateful to the contributors and reviewers of this text. Additionally, we would like to acknowledge Shirley Steinberg, series editor, and Chris Myers, Managing Director at Peter Lang Publishing, for their patience throughout this evolving project. Additionally, this book would not have been possible without Bernadette Shade, Production Manager.

Our colleagues in the Department of Curriculum and Instruction at the Neag School of Education at the University of Connecticut and in the Division of Curriculum and Teaching at Fordham University have been very encouraging—we are lucky to work with such talented and dedicated colleagues. We especially thank Mary Rinaldo-Ducat for her administrative brilliance and enduring good nature. And finally, we thank our families for their patience and support during an often time-consuming process.

Introduction

Considering Resistance

DAVID M. MOSS & TERRY A. OSBORN

In Walt Whitman's poem, *When I Heard the Learn'd Astronomer*, the narrator struggles with coming to understand the beauty and essence of the cosmos as academic discourse, in its many forms, seems to obscure it.

> When I heard the learn'd astronomer;
> When the proofs, the figures, were ranged in columns before me;
> When I was shown the charts and the diagrams, to add, divide, and measure them;
> When I, sitting, heard the astronomer, where he lectured with much applause in the lecture-room,
> how soon, unaccountable, I became tired and sick;
> Till rising and gliding out, I wander'd off by myself,
> in the mystical moist night-air, and from time to time,
> look'd up in perfect silence at the stars. (1965, p. 271)

In preparing a text on resistance in education, we find ourselves in a similar predicament. Resistance related to education and educational settings has been extensively addressed across a broad continuum of research and policy. Yet its very nature remains elusive and poorly understood.

Educational programs such as drug abuse resistance education (DARE) have appropriated the concept (or term) of resistance as a way of encouraging children to, in the words of former First Lady Nancy Reagan, "Just say no" to drugs. Paul Willis' famous study, *Learning to Labour* (1977) has been widely cited and seen as seminal in the field as he has carefully documented how resisting authority in school settings essentially prepared, even destined, boys for working class jobs in society. McRobbie (1978), in a perhaps lesser-known study, examined in part the role of resistance in working class girls as they assumed the social roles of women in their own culture. Likewise, much of critical pedagogy and critical theories in education focuses on resistance in education, especially those in introductory texts such as Wink's (1997) *Critical Pedagogy: Notes from the Real World.* Additionally, the work of the Highlander Folk School in preparing those who would resist the oppression of minorities in the southeast United States during the Civil Rights movement of the sixties and seventies, has been discussed and documented at length. (Adams & Horton, 1975; Horton, 1989; Horton & Freire, 1990). Finally, Cole and Hill (1995) examined the "strands of postmodernism" in education, concluding that a postmodernism of reaction and resistance discourses have more in common than they do that delineate them.

In much of the analysis, however, there emerges no clear understanding or description of the multiple roles—and numerous contexts—that resistance plays in educational settings, both in ways that oppress and in ways that liberate. In this work we choose to look at the multiple contradictions of resistance in education, and to appreciate them for the complex phenomena they are. We recognize in all educational endeavors the tension that Giroux (2001) captures regarding literacy:

> [W]hile resistance to literacy exposes an exploitive moment in the logic of the dominant culture, it also fails to understand how skills such as reading and writing can be used in the service of critical analysis and social construction. Students must be given critical literacy skills that not only help them understand why they resist but also allow them to recognize what this society has made of them and how it must, in part, be analyzed and reconstituted so that it can generate the conditions for critical reflection and action rather than passivity and indignation. (p. 231)

It is this same tension we seek to illuminate and appreciate. Resistance in education creates, or reflects, the multiple counter-discourses that arise to challenge the one or more dominant discourses in any given educational setting. But they simultaneously provide freedom and oppression as they do so. Much like a drawing by M. C. Escher, the staircase of resistance leads back to itself, the one hand draws its counterpart.

In Chapter One, *Planting the Seeds of Resistance: The Times They Have a-Changed,* Terry A. Osborn explores the need to plant the seeds of resistance in future generations of teachers. He argues that teachers must see education as taking place in a larger, complex, socio-political, and cultural landscape beyond that of a classroom or school. Addressing the notion of advocacy, he concludes teachers should begin to connect both curriculum and instruction to the individual settings in which their practice takes place, incorporating the local political, economic, and cultural factors that impact their students' lives and their own work.

INTRODUCTION: CONSIDERING RESISTANCE | 3

In Chapter Two, *Resisting Traditional Notions of Teacher Certification: Reflecting on Teach For America*, Molly Ness addresses the controversial and much debated issue of alternate routes to teacher certification. Here she addresses the numerous forms of resistance seen across the continuum of professional education with regard to teacher education, offering a comprehensive and timely treatment of this issue. She concludes Teach for America may not be a long-term solution to the vast and complex problems that exist in our public schools, but considers the pros to outweigh the cons in an era when so many schools are in such dire need.

Addressing issues of curriculum and power in Chapter Three, *Resisting the State: Christian Fundamentalism and A Beka*, Dina C. Osborn explores the resistance of Christian fundamentalists to secular humanism through an analysis of A Beka history texts, a widely used curriculum in Christian schools. The chapter is contextualized within the broader social and political milieu of the Christian Right regarding their perceptions on America's identity, the citizen's role in preserving that identity and conceptualizations of diversity.

In Chapter Four by Timothy Reagan titled, *Critical Pedagogy in the Foreign Language Education Context: Teaching Esperanto as a Subversive Activity*, he asserts resistance theories in education are concerned with articulating the moral and political potentials of opposition to schooling as it is currently constructed both in American society and in other societies around the world. Resistance theory is thus concerned, ultimately, with challenging oppression: oppression as cultural hegemony, oppression as capitalist accumulation, and oppression as discursive effect. Oppression with respect to language in educational settings, he concludes, occurs in a number of ways, including the failure to recognize the language rights of minority children.

David I. Smith authored Chapter Five, titled *Teaching (and Learning from) the White Rose*. Here he addresses how various specifically contextualized forms of resistance may intertwine in an intermediate language class. He illustrates how a story of resistance paired with attempts to resist the utilitarianism and secularity of typical language classroom discourse opens spaces to provoke students to consider what is affirmed and what is resisted in their own learning and speaking. He concludes that resistance is bound up with submission as certain words, convictions, and norms must be submitted to in order to resist others.

In Chapter Six, *Dialogic Resistance in Education: Tsunesaburo Makiguchi, Daisaku Ikeda and Transformative Language Learning*, Jason Goulah calls for transformative language learning as resistance pedagogy against the forces of neoliberal competitiveness in language education under the influence of No Child Left Behind. He contextualizes his argument in Tsunesaburo Makiguchi and Daisaku Ikeda's Buddhist-influenced philosophies of value-creation pedagogy, humanitarian competition, human revolution, dependent origination, and dialogue.

Chapter Seven by Marshall A. George, titled *Resisting Mandated Literacy Curricula in Urban Middle Schools*, asserts the first decade of the 21st century has seen the development of an unprecedented emphasis on the testing of America's school children. He concludes acts of resistance related to mandated or scripted literacy curricula can and must occur at all levels from the individual classroom, at the local, district, and state levels, and even in the national arena.

Continuing the theme of testing in Chapter Eight, Kristen Hawley Turner in *Fighting the Fear of Failure: Resisting the Effects of THE TEST in a Thinking-based Writing Class* argues that such prescriptive assessment models encourage reductive teaching that focuses more on test scores than actual learning. By fighting the fear of failure that can dominate a school culture, teachers and administrators can resist these effects of testing and promote effective teaching within their classrooms. She concludes educators should resist the emphasis on test-driven instruction that does little to encourage real thinking and as such will reap the rewards of educating students who become thoughtful learners—and ironically—who succeed on the test.

In Chapter Nine, titled *"A Small Group of Thoughtful, Committed Citizens": Social Studies Classrooms as Communities of Practice that Enable Social Action*, Thomas H. Levine asserts that social studies teaching may at times be viewed as social control or indoctrination. This chapter opens by arguing that at present, much social studies instruction may actually inhibit future citizens' capacity to engage in social action but considers how instruction in a community of practice could indeed help future citizens acquire the knowledge, skills, and dispositions needed to thoughtfully decide when and how to engage in such action. Resisting the norm, this chapter closes by presenting four specific approaches to social studies education that model—and foster—the work of small groups of thoughtful, committed citizens seeking to accomplish change.

Jo Ann Freiberg authored Chapter Ten, *The Challenge of Bullying in U.S. Schools: Resistance and Reaction*, in which she emphasizes that every adult school community member has an obligation to make each and every child in school physically, emotionally and intellectually safe. Describing the historical "resistance" to bullying as finger pointing at every place other than inward at the school, including parents and guardians, the media and technology, communities, the wider culture, a weapons-rich country, etc…she concludes educators must resist the urge to assume all of the causes of bullying are out of their control and make schools safer for children. Resisting bullying requires an assumption and acceptance of responsibility at a systemic level. No one person or constituency is singularly responsible, but everyone collectively must share the burden of resistance.

In Chapter Eleven, titled *"We Want to Be Heard": Using Instructional Technology to Resist Student Silence* by Kathleen P. King, she provides a "resistance perspective" on innovative technologies, specifically new media technology applied to teaching perspectives and practice. Here she describes and demystifies new media technology, while at the same time illustrating practical classroom examples and applications. She notes 21st century living and learning is about *constant* change, and nowhere is the need for responsive change more evident than in education. Older methods of teaching will not work without substantial transformation to reach deeper and wider across diversity lines and dimensions of content and learning. She concludes we must resist the vocal remnant who are hanging onto the last threads of archaic classroom power structures and embrace the means of equal voice, empowerment, and validation. Digital media which embraces all abilities and perspectives stands to offer greater democratization of education, if we as educators will challenge the status quo of education and appropriate its transformation to inclusiveness.

Resisting an Unbecoming Science is the focus of Chapter Twelve by John Craven and Tracy Hogan. Here they assert that science education has seen little change in form and function over the years, and all too often if one were to walk into science classrooms today you would find students sitting in their chairs being fed an irrelevant curriculum. However, they find hope in an expanding community of science educators resisting the norm and seeking to use science education as a vehicle to tap into the vitality, creativity, and capacity of young minds to teach how the phenomenological world operates (science) in the context of understanding and solving the messy, technologically based problems brought about both inadvertently and intentionally by human design.

In Chapter Thirteen, *Being at Crossroads: Resisting the Typical Conference Format to Rekindle Passions and Priorities in Science Education* by Julie M. Kittleson and Robert J. Ceglie, science education serves as the context in which the very essence of the long-standing tradition of academic conferences is questioned. They view alternative models of discourse as modes of resistance in which scholar activism, pragmatism, and orchestration may be fostered to promote new alliances essential to address pressing issues in science education and beyond.

Finally, in Chapter Fourteen titled *Should We Teach Resistance?* David M. Moss offers concluding perspectives regarding the many diverse ways resistance is essential for education. He argues that educators should be strategically evaluating and assessing their professional circumstances to see where their efforts may be needed to either resist or advance certain agendas. He concludes resistance must be planned and purposeful and that academics must live a life engaged to most effectively promote the ideals of reform and justice.

Thus, we invite you to explore with us the many and varied perspectives on resistance in education. Like many contributed volumes, there is potency in the plurality of the varied—and sometimes controversial—ideas discussed in the book.

Although each chapter stands alone as an exploration of this central theme of the book, taken together they offer a timely portrait of the complexity of issues at the very core of education today.

REFERENCES

Adams, F. & Horton, M. (1975). *Unearthing seeds of fire: The idea of Highlander*. Winston-Salem, NC: John F. Blair, Publisher.
Cole, M. & Hill, D. (1995). Games of despair and rhetorics of resistance: Postmodernism, education, and reaction. *British Journal of Sociology of Education* 16(2), 165–182.
Escher, M.C. (Artist). (1953). *Relativity* [Lithograph]. Holland.
Giroux, H. (2001). *Theory and resistance in education: Towards a pedagogy for the opposition* (Rev. ed.). Westport, CT: Bergin & Garvey.
Horton, A. I. (1989). *The Highlander Folk School: A history of its major programs, 1932–1961*. Brooklyn, NY: Carlson Publishing Inc.
Horton, M. & Freire, P. (1990). *We Make the Road by Walking: Conversations on Education and Social Change*. Philadelphia: Temple University Press.
McRobbie, A. (1978). Working class girls and the culture of femininity. In *Women take issue* (ed.) Women's Studies Group, 96–108. London: Hutchinson.
Whitman, W. (1965). When I heard the learn'd astronomer. *Leaves of Grass*. In Harold W. Blodgett & S. Bradley (Eds.). New York: Norton.
Willis, P. (1977). *Learning to Labour*. Lexington: D. C. Heath.
Wink, J. (1997). *Critical pedagogy: Notes from the real world*. New York: Longman.

CHAPTER ONE

Planting the Seeds of Resistance

The Times They Have a-Changed

TERRY A. OSBORN

I was somewhat surprised, perhaps also naïve, to discover the students' answer to a question asked in my foundations class, "As a government institution in a democracy, do public schools have any obligation to the disenfranchised in society?" "No," the students responded resoundingly. Their position was, in essence, that it should be "every man for himself." And so, the group of students known by many as the "entitlement generation" believed in entitlement, but only for themselves.

The vignette that starts this chapter is from the author's own experience and illustrates how far we need to go in planting the seeds of resistance. Many teacher educators may believe that the next generation of teachers is in danger of becoming mere technicists of a craft, that is, those who merely apply lesson planning principles in an attempt to meet standards and prepare students for the next standardized, high-stakes test. I would argue that danger has passed—the next generation of teachers is fully in that mode—the danger has become reality.

In this chapter, I will explore the need to plant the seeds of resistance in future generations of teachers. Merriam-Webster defines resistance as an act or instance of resisting. In turn, resist is from the Middle English, from Anglo-French or Latin; Anglo-French *resiste*, from Latin *resistere*, from *re-* + *sistere*, to take a stand and akin to the Latin *stare*, to stand. As an intransitive verb, it means to "exert force in opposition" and as a transitive verb, "to exert oneself so as to counteract" or "defeat or to withstand the force or effect of" (see www.merriam-webster.com). Planting the seeds of resistance involves developing a critical consciousness, introducing teaching as advocacy, and exploring avenues of resistance available to teachers.

FROM CRITICAL CONSCIENCE TO ADVOCACY

The springboard to developing critical conscience, or an awareness of the power relationships that shape education, lies in reflective practice—still popular, though misunderstood, in contemporary teacher education. Reflective practice, as I hear how teacher educators and teachers use it, has grown to mean something different to almost everyone who uses it (see Brookfield, 1995; Smyth, 1992; Zeichner, 1994). Reagan, Case, and Brubacher (2000) argued that reflective practice can be understood in multiple levels, from looking at specific methods and strategies to understanding the moral and political dimensions of practice. It is this third level, I contend, that allows for a segue into the elements of resistance. As Brubacher, Case, and Reagan (1994) in their text on building a culture of inquiry in the schools have argued:

> In developing transformational curricula, it is essential that teachers go beyond traditional teaching methods and materials. Textbooks, for instance, should at best be seen as points of departure for the curriculum rather than as curricular guides themselves. The distinction between curriculum and instruction is at best misleading; there is a symbiotic relationship between them that the teacher must take into account. (p. 74)

Critical reflection is described by Brookfield (1995) as follows:

> Critical reflection is inherently ideological. It is also morally grounded. It springs from a concern to create the conditions under which people can learn to love one another, and it alerts them to the forces that prevent this. Being anchored in values of justice, fairness, and compassion, critical reflection finds its political representation in the democratic process.... encouraging] us to create conditions under which each person is respected, valued, and heard. (p. 26–27)

In my own work (Osborn, 2005), I have suggested that

> Critical reflection involves challenging the boundaries of our educational thought and practice and rearranging or dissecting the constructs that we employ in an effort to understand the relations of power which underlie them. It is ideological and moral, yes, but it is also disquieting. Critical reflection should not result in lengthy, complex lists of the essential or base elements of equitable praxis in the....classroom, but ideally should lead us to discover that the parameters of our theory and practice, our curriculum and instruction, our language and culture are inherently *context dependent*. The aspects of this context include social, cultural, political, economic, historical, and other categories associated with the interaction of human beings within a society. Those who crave simple, unchanging formulas within which to struc-

ture their teaching or thought will not find critical reflection comforting. Those who recognize the social conditions placed on the production of knowledge may find it empowering. (p. 66)

In working to develop critical reflective skills with foreign language teachers (see e.g., Osborn, 2005), I developed a framework intended only to provide a point from which critically reflective skills should grow. To engage in critical reflection in the classroom, teachers should

1. Describe elements of theory or practice as they are found, at first without attribution of suspected power relationships involved.
2. Examine the role of the elements in terms of the classroom. Why is this element found within the classroom? Which broader educational objectives does it advance?
3. Ask, within the United States, what relevance might these elements have for specific cultural, ethnic, gender, racial, socioeconomic or other groups?
4. Ask, given the premise that schools mediate between segments of society, how do these descriptions of the classroom and the societal context reflect that mediation? Do certain segments benefit from the educational results?
5. Understand, what could be changed in and beyond the classroom such that the ideological underpinnings are effectively challenged.

To begin, pre-service teachers can journal a description of the point or points of analysis, usually a theoretical construct, textbook presentation, or classroom practice, providing an opportunity to segue from the role of active participant to participant observer. At this stage of critical reflection, the pre-service teachers build on the "clinical" skills that they have developed in describing the event, point, or theory. The second phase of critical reflection, an analysis of the classroom rationale for elements of practice, involves questioning those practices that are taken for granted. For example, "Why do we ask students to solve word problems in math?" The student should be encouraged to look beyond the truth that mathematical problems in life are rarely found already in equation form, which though true, is not the only reason. Math classes also include word problems because students are required to complete such items on high stakes assessments, which in turn are developed by humans who attempt to quantify student skills in mathematics and, more recently, teacher effectiveness in teaching those skills. Additionally, math and science skills are significant aspects of international competition, in terms of technological and other forms of advanced development.

Next, critical reflection must then move beyond the classroom for analysis. Students should examine the role of the subject matter, the applicable theories and practices of the educational process, and the roles differing segments of societies take as these elements are interrelated. Rather than simply looking for cause-effect relationships, however, we need to focus on contributions to cultural struggle while understanding the school as mediator of value in terms of cultural capital along with the competing pressures from society on the actors within the school. Returning briefly to mathematics, students consider the role of mathematics in scientific careers, the advances in technology that place the United States in global competition with other nations, the salaries associated with scientific careers, and the value placed by society on these factors as a context within which mathematics education operates. How then, do gender and ethnic differences, for example, play out in mathematics classes—are females and males, whites and blacks, equally encouraged to enter mathematics professions?

Advocacy

If the analyses gathered in the exercises above have developed in teachers an awareness of the issues of power in education, they can now move toward an understanding of the need for advocacy in the teaching profession. In critical terms, teaching can serve to disrupt the hegemony as it currently exists? We often contrast the role of a teacher-dominated and student-centered classroom with adages such as "Don't be the sage on the stage, but be the guide on the side." Perhaps it is time to simply point out to would-be teachers that "Your role is to be an advocate for children." In terms of the society in which the children live, that advocacy can take the form of resistance to hegemony. To challenge hegemony, in turn, teachers can engage in behaviors which point out the power basis underlying educational practices and/or constructs accepted as neutral or natural.

At the same time, teachers want more than just rhetoric. They need concrete ideas and solutions to very real problems. If we add "resistance" to the repertoire, we also need to develop specific steps one can implement. The work of Myles Horton, whose Highlander Folk School trained many of the workers in the civil rights movement, can provide direction. Horton (1989) notes Highlander's programs had specific features:

> There were two kinds of pre-conditions, the School believed, to developing an educational program which could basically influence community life. First, there was the relationship between the school and the community. The school and its teachers, it was emphasized, needed to be "a natural part of community life."...The other necessary pre-condition had to originate within the community: some generally perceived crisis situation which could rouse people to want to do something....The community program was to include, henceforth, not only discussion of subjects of concern and social and recreational activities, but direct participation in achieving an improved (if not a new) local social order. (p. 47)

Horton (1989) points to other salient features as well:

- Activities included functioning together as a group to analyze situations (p. 50);
- Members of the communities learned to work together to bring about social change (p. 52);
- Personal accounts are an important component (p. 121);
- The problems of local communities provided the basic content and focus for the educational activities (p. 205); and
- For the program to be effective, it needed to be part of a larger social movement (p. 258).

One can readily see that within teacher education, there are both opportunities as well as dangers. The opportunities are in our increasing interaction with the schools—we can work in partnership with local schools to identify and work on specific and real problems within the communities served by both schools and teacher education programs. The danger, of course, is that in working with the schools, one can substitute standards for justice, technicist teaching for advocacy, and accountability for a social movement. Teachers need to understand how to resist the programs of the schools when necessary.

Curricular Nullification

I have written rather extensively on the issue of curricular nullification as a form of activism (see Osborn 2000, 2005, 2006; Reagan and Osborn, 2002). Curricular nullification resembles the phenomenon in courtrooms known as jury nullification, when the jury, though aware of the legal mandates before them as applied to a particular case, chooses to apply a standard of judgment in substitution of what the law and the evidence would compel. Teachers nullify the curricular mandates as well when they act or fail to act in a way, the effect of which stands in opposition to explicit or implicit curricular mandates or goals. Curricular nullification can be further analyzed utilizing several distinct dichotomies: subtractive/additive, ethical/unethical, harmonious/dissonantal, and intentional/consequential. These dichotomies can aid teacher educators in utilizing curricular nullification as a strategy for teaching resistance.

Subtractive curricular nullification occurs when one fails to engage in behaviors that are mandated by the curriculum or institution. If a teacher refuses to teach part of the text or standards that s/he deems improper, reductionist, misleading, or irrelevant, s/he is engaged in subtractive curricular nullification. It is important to contrast subtractive curricular nullification with individualization or modification. If a teacher modifies or eliminates course content for a student with special needs, for example, that teacher is attempting to meet, not thwart, curricular mandates. Subtractive curricular nullification, by definition, stands to resist by way of an omission. Of course, some acts of subtractive curricular nullification would be unethical or even constitute professional malpractice, as in the case of a sex education teacher who fails to provide students with information regarding sexually transmitted diseases.

Additive curricular nullification by contrast, occurs when one engages in behaviors beyond those mandated in the curriculum with the intent of resisting curricular mandates. Perhaps the best example of this is shared by my colleague and friend Timothy Reagan who observed an elementary teacher share a creative and well-designed lesson on evolution. She concluded this "perfect" lesson with the addition of, paraphrasing, "And children, that is what I teach you because the state tells me to. You can believe you came from monkeys if you want to. I know we were created in the image of God."

If a social studies teacher, when finishing a discussion on tolerance of diversity, closes with the comments, "And that's why the country has gone downhill," that teacher has engaged in additive curricular nullification. The unit was taught, but the addition of the comment was contradictory to curricular mandates. Another example might be a teacher who, in adding units on the diversity of language in the United States resists a hidden curriculum in the foreign language classroom of "foreignness" (see Osborn, 2005).

Curricular nullification can be ethical or unethical in the sense that it mirrors professionally recognized and appropriate behavior. As Strike and Soltis (1992) assert:

> We believe that a kind of rational ethical thinking that goes beyond personal beliefs and values is essential both to professional ethics and to the moral education of all members of society. Ethics is a public as well as a personal matter. If we are correct, then it would seem to follow that teachers have a special obligation to help their students see and share the potential objectivity and rationality of ethical thinking so that we can all lead morally responsible lives together. (p. 5)

Clearly, we should direct teachers to engage in ethical curricular nullification. Further, curricular nullification can either be dissonant or harmonious with one's own value commitments. The concept of cognitive dissonance, outlined by Wicklund and Brehm (1976), provides with the following understanding:

> Any bit of knowledge that a person has about himself or the environment is a "cognition," or "cognitive element."

> The relationship between two cognitive elements is *consonant* if one implies the other in some psychological sense. Psychological implication can arise from cultural mores, pressure to be logical, behavioral commitment, past experience, and so on....If having cognition *A* implies having cognition *B*, a dissonant relationship exists when the person has cognitions *A* and the obverse or opposite of *B*. (p. 2)

It is important to note that if a teacher seeks the goals of social justice and discovers that a particular curriculum or curricular element supports hegemony, an act of resistance through curricular nullification may be harmonious with her or his own value commitments or dissonant. For some, it may be the case that all curricular nullification is dissonant and for another, all may be harmonious. Finally, one should note that curricular nullification can occur as the result of intentional action or inaction or can simply be the effect of circumstances. If one seeks to employ curricular nullification as resistance, then causation is an essential element of this approach, since only intentional acts can be included as part of a strategy.

Though the forms presented are all examples of curricular nullification, it is the intentional, harmonious, and ethical forms that should be utilized as a strategy of resistance by teachers. They should be directed to incorporate curricular nullification into their practice with the intent of challenging the ideological boundaries of educational concepts and practices.

Speaking Concretely

As indicated earlier, teachers desire concrete examples. I offer a few glimpses, but recognize that limitations of space and of my own expertise will leave the reader still wanting more. I encourage her or him to add the following examples to their list.

In history classes, instead of teaching merely about the concept of manifest destiny, or a belief that God intended for European Americans to expand the colonies to the western coast of North America, one could share that concept in juxtaposition with the imperialism of the Axis powers in World War II. Though these two do not normally appear together in a history class, the addition of the same impulse by the nation's "enemy" serves to resist reductionist views of U.S. history. There is a tendency to utilize terminology to "sanitize" ambitions that may not be noble. The teacher could ask students how the terms themselves serve to defend actions which might be deemed objectionable or have students explore other concepts which seem historically neutral, but are in themselves reflecting the interests of the dominant culture.

History, or the presentation of history in textbooks, has drawn much criticism and examination, such Jean Anyon's (1979) study of history textbooks two decades ago, when she concluded:

> The school curriculum has contributed to the formation of attitudes that make it easier for powerful groups, those whose knowledge is legitimized by school studies, to manage and control society. Textbooks not only express the dominant groups' ideology but also help to form attitudes in support of their local position. Indeed the importance of ideology to the power of dominant groups increases as the use of overt social coercion declines....Inasmuch as social choices are likely to be made on the basis of the social knowledge and symbolic meanings that are available, what one knows about social groups and processes is central to one's decisions. The perceived legitimacy of certain ideas increases their acceptance and utilization....If the views embedded in the information disseminated by these agencies [schools] predispose people to accept some values and not others, support some groups' activities and not others, and exclude some choices as unacceptable, then they provide invisible intellectual, internalized, and perhaps unconscious boundaries to social choice. (pp. 382–383)

A teacher of language arts, in addition to the "greats of literature" from known authors, may choose to include lesser known selections from local authors. Though much has been accomplished in moving away from the canon, even "multicultural literature" is reified as meeting certain global criteria and assuming that literature written by those who speak a certain language is representative of the voices of all who speak the language. A Spanish student, for example, who has spent most of her life in the United States, may not find Spanish or Mexican literature to be more meaningful to her than Shakespeare. By moving to local examples, the communities' struggles and perspectives may be more readily incorporated in the classroom. In any case, the presentation of literature in a classroom can be powerful and motivating, but a caution issued almost two decades ago by Wong (1993) should still resonate:

> A key instructional means of eliciting insight being comparison and contrast, at every turn we need to decide what to compare a marginalized literature to, and to what end. If this is done from a fallacious assumption of one's impartiality, however well-intentioned, the purpose of broadening the curriculum, namely, to honor the articulation of previously suppressed subjectivities, will be seriously undermined. (p. 112)

CONCLUSION

At the heart of planting the seeds of resistance lies the reality that teachers must begin to see education as taking place in a larger, complex, sociopolitical and cultural landscape than we currently show students. Teachers should begin to connect both curriculum and instruction to the individual settings in which their practice takes place, incorporating the local political, economic, and cultural factors that impact their students' lives and their own work. Beyond current goals of utilizing the best practices or meeting the latest standards, teachers can engage what Giroux and McLaren (see McLaren, 1998) have discussed as micro-objectives and macro-objectives, with the latter related to connecting classroom objectives to external social realities. In my previous work on foreign language education, I have termed this shift in practice *macrocontextualization*. Schooling must always be seen as part of a social struggle and teaching as a political act. Once teachers embrace that reality of their contexts and their activities, then their daily choice is clear: compliance or resistance.

Resistance, then, is taught by teacher educators as part of a teacher's practice. New teachers learn not to simply become technicians of a craft nor artists, but participants in the formation and reformation of social and cultural patterns in society. In doing so, they likewise resist seeing the social realities as a *fait accompli* and see themselves as part of a broader movement to reshape them in line with the greatest ideals of democratic education.

REFERENCES

Anyon, J. (1979). Ideology and United States history textbooks. *Harvard Educational Review*, 49 (3), 361–386.

Brookfield, S. D. (1995). *Becoming a critically reflective teacher.* San Francisco: Jossey-Bass.

Brubacher J. W., Case, C. W., and Reagan T. G. (1994). *Becoming a reflective educator: How to build a culture of inquiry in the schools.* Thousand Oaks, CA: Corwin Press.

Horton, A. I. (1989). *The Highlander Folk School: A history of its major programs, 1932–1961.* Brooklyn, NY: Carlson Publishing Inc.

McLaren, P. (1998). *Life in schools: An introduction to critical pedagogy in the foundations of education.* New York: Longman.

Osborn, T. A. (2000). *Critical reflection and the foreign language classroom.* Westport, CT: Bergin & Garvey.

Osborn, T. A. (2005). *Critical reflection and the foreign language classroom.* Rev. ed. Greenwich, CT: Information Age Publishing.

Osborn, T. A. (2006). *Teaching world languages for social justice: A sourcebook of principles and practices.* Mahwah, NJ: Lawrence Erlbaum Associates.

Reagan, T. & Osborn, T. A. (2002). *The foreign language educator in society: Toward a critical pedagogy.* Mahwah, NJ: Lawrence Erlbaum Associates.

Reagan T. G., Case C. W., & Brubacher, J. W. (2000). *Becoming a reflective educator: How to build a culture of inquiry in the schools.* 2d ed. Thousand Oaks, CA: Corwin Press.

Smyth, W. J. 1992. Teachers' work and the politics of reflection. *American Educational Research Journal*, 29 (2): 267–300.

Strike, K. A. & Soltis, J. F. (1992). *The ethics of teaching.* (2d ed.). New York: Teachers College Press.

Wicklund, R. A. & Brehm, J. W. (1976). *Perspectives on cognitive dissonance.* Hillsdale, NJ: Lawrence Erlbaum Associates.

Wong, S. C. (1993). Promises, pitfalls, and principles of text selection in curricular diversification: The Asian-American case. In T. Perry & J. Fraser (Eds.), *Freedom's plow* (pp. 109–120). New York: Routledge.

Zeichner, K. M. (1994). Research on teacher thinking and different views on reflective practice in teaching and teacher education. In I. Carlgren, G. Handal, & S. Vaage (Eds.) *Teachers' minds and actions: Research on teachers' thinking and practice*, 9–27. Washington, D. C.: Falmer Press.

CHAPTER TWO

Resisting Traditional Notions of Teacher Certification

Reflecting on "Teach For America"

MOLLY K. NESS

Today's public schools face enormous challenges, one of which is the placement and retention of high-quality teachers. According to the National Commission on Teaching and America's Future (NCTAF), 2.8 million new teacher hires will be needed by the year 2015 (Wehligh, 2007). To complicate the matters, 30% of new teachers quit the profession in the first three years, citing lack of time to prepare, heavy teaching loads, large class sizes, poor salary and/or benefits, and students' behavioral problems as the top reasons for quitting. As our schools scramble to find quality candidates to fill classroom vacancies, we must look to innovative pathways to secure our teachers. One such approach is Teach For America, perhaps the most recognizable alternative route to certification. Since its 1990 inception, Teach For America has prepared more teachers in low-income areas than any other institution in the country. In nearly two decades, Teach For America has placed 17,000 teachers, who have in turn taught nearly 2.5 million K-12 students.

Teach For America, as a selective and controversial program, has become a key player in the landscape of public education reform. Presidents—past and present—refer to Teach For America as an exemplar of young citizens making a difference in our nation today, and CNNMoney.com lists Teach For America as a top employer of recent grads. In an October 2009 speech at Columbia University, Secretary of Education Arne Duncan reported "Now I am all in favor of expanding high-quality alternate certificate routes like…Teach for America." Early in its history, many questions focused on the mere existence of Teach For America

(Darling-Hammond et al., 2005; Laczko-Kerr and Berliner, 2002). Over time, these questions have shifted in their nature and now focus on how best to constructively critique, support and even integrate these programs; as such, programs such as Teach For America have prompted traditional schools of education to re-envision their own efforts in recruiting, preparing, and supporting teacher candidates.

Understanding the History of and Trends in Alternative Routes to Certification

Since 1985, the hiring of teachers who are not certified by government agencies through traditional university-based teacher training has rapidly increased. Alternative teacher certification can be defined as "a program leading to a teaching certificate, designed for persons who have not earned a bachelor's degree or who have not followed a traditional path through pre-service teacher training programs" (Glass, 2008, p. 4). According to Glass (2008), nearly 60,000 alternatively certified teachers are currently employed in our public and private schools. Additionally, more than 140 alternative routes to certification or provisional certification exist today (Feistritzer & Chester, 2003). Glass (2008) posits that the growth in alternatively certified teachers is due to two factors: (1) the shortage of teachers in low-income urban and rural schools and (2) a political opposition to the regulation of teacher education programs by government agencies. The increasing popularity of alternative routes to certification prompted the National Center for Educational Information (NCEI) to create the National Center for Alternative Certification (NCAC) in 2003, a one-stop, comprehensive clearinghouse for information about alternative certification routes.

Alternative certification routes often appeal to candidates for whom traditional pathways to teaching may not otherwise be available. A 2005 study of alternatively prepared teachers in New York, Florida and Texas indicated that nearly half (47%) of respondents indicated that they would not become a teacher if an alternative certification route were not available (Feistritzer, 2005). Furthermore, alternative certification route appears to be more likely to attract potential candidates who are traditionally underrepresented in teaching. The North Central Regional Educational Laboratory (Legler, 2002) reported that alternative certification programs increased the number of male teachers and attracted both older teachers with life experiences and people with business experience. Furthermore, approximately 32% of new teachers who have pursued alternative certifications are non-white, whereas nationally 10% of the teaching force is non-white (Feistritzer & Chester, 2003). Research (Haycock, 2004; Keller, 2007; Podgursky, 2006) indicates that teachers who pursue alternative certifications are highly likely to teach poor and minority children.

THE NEW TEACHER PROJECT AND THE TEACHING FELLOWS

Though Teach For America is perhaps the most recognizable alternative initial teaching training program, there are certainly other models. Another strikingly similar one is the Teaching Fellows, created by The New Teacher Project (TNTP). Founded in 1997, TNTP is a national non-profit organization dedicated to closing the achievement gap by ensuring quality teachers in every classroom. TNTP partners with school districts to address issues of teacher quality and placement. Since its creation, TNTP has trained or hired 33,000 teachers and benefited approximately 3.8 million poor and minority students. TNTP recruits, hires, and trains "Teaching Fellows," high-achieving individuals who do not have backgrounds in education. These Teaching Fellows are placed in hard-to-staff schools in more than 20 locations nationwide. In fact, nearly 10% of New York City school teachers have come to the classroom through the alternative certification program of the New York City Teaching Fellows (NYCTF), which recruits and trains both recent college graduates and mid-career switchers. In addition to its multiple routes to certification, TNTP has created other recruitment initiatives, specifically geared to attract and hire already certified high-quality teachers. These recruitment initiatives currently run in three locations: the Newark TeacherNex, the Oakland City Teacher Corps, and TeachNOLA (New Orleans, LA).

Other Alternative Routes to Teacher Certification

Online teaching credential programs, including Walden University, the University of Phoenix, and Western Governors University, are also growing in popularity. Another program, Troops to Teachers, was created in 1994 to bring former military personnel into K-12 classrooms. Since its inception, it has placed nearly 10,000 teachers in classrooms. Alternative routes to the classroom have also been adopted by various states, such as Teach Kentucky and the Mississippi Teacher Corps, in which college graduates are selected to teach in public schools, while receiving full salary, benefits, credentialing, and a subsidized master's degree. A program founded by Yale alumni concentrated in the greater Louisville area with great peer and community support.

The Characteristics of Alternative Routes

Across the diverse offerings of alternative routes to certification, there are several common features. All the candidates who get licensed to teach through alternative routes should possess at least a bachelor's degree. They all must pass a screening process, which includes tests, interviews, and mastery of the content they are likely to teach. All candidates begin on-the-job training early in their programs and are led by a mentor teacher. They all complete some sort of coursework or equivalent experiences in professional education studies during their teaching. Lastly, all candidates must meet high performance standards.

Teach For America as an Alternative Route to the Classroom

Of the vast array of alternative routes to teacher education, none is more visible than Teach For America. Created in 1990, Teach For America is the national corps of recent college graduates who commit two years to teach in our nation's low-income rural and urban school districts. Teach For America's mission is to address the profound achievement gap that affects the 13 million children who live in poverty by ensuring that all children have quality teachers in their K-12 classrooms. Teach For America is the brainchild of Wendy Kopp, who created the program as a part of her senior thesis at Princeton University. Kopp envisioned an innovative solution to the achievement gap: The nation's most outstanding recent college graduates would put their degrees to work by teaching in our nation's low-income communities. The result of her vision was Teach For America, which pursues educational equity for students of low-income neighborhoods.

Teach For America is a comprehensive two-year program, in which teachers—also called corps members—are actively recruited and selected through a competitive process, trained in summer institutes, placed as full-time paid teachers, and supported in two years of teaching through an elaborate support network of graduate schools, mentor teachers, and collaborative learning teams. Teach For America attracts college graduates who develop ambitious visions for social change, who work to overcome the obstacles inherent in underresourced schools, and who are passionate about the organization's mission that "one day all children in the nation will have the opportunity to attain an excellent education."

Teach For America envisions itself as more than an organization which merely fills teaching vacancies; instead Teach For America hopes to build a movement of past and present teachers who work toward eliminating educational inequity. The organization was founded on the belief that the educational gap that exists between students of high and low socioeconomic backgrounds is our nation's greatest injustice; Teach For America points to sobering statistics about the educational inequity which persists along socioeconomic and racial lines. Consider the following statistics from the National Center for Children in Poverty (Chau & Douglass-Hall, 2008):

~ Nine-year-olds growing up in low-income communities are already three

- grade levels behind their peers in high-income communities.
- Half of these nine-year-olds in low-income schools won't graduate from high school by the time they're 18. Those who do graduate will, on average, read and do math at the level of eighth graders in high-income communities.
- Furthermore, only 1 in 10 will graduate from college.
- African American and Latino children are three times as likely to live in a low-income area.

Teach For America believes that the elimination of educational inequity will require a cadre of committed individuals who work at the problem in several arenas. In their two-year teaching commitment, corps members are expected to lead their students toward significant academic gains in spite of the institutional and systemic challenges inherent in schools and communities of poverty. The organization's mission does not stop after the two-year teaching commitment; instead, Teach For America holds its 12,000 alumni to the long-term goals of affecting fundamental changes in every sector, as explained below by founder Wendy Kopp:

> We believe our best hope for a lasting solution is to build a massive force of leaders working from inside and outside education who have the conviction and insight that come from teaching successfully in low-income communities. We need such leadership working at every level of our school systems, working outside the system to address the socioeconomic factors that contribute so significantly to the problem, and working in policy and the sectors, such as journalism and business, that influence policy (Kopp, 2008, p. 735).

THE TEACH FOR AMERICA EXPERIENCE: WHO JOINS TEACH FOR AMERICA?

Teach For America corps members are recent college graduates and young professionals who have proven to be leaders in the classroom, workplace, and community. Teach For America is both highly competitive and selective. Corps members have an average GPA of 3.6 and 95% held leadership positions on their college campuses. In 2007, 2900 new teachers were selected from over 18,000 candidates, with an acceptance rate of 17%. In its extensive recruiting and application process, Teach For America seeks applicants from all backgrounds and career interests. More specifically, Teach For America seeks candidates who have demonstrated measurable achievement, have persevered in instances of adversity, possess strong critical thinking skills, can influence and motivate others, operate with organizational ability, and who respect the low-income communities in which they will teach. The majority of corps members do not have either a degree in education nor a prior teaching experience. To apply for Teach For America, applicants must possess a bachelor's degree from an accredited college or university, demonstrate an undergraduate grade point average of at least 2.5, and be an American citizen or a permanent resident.

In its recruitment and hiring processes, Teach For America remains strongly committed to candidates from diverse ethnic, racial, and socioeconomic backgrounds. In 2007, over 28% of incoming corps members were from minority backgrounds. Because Teach For America is an alternative route to teacher certification, corps members teach in conjunction with completing state requirements toward state certification as mandated by No Child Left Behind's push for highly qualified teachers.

TEACH FOR AMERICA'S APPROACHES TO TRAINING AND CERTIFICATION

Upon acceptance, Teach For America corps members are placed in rural or urban districts. Urban regions include Atlanta; Baltimore; Bay Area (California); Charlotte, North Carolina; Chicago; Denver; Houston; Indianapolis; Jacksonville; Kansas City; Las Vegas; Los Angeles; Memphis; Miami; New Haven, Connecticut; Newark and Camden, New Jersey; greater New Orleans; New York City; Philadelphia, Phoenix; St. Louis; and Washington, DC. Rural sites include the Mississippi Delta, rural Hawaii, New Mexico, North Carolina, the Rio Grande Valley, South Dakota, and South Louisiana. Prior to their actual placement, all incoming corps members receive five weeks of intensive training at one of the summer institutes in Atlanta, Houston, Los Angeles, New York City, Philadelphia, and Phoenix. Institute coursework consists of six content strands:

1. Teaching as Leadership, which focuses on the how successful teachers approach low-income communities
2. Instructional Planning and Development, including student assessment and diagnosis, lesson planning, and instructional delivery
3. Classroom Management, which helps teachers maximize student learning in productive environments
4. Diversity, Community, and Achievement, which examines the diversity-related issues which novice teachers may experience
5. Learning Theory, which presents instructional planning to meet student needs
6. Literacy Development, including both elementary and secondary methods

During these intense and rigorous summer institutes, corps members teach in a district summer school program. They are closely monitored by veteran teachers; through observations, written feedback, and debriefing, corps members are taught to become reflective practitioners. Corps members also receive additional preparation through interactive clinics and courses, focusing on instructional planning, classroom management and culture, learning theory, and literacy development. By no means does Teach for America consider the summer institute exhaustive and sufficient in the complexities of teacher preparation. At the end of the five weeks of training, corps members are reminded to continue professional development and state certification in their schools and communities. Once in their placement regions, corps members are grouped in schools with other Teach for America teachers, are paired with mentor teachers, and attend frequent meetings to plan curriculum and classroom problem-solving issues. The vast majority of corps members are teaching students: the nation's most disadvantaged students, who begin the school year on average at the 14th percentile against the national norm (Kopp, 2008).

Teach for America corps members are neither volunteers nor interns; they are full-time, fully paid classroom teachers. Most are placed in schools which qualify for funding under Title I of the Elementary and Secondary Education Act. School districts, who face teacher shortages particularly in the bilingual, secondary science, and special education classrooms, hire Teach for America corps members through state-approved alternative certification programs. These programs meet No Child Left Behind's provision for highly qualified teachers by requiring corps members to meet specific requirements and to demonstrate proficiency in the grades and content matter that they will teach. Certification requirements vary by states and by teaching positions, but the majority of incoming corps members must pass subject-area tests before teaching and continue ongoing graduate level coursework during the school year. Teach for America works with regional graduate schools of education and school districts to provide corps members with access to the necessary coursework and testing to meet certification requirements. In addition to a full teaching salary, corps members receive nearly $10,000 of Americorps vouchers.

According to the organization's self-reported statistics, 88% of corps members complete their two-year commitments. In fact, 89% of corps members finish their first year of teaching: a figure slightly higher than the national average of 82% of first-year teachers in low-income schools who complete one year of teaching. Those corps members who do not finish their commitment provide a number of reasons for leaving the classroom, including dissatisfaction with their teaching placements and family and medical issues. Almost all Teach for America corps members earn their certification and/or master's degree within their two-year commitments (Boyd, Grossman, Lankford, Loeb, Michelli, and Wyckoff, 2006).

Teachers as Leaders: Teach For America's Definition of Teacher Effectiveness

Teach for America believes that when children in low-income communities are given educational opportunities, they excel and that effective teachers are a key factor in ensuring academic achievement. Embedded through Teach for America's recruitment and training is its vision of successful leaders. Teach for America believes that effective teachers excel in the following contexts:

> They set big goals for where students will be academically at the end of the year, invest students, parents, and others in working hard to realize that vision, plan purposefully and work relentlessly with a sense of urgency to maximize class time in pursuit of the vision, and continuously increase effectiveness to reach the vision in spite of the multiple challenges and obstacles along the way (Teach for America, 2009).

To ensure that all corps members demonstrate the qualities of effective leadership, Teach for America leads corps members in setting measurable long-term goals for student achievement. In fact, corps members are expected to move their students forward at least a year and a half's worth of progress in one academic year. This goal-driven approach, in turn, impacts all instructional decisions and classroom management. To ensure that students are on board with these ambitious goals, Teach for America encourages corps members to communicate effectively with students' families and school communities. Teach for America also acknowledges that low-income school communities are challenging contexts, which force successful teachers to overcome roadblocks. Successful corps members "recognize the massive challenge before them, but resolutely determine what is in their control, focus all their efforts on those factors, and assume responsibility for their students' achievement in spite of the challenges that remain out of their control" (Teach for America, 2009). Finally, in an era of accountability, Teach for America guides corps members in using data-driven self-analysis to measure progress and student growth. Data indicates that many corps members take on leadership positions within their first few years in the profession and generate proposals for charter schools, pre-schools, and summer or after-school academic programs (Olson, 2007).

Life After Teach For America

At the end of their two-year commitments, corps members pursue many different career paths, both within and beyond the field of education. Teach for America self-reports that two-thirds of its corps members remain in the field of education at the completion of their two-year commitment. Alumni within the field of education hold very different roles; some remain in their original placements, while others take on positions as curriculum coaches or pursue paths of school and district leadership. Many alumni have gone on to open charter schools; in fact, approximately 360 Teach for America alumni serve as school leaders in 35 states. In Washington, DC, more than 10% of the city"s schools are now run by Teach for America alumni. To support alumni efforts to become successful school leaders, Teach for America created a School Leadership Initiative in 2006. Yet, other alumni remain connected to the field of education in policy positions. For example, Michelle Rhee, a Baltimore corps member in 1992, now serves as the chancellor for the District of Columbia Public Schools and holds a significant voice in conversations about urban public school reform.

As for the alumni who leave the field of education at the end of their two years of teaching, they are challenged to take on the second part of Teach for America's mission: to affect long-term change from a variety of professional fields, including politics, business, medicine, law, advocacy, social services, and policy. Teach for America self-reported data reveals that 93% of alumni report that they are supporting Teach for America's mission through career, philanthropy, volunteer work, and/or graduate study (Teach for America, 2009).

THE EFFECTIVENESS OF TEACH FOR AMERICA: CONFLICTING REPORTS

Throughout its history, Teach for America has been in the national spotlight and has been the recipient of much praise (Decker, Mayer, and Glazerman, 2004; Raymond and Fletcher, 2002) and also of critique (Darling-Hammond, 1994; Darling-Hammond et al., 2005; Laczko-Kerr and Berliner, 2002; Popkewitz, 1998). Comprehensively, the existing research base does not provide conclusive answers about whether Teach for America is detrimental or beneficial to our nation's public schools and children.

Research in Support of Teach for America

Several research articles, both from independent sources and commissioned by Teach for America, support Teach for America as a viable source of effective teachers (Boyd et al., 2006; Decker, Mayer, and Glazerman, 2004; Glazerman, Mayer, and Decker, 2006; Kane, Rockoff, and Staiger, 2008; Raymond and Fletcher, 2002; Xu, Hannaway, and Taylor, 2008). In 2002, an independent non-partisan research group at the Hoover Institute of Stanford University released the first evaluation of Teach for America's effectiveness (Raymond and Fletcher, 2002). Researchers undertook the study to explore how Teach for America teachers performed when compared with other beginning teachers. Data collection occurred in Houston Independent School District, which was the nation's seventh largest school district at the time of the study. In looking at teacher's effectiveness, researchers used year-end learning gains from the students of Teach for America teachers versus those from students taught by non-Teach for America teachers. More specifically, individual scores on the annual Texas Assessment of Academic Skills (TAAS) in math, reading, and English language arts measured student performance. Results indicated that students taught by Teach for America corps members learned more than students of other new teachers, with Teach for America recruits producing gains in student achievement at 12% of a standard deviation higher in elementary school math and 5.8% higher in reading. Furthermore, the lowest performing teachers in this study were consistently not TFA teachers, and TFA teachers made up a disproportionate amount of high performers. The researchers used these results to "dispel the notion that only the traditional route to teaching can produce good teachers" (p. 68).

Subsequent research conducted by Mathematica (Decker, Mayer, and Glazerman, 2004) compared student achievement in grades 1 through 5 among students taught by Teach for America teachers and other teachers in the same schools and in the same grade levels. Student performance on math and reading tests at the beginning and the end of the academic year served as measurements. The study found that Teach for America teachers outperformed the control group, which included both certified and veteran teachers, in math achievement. Researchers found no significant differences when looking at reading achievement.

Additional research (Boyd, Grossman, Lankford, Loeb, and Wyckoff, 2006) found similar results when looking at Teach for America in New York City, one of the largest placement sites. Kane, Rockoff, and Staiger (2008) used six years of student achievement data and found a small positive effect of 0.02 standard deviations for TFA on student math achievement relative to certified teachers. These researchers concluded that the certification status of a teacher has at most a small impact on student performance.

In 2007, Teach for America commissioned Policy Study Associates (Policy Study Associates, 2007), an external independent reviewer, to conduct a survey of school principals where corps members have taught. The survey asked 785 school principals in 25 school regions to evaluate the performance of their respective corps members. The results indicated very high levels of principals' satisfaction with corps members; 94% of principals reported that Teach for America corps members have positively impacted their schools and 90% of principals would hire corps members again. Furthermore, 95% of participants rated corps members as effective, if not more effective than, other beginning teachers. In fact, 61% reported that Teach for America teachers were more effective than other beginning teachers in terms of impacting student achievement. Principals also expressed satisfaction with Teach for America corps members' training and preparation; 93% reported that corps members' training is as good as the training of other beginning teachers, while 63% reported that Teach for America's training is better than that of other beginning teachers. Principals were also overwhelmingly positive on other measures, rating corps members as good or excellent in their subject matter knowledge (90%), in their purposeful planning to meet ambitious goals of student achievement (90%), and in their ability to foster positive relationships with colleagues and administrators (89%).

The most recent independent study of Teach for America's effectiveness was released in 2008 from the National Center for the Analysis of Longitudinal Data in Educational Research (CALDER) (Xu, Hannaway, and Taylor, 2008). Conducted in North Carolina, the study represents the first one conducted specifically at the high school level. Data sources consisted of student scores in end-of-course exams in eight core subject areas as data sources. Findings indicate that Teach for America corps members' impact on student learning exceeds that of other teachers—both novice and experienced certified teachers. In fact, researchers found that TFA teachers had three times the positive effect of experienced teachers. Through these findings, researchers conclude that "disadvantaged students would be better off with TFA teachers, especially in math and science, than with fully licensed in-field teachers with three or more years of experience" (p. 24).

In sum, these research findings seem to dispel the notion that only traditional routes to teacher certification can produce good teachers who positively impact student performance. The general pattern of research findings indicate that Teach for America teachers produce student achievement results as strong as or better than their peers.

Critiques of and Research against Teach for America

Since its inception, Teach for America has been under much scrutiny, resulting in some vocal critics. The criticisms of Teach for America fall along two lines. First, critics point out that the five weeks of training is insufficient, leaving these teachers ill prepared for the demands of their teaching placements. Critics claim that Teach for America teachers lack pedagogical training and fail to connect classroom practice with child development theories. Other critics of Teach for America point out that two-year commitment is too short and often causes problematic teacher turnover in already troubled schools. In fact, the American Federation of Teachers has referred to Teach for America as a "band-aid." Others believe that Teach for America demeans teaching by treating it as a "Peace-Corps style rescue mission rather than a true profession" (Raymond and Fletcher, 2002, p. 64). A final point of contention concerns Teach for America's "rescuer role in high-poverty urban and rural communities" (Veltri, 2008, p. 533). Popkewitz (1998) notes that Teach for America focuses on a missionary discourse of saving or rescuing children from low-income urban or rural communities. In perhaps its earliest and most scathing attack, Linda Darling-Hammond (1994) called Teach for America "a frankly missionary program" which puts "ill-prepared recruits in classrooms for a revolving-door trip into and out of teaching" (p. 23).

Though there are several research studies which highlight the positive impacts of Teach for America, there are also others that raise serious concerns. Research from Linda Darling-Hammond and her colleagues (Darling-Hammond et al., 2005) indicates that regularly certified and experienced teachers have a stronger positive impact on student learning than uncertified, alternatively certified, or provisionally certified teachers. Using regression analyses, looking at fourth- and fifth-grade student test scores on six years of reading and mathematics state assessments, certified teachers produced stronger student achievement gains than uncertified teachers. In additional research, Darling-Hammond and colleagues (Darling-Hammond, Chung, and Frelow, 2002) reported that teachers who were prepared in teacher education courses felt better prepared than those who entered the field through alternative programs. Darling-Hammond et al. (2005) also investigated retention rates of Teach for America and found that Teach for America corps members left the classroom at rates higher than traditionally certified teachers; between 57% and 90% of Teach for America teachers left the classroom after two years, and between 72% and 100% left after three years. Additional research from Lackzo-Kerr and Berliner (2002) revealed that students of Teach for America teachers show about 20% less growth than students with beginning but fully certified teachers. Researchers matched traditionally certified teachers with alternative certified teachers on three criteria: (1) within the same school, (2) within the same school district, and (3) between similar school districts. Using four different statistical analyses, Lackzo-Kerr and Berliner (2002) concluded that "in reading, mathematics, and language, the students of certified teachers outperformed students of under-certified teachers, including the students of TFA teachers, by about 2 months of a grade equivalent scale" (p.2).

Lastly, a recent ethnographic study (Veltri, 2008) of 300 Teach for America participants over eight years concludes that many TFA teachers "lacked pedagogy, school law, child and adolescent development knowledge, and realistic clinical experiences in classrooms" (p. 512). Citing that corps members learn the complex nature of schools and low-income communities on the job, Veltri questions TFA's current model and mission and provides alternative solutions including extending the length of the Teach for America commitment, improving the training model by both extending the duration of summer institutes and providing extensive district-based summer school teaching, and hiring effective veteran teachers to model effective teaching practices in a comprehensive manner in the first year of teaching.

FUTURE DIRECTIONS FOR TEACH FOR AMERICA

Today, nearly 5,000 corps members teach in over two dozen low-income rural and urban districts nationwide. In an ambitious growth plan, Teach for America aims to address educational inequity by becoming both bigger and better. Teach for America has set several key priorities in its plan. First, the organization aims to increase the racial, ethnic, and economic diversity of the corps. The goal is that the 2010 corps will include approximately one-third people of color. Another priority is maximizing the impact of corps members on student achievement. To meet this expectation, Teach for America intends to rigorously evaluate its teacher training and support, as well as measure the percentage of corps members who move their students forward a year and a half's worth of academic progress in one academic year. In its third priority, Teach for America looks to its alumni network as leaders in education and social reform. In particular, Teach for America is focused on three areas to foster alumni leadership: school leadership, political leadership, and social entrepreneurship. In its final priority, Teach for America aims to build itself as an enduring institution which thrives as long as the need exists. Steps to ensure sustainability include building public recognition, securing a diverse funding base, enlisting alumni to support the organization, and increasing the quality and quantity of staff nationwide.

RESISTING TRADITIONAL NOTIONS OF TEACHER PREPARATION: TEACH FOR AMERICA AS A MODEL OF RESISTANCE

Of all alternative routes to the classroom, Teach for America is by far the most visible. Interestingly, Teach for America accounts for a very small proportion— approximately 5%—of all alternatively certified teachers nationwide. Nevertheless since its creation nearly two decades ago, Teach for America became—and in many senses still remains—a key player in conversations about teacher recruitment and training. With Teach for America accounting for such a relatively small percentage of nationwide teachers, it is logical to question why the organization has been met with such resistance and continues to draw much criticism. The opposition to Teach for America seems to stem largely from graduate schools of education, who look at the organization as a challenge to the status quo in teacher preparation. However, the relationship between Teach for America and traditional graduate schools of education need not be a confrontational one. The enormous popularity of Teach for America, its support from educational policy makers, and its continued sources of funding indicate that Teach for America is a strengthening, rather than weakening, force. As such, we must look at Teach for America not as being pitted against graduate schools of education but rather help the two forces engage in mutually beneficial conversations. Both Teach for America and graduate schools of education can learn a lot from each other, with the end result being a cadre of better prepared teachers who embrace the challenges of teaching in low-income urban and rural school districts.

We must begin by examining the valuable lessons that Teach for America can offer to traditional avenues of teacher preparation. Firstly, Teach for America has become an enormously popular avenue to recruit young teachers into public schools which traditionally are difficult to staff. Teach for America taps into an unconventional pool for teachers and recruits teachers with stronger than usual academic records. In the 2008–2009 academic year, Teach for America was flooded with 35,000 applications, 11% of the graduating class from Yale, 10% from Georgetown, and 9% from Harvard (Dillon, 2008). Teach for America was the number one postgraduation employer on many campuses, including Duke, Emory, George Washington, New York University, and Spelman. As such, Teach for America has made teaching in low-income school districts both highly attractive and incredibly competitive to recent college graduates.

In addition to its revolutionary recruitment practices, Teach for America seems to offer important ideas about how teachers can be effective immediately upon entering the classroom. Graduate schools of education operate with the belief that teachers need semesters of preparation in educational theory, child development, classroom management, and instructional practices before becoming effective teachers. After completing the multi-week summer institute, the majority of Teach for America corps members are able to be successful teachers in their first year in the classroom. It is important to note that Teach for America teachers are enrolled in traditional graduate education coursework in their first semesters of teaching; therefore, somehow the partnership of an intensive short-term preparation and ongoing coursework merge together in making Teach for America corps members stronger teachers with the knowledge, reflection, and understandings essential in becoming effective teachers. Both parties—Teach for America and graduate schools of education—must recognize and appreciate this partnership.

Just as graduate schools of education can learn from Teach for America, the reverse is true in that Teach for America must take important lessons from traditional avenues of teacher preparation and other vocal critiques. As Teach for America candidates are too often unprepared for the cultural and often linguistic diversity of their classroom, some crucial elements of teacher education appear to be lacking in the organization's training model. Additionally, a legitimate critique of Teach for America concerns the two-year commitment and the resulting teacher turnover in high-needs schools. Here, Teach for America must engage in conversations with other teacher preparation routes who successfully mentor and track their alumni through multiple years in their teaching careers.

In short, the resistance to Teach for America must be welcomed as positive element which will challenge the organization to critically reflect upon its recruitment, training, and ongoing support. The organization must continue to embrace the resistance and see such resistance as a crucial factor which will better serve its corps members and the K-12 public school students in their classrooms. When such resistance is viewed not as obstructionist but rather as critical, reflective, and advantageous, multiple forces in teacher education will regard each other as key players and contributors to educational reform.

Conclusion

The success of Teach for America teachers on student achievement seems to indicate that multiple pathways to teaching are both possible and beneficial. The research pointing out the effectiveness of Teach for America suggests that the organization is a valuable contribution to the ongoing debate of how to fix our nation's schools and how to raise the achievement levels of our nation's poor and minority students. Teach for America may not be a long-term solution to the vast problems that exist in our public schools, but the net pros of the program seem to outweigh its cons (Ness, 2004).

In debates about teacher quality and public school reform, Teach for America has emerged as a major player; Cochran-Smith (2004) explains that Teach for America "has been constructed as both the poster child for alternative routes into teaching…and a major battleground for larger discussions about who should teach, what they should know, how and where they should be prepared, and who should decide" (p. 3).

As one of the nation's largest suppliers of alternatively certified teachers, there can be no doubt that Teach for America is effective in its model of recruiting and hiring novice teachers. Teach for America, therefore, represents not a threat to traditional teacher education programs, but a mirror which forces graduate schools of education to reflect about their relevancy to current teaching practices, to be adaptive and relevant to the needs of teachers in low-income schools, and to remain practically rooted to today's diverse classrooms.

REFERENCES

Boyd, D., Grossman, P., Hammerness, K., Lankford, R. H., Loeb, S., McDonald, M., Reininger, M., Ronfeldt, M., & Wyckoff, J. (2008). Surveying the landscape of teacher education in New York City: Constrained variation and the challenge of innovation. *Educational Evaluation and Policy Analysis*, 30 (4), 319–343.

Boyd, D., Grossman, P., & Lankford, R. H. (2006). Complex by design: Investigating pathways into teaching in New York City schools. *Journal of Teacher Education*, 57 (2), 155–156.

Chau, M. & Douglass-Hall, A. (2008). *Low-income children in the United States: National and state trend data, 1997–2007.* New York, NY: National Center for Children in Poverty. Retrieved January 9, 2008 from http://www.nccp.org/publications/pdf/text_851.pdf.

Cochran-Smith, M. (2005). Taking stock 2005: Getting beyond the horse race. *Journal of Teacher Education*, 56 (1), 3–7.

Darling-Hammond, L. (1994). Who will speak for the children?: How Teach for America hurts urban schools and students. *Phi Delta Kappan*, 76 (1), 21–34.

Darling-Hammond, L. (2000). Reforming teacher preparation and licensing: Debating the evidence. *Teachers College Record*, 102 (1), 28–56.

Darling-Hammond, L., Chung, R., & Frelow, F. (2002). Variation in teacher preparation: How well do different pathways prepare teachers to teach? *Journal of Teacher Education*, 53 (4), 286–302.

Darling-Hammond, L., Holtzman, D., Gatlin, S., & Heilig, J. (2005). Does teacher preparation matter? Evidence about teacher certification, Teach for America, and teacher effectiveness. *Education Policy Analysis Archives*, 13 (42). Retrieved January 11, 2009, from http://epaa.asu.edu/epaa/v13n42.

Decker, P. T., Mayer, D. P., & Glazerman, S. (2004). *The effect of Teach for America on students: Findings from a national evaluation.* Princeton, NJ: Mathematica Policy Research.

Dillon, S. (2008, May 14). Teach for America sees surge in popularity. *The New York Times*, p. A18.

Feistritzer, C. E. & Chester, D. T. (2003). *Alternative teacher certification: A state-by-state analysis, 2003.* Washington, DC: National Center for Education Information.

Feistritzer, C. E. (2005). *Profile of alternate route teachers, 2005.* Washington, DC: National Center for Educational Information. Retrieved from http://www.ncei.com/PART.pdf.

Glass, G. (2008). East Lansing, MI: The Great Lakes Center for Educational Research & Practice. *Alternative sources of teachers*, Retrieved January 10, 2008, from http://epicpolicy.org/publication-/alternative-certification-of-teachers.

Glazerman, S., Mayer, D. & Decker, P. (2006). Alternative routes to teaching: The impacts of Teach for America on student achievement and other outcomes. *Journal of Policy Analysis and Management*, 25 (1), 75–96.

Haycock, K. (2004). Thinking K-16. *Education Trust*, 8 (1), 1–36.

Kane, T., Rockoff, J., & Staiger, R. (2008). What does certification tell us about teacher effectiveness? *Economics of Education Review*, 27 (6), 615–631.

Kane Parsons & Associates (2005). "A survey of principals in schools with Teach for America corps

members."
Keller, B. (2007). NCLB rules on "quality" fall short: Teacher mandate even disappoints supporters. *Education Week,* 26 (37), 1, 16.
Kopp, W. (2008). Building the movement to end educational inequity. *Phi Delta Kappan,* pp. 734–738.
Laczko-Kerr, I. & Berliner, D. (2002). The effectiveness of "Teach for America" and other under-certified teachers on student academic achievement: A case of harmful public policy. *Education Policy Analysis Archives,* 10 (37). Retrieved January 11, 2009, from http://epaa.adu.edu/epaa/v10n37.
Legler, R. (2002). *Alternative certification: A review of theory and research.* Washington, DC: North Central Regional Educational Library. Retrieved March 23, 2010, from http://www.ncrel.org/policy/pubs/html/altcert/.
Mathematica Policy Research. (2009). *An Evaluation of Teachers Trained Through Different Routes to Certification.* Washington, DC: National Center for Education Evaluation and Regional Assistance, Institute of Education Sciences, U.S. Department of Education.
Ness, M. (2004). *Lessons to learn: Voices from the front lines of Teach for America.* New York: Routledge.
Olson, L. (2007). TFA Teams with districts to groom aspiring principals. *Education Week,* 27 (6).
Podgursky, M. (2006, Spring). Is there a "qualified teacher" shortage? *Education Next,* pp. 27–32.
Policy Study Associates. (2007). Teach for America 2007 National Principal Survey.
Popkewitz, T. (1998). *Struggling for the soul: The politics of schooling and the construction of the teacher.* New York: Teachers College Press.
Raymond, M. & Fletcher, S. (2002). The Teach for America evaluation. *Education Next. 2,* 62–68.
Raymond, M., Fletcher, S., & Luque, J. (2001). Teach for America: An evaluation of teacher differences and student outcomes in Houston, Texas. Stanford, CA: The Hoover Institute, Center for Research on Educational Outcomes.
Teach for America. (2009). *Teach for America.* Retrieved from www.teachforamerica.org
The New Teacher Project. (2009). *The New Teacher Project* Retrieved from http://www.tntp.org.
Veltri, B.T. (2008). Teaching or service?: The site-based realities of Teach for America teachers in poor, urban schools. *Education and Urban Society,* 40 (5), pp. 511–542.
Wehligh, B. (2007). *Building a 21st century U.S. education system.* Washington, DC: National Commission on Teaching and America's Future (NCTAF). Retrieved January 7, 2009, from http://www.nctaf.org/resources/research_and_reports/nctaf_research_reports/Buildinga21stcenturyu.s.educationsystem.htm.
Xu, Z., Hannaway, J., & Taylor, C. (2008). Making a difference: The effects of Teach for America in high school. Report from the Urban Institute and CALDER.

CHAPTER THREE

Resisting the State

Christian Fundamentalism and A Beka

DINA C. OSBORN

SECULAR HUMANISM, THE GREAT ENEMY

The purpose of establishing fundamentalist Christian schools, and the curricula that support them, has historically been to procure a safe haven for children from the secularization of public schools (Peshkin, 1986). The popular Christian Right theologian Francis Schaeffer, author of *A Christian Manifesto* claimed that secular humanism is the greatest threat to Christianity the world has ever known. He reportedly said

> Today we live in a humanist society. They control the schools. They control public television. They control the media in general....(Koepsell, n.d., n.p.)

Similarly, Geisler (1983) argues

> Secular humanism presents one of the greatest threats to the survival of Christianity in the world today. (pp. 7–8)

Secular humanism is viewed by Christian fundamentalists as a malevolent worldview that impacts society, particularly the public education system in licentious ways.

Guinness (1983) defines secularization as "the process through which...sectors of society and culture have been freed from the decisive influence of religious ideas and institutions" (p. 51). Fundamentalists would agree but point to the idea that humanism is in itself a religion in that it shapes its followers' beliefs. The public schools, they argue, teach a form of religion called secular humanism, a by-product of the modernism that entered the United States beginning in the 1920s and has infiltrated the public schools. Brannon Howse, president and founder of Worldview Weekend Conferences and radio host argues

> Modern-day liberalism is in fact the *religion* of secular humanism, but no one screams "separation!" when liberal, humanistic curriculum is continually used in American schools and funded by U.S. taxpayers. (2005, p. 60)

Most Christian fundamentalists take a stance on separation of church and state that underscores their deep conviction on the immorally entrenched status of public schools. They view separation of church and state as a way of ensuring that government stays out of religious matters, not vice versa. Howse (2005) states, "Jefferson declared that a wall of separation between church and state should be maintained in order to keep the government from interfering with the free exercise of religion" (p. 36). He further notes, "The Federal government has no constitutional authority to tell the states what they can and cannot do when it comes to the free exercise of religion" (p. 38). This position typifies those who believe public schools should allow prayer and bible reading in the curriculum and exclude other topics that reflect a humanistic worldview, such as evolution, moral relativism and sex education.

In this chapter, I report on a study that sought to better understand the resistance of Christian fundamentalists to secular humanism through an analysis of A Beka history texts, a widely used curriculum in Christian schools. It has grown from use in 9,000 schools as of 1998 (Paterson, 2000b), to 10,000 schools most currently (Bartlett, 2006) The study is contextualized within the broader social and political milieu of the Christian Right regarding their perceptions on America's identity, the citizen's role in preserving that identity and conceptualizations of diversity. The analysis was conducted on approximately 1,775 pages of text for use in grades in kindergarten through six. When speaking of the same or closely related group, the following terms will be used to identify its constituents: Christian fundamentalists, the Christian Right, and conservative Christian.

Conservative Christian movements in education have been the subject of inquiry and critique by critical theorist Michael Apple (1995, 2006). Additionally, the works of Peshkin (1986) and Rand (2003) are ethnographies of the Christian school subculture regarding the integration of faith and learning and conservative views on literature. Other ethnographic studies of conservative Christian school cultures and textual analyses have been done by Paterson (2003), Menendez (1993), Parsons (1987), Flemming and Hunt (1987), and Rose (1990). These studies reveal, in essence, that the infrastructure of the conservative Christian school subculture exists and operates within a separatist ideology. Apple (1995, 2001) refers to this as an elitist reputation that characterizes the Christian Right.

In the interests of U.S. democracy, it is important that we more closely examine the views and attitudes expressed in texts that may contribute to a mindset of elitism and intolerance to diversity. Moreover, it is increasingly significant to do so with a critical lens, deconstructing the discourse in order to promote awareness on issues related to social inequalities, the reification of dominant paradigms, and the existence of cultural reproduction in textbooks.

Preservation as Resistance

Schooling in the United States has historically been an attempt to dominate and "civilize" certain groups of people, particularly those seen as deviating from the idealized White Anglo-Saxon Protestant norm. Michael Apple (1995) suggests that in contemporary society, schools continue to be sites of the attempted transmission of cultural values through a complex system of policies, practices, and curricula. Related to this, Apple (2001) further suggests that assumptions of cultural superiority consist of ignoring groups that compose the American population and focusing on small groups seen as archetypes of "tradition" for everyone. Alongside other traditionalists, it is apropos as to whether Christian fundamentalists should be considered in this category in light of their viewpoints on American history and diversity.

In the United States, fundamentalist school curriculum is crafted in resistance to what is viewed as the dominant, secular ideology and in light of the strong conviction that America has turned away from God (Parsons, 1987; Thiessen, 1993). The firm belief that turning away from a providential, God-centered past has caused the moral and economic decline of America has led the Right to reconcile this failing through the creation of fundamentalist educational programs and broader political coalitions that impact educational policy. Apple (2001) has affirmed that in the United States, the Christian Right appeals to a kind of lost innocence in which the nation's educational institutions have turned away from the fundamentalist principles upon which the nation was founded. He argues that one of the driving ideologies of the Christian Right includes a belief that the public schools have abandoned their heritage of a common and classical education in favor of liberalism and social engineering. He sees the pining for an edenic past and the restoration of a traditional common culture as a major focus of today's Christian community.

Indeed, the quest to preserve culturally elite ideals is not a new one. The notion that a just society may be established and sustained by an educational program has appeared many times in the history of thought, including Plato's *Republic* and

Comenius' *Great Didactic* (Reitman, 1992). Avenues of preservation have often taken the route of cultural domination of the less fortunate creating diversity-unity tensions. The Common School Movement of the 1830s and 1840s was a prime example of the cultural domination and oppression of certain groups that created racial tension and cultural wars (Spring, 2001). Feelings of cultural superiority fueled the attempts of English descendants to sustain a united society. Themes of cultural dominance and oppression in the history of the Common School Movement can be seen in specific cases (Spring, 2001).

During the Common School Movement, preservation of the White Anglo-Saxon Protestant ideal was achieved through the educational system that essentially functioned as a tool for Americanizing all groups of people in the United States, including British children. The *Blue Back Speller* by Noah Webster first published in 1783 was an effort to transition British English to a uniquely American English. The first Secretary of State, Horace Mann, believed America was divinely favored and destined for greatness (Gutek, 2001). Mann campaigned for a non-sectarian school system, arguing for a "common school" where children of all races and class attended. Cremin (1964) notes it was the duty of schools to assimilate the incoming immigrants to become part of the "American race."

There exists a similarity between early school reformers and that of contemporary Christian educators in the rationale that curricula can serve as a powerful tool in the reproduction of cultural ideology. In A Beka, the effort to preserve "eden" is channeled through the transmission of a conflated value system in these texts. As noted

> The intertwining of language and politics is readily seen in learning materials consisting of not only dialogue and oral language but written texts and manuals as well. (Wodak and Meyer, 2001)

THE A BEKA CURRICULUM

In distinctive fundamentalist manner, the A Beka social studies curriculum is presented to children in an integrative style of faith and learning. It describes history as a spiritual narrative in linear fashion beginning from America's pristine spiritual condition at its birth, its fall in the mid-20th century on account of secularization, to the current day struggle to restore America to its former condition (Osborn, 2006). Inherent in this struggle is resistance of influences of secular humanism in the lives of students. The narrative unfolds within the context of Englishmen who came to America primarily for the establishment of religious freedom. The linguistic descriptions of America are of a place of divine destiny, a redeemer nation with a God-given purpose to fulfill. Its people, as well, were to be separated, in a spiritual sense unto God for the fulfillment of the nation's destiny—to be a nation under God, a "City on a Hill" and a beacon of Protestant ideals. The founders of the United States believed their destiny to be the achievement of a Republic primarily composed of White Anglo-Saxon Protestant values. Moreover, the texts suggest that the very identity of this land and its people became part of what is called the "Christian heritage" of America, an identity that has become threatened by secular humanism. This providential argument sets up the foundation for subsequent positions regarding the United States as a Christian nation and the political obligations of its citizens.

The texts note with repetition that English colonists were victims of the Anglican Church, and their victimization therefore justified their need to establish a Christian nation. Related to this, A Beka makes references to the divine purpose for which America is called and how God's hand was upon America's discovery and struggle for freedom from British domination. Attention is called to the religiosity of Christopher Columbus and portrayed in this manner: "Christopher Columbus prayed to God" (Moore, 1997, p. 3) and "Columbus thanked God for finding land" (Moore, 1997, p. 12). Implicit within the literature is the idea that Columbus, a devout Christian, became a God-entrusted instrument for the purpose of creating a religious haven for those fleeing persecution—again, a basis for the Christian nation argument.

The additional references in the texts often conflate history and scripture in a developing pattern. The scriptural reference from Psalm 33:12 "Blessed is the nation whose God is the Lord" (NIV) is used repeatedly to support the claim that there exists a union between nation and religion. It is further presented that the greatness and fortitude of a nation or government is based on its dependence on God. When taken within the context of the writings, the following implications can be taken from the references: (1) God blesses countries that follow the Bible and punishes countries that don't; (2) countries or governments that do not believe in certain "Christian" values fail; (3) those who forget God lack good judgment in government matters (Osborn, 2006). A Beka texts are based on the premise that resistance to secularism unleashes the favor of God and consequently the security and prosperity of the nation.

The struggle against secular humanism and the preservation of America's heritage also presented in light of the duties of good citizenship. A Beka maintains that it is the Christian's duty to be actively involved in Republican politics in order to support the traditional values that are a part of America's founding. These passages are taken from the grade six text: "Christians became politically active in 1980 as Reagan took office," "Reagan helped America return to traditional and family values before America became washed away by immorality," "Reagan believed America was meant to be 'a city on a hill,'" and "Reagan appointed three conservative justices to the Supreme Court. Conservative justices interpret the Supreme Court more in line with the traditional values of our founding fathers" (Hicks and Moore, 1992, pp. 395–396).

A Beka generally traces the rise of secularism to the 1920s humanistic movement, the Enlightenment: "Humanism and Modernism have caused great harm to every nation," "England's decline during the 20th century was a result of humanistic thought," "Modernism is the result of a humanistic movement in the 1900s called the Enlightenment" (Hicks, 1999, p. 277). However, Christian fundamentalist believe that the decline of America's spiritual condition has occurred in light of the shift from America's conservative Christian identity to its secularization which began in the 1950s. During this era, these Christians felt especially victimized by the Supreme Court decisions to include evolution in the curriculum and to take prayer and Bible reading out of schools; thus, the ensuing struggle marked a reaction to save the figurative eden via the emergence of fundamentalist schools and curricula. The early separatist values of the Common School era increasingly manifested themselves within the rise of the Christian School Movement which rose to its height in the 1980s. A Beka describes the movement as a necessary action of resistance taken by those who felt they had no choice but to protect their children from the secularization of public schools.

> The Christian School Movement saw tremendous growth in the 1960s and 1970s because of the Supreme Court's decision to ban prayer….Many parents enrolled their children in Christian schools in the 1960s and 1970s. (Hicks and Moore, 1992, p. 392)

MERITOCRACY AND THE LIBERAL AGENDA

The connection to resistance also presents itself in A Beka's position on the Protestant work ethic, essentially represented as a virtuous principle embraced by the early settlers and to be emulated by all Americans (Osborn, 2006). This is explicitly stated in passages about colonial history, the American dream, capitalism and the free enterprise system. The texts support the idea that those nations which abide by the work ethic achieve wealth and prosperity. Conversely, the perceived demise of America's prosperity is attributed to welfare, a by-product of the liberal policies of the Democratic Party which substitute welfare for hard work. A Beka texts define the terms, liberal and democrat:

> A liberal is a person who believes government should provide for people's everyday needs. Democrats promise people prosperity without hard work. (Hicks and Moore, 1992, p. 391)

A Beka texts generally attribute America's spiritual decline to the secularization inherent in the economic policies of the Democratic Party. The inference that Democrats are in opposition to the Christian work ethic indicates a sense of disruption to God's plan for America. The association to the Democratic Party and welfare is made further, as is the anti-Democrat sentiment,

> The government is not responsible for individual success or failure. In America, everyone is responsible for his/her own success or failure. (Hicks and Moore, 1992, p. 389) By the 1960s, *some* politicians said the government should provide food and shelter for large number of people. (Hicks and Moore, 1992, p. 390, emphasis added)The responsibility of earning money lies with individuals, not the state. (Hicks, 1999, p. 278)

Additionally, A Beka texts view welfare as causing a number of problems economically including the weakening of the American family, debt, and irresponsibility in people (Hicks, 1999, p. 320). The texts continue to impugn the liberal agenda

> Welfare and Democrats take away self-respect, initiative and civil liberties…Welfare causes higher taxes from hard working citizens…Welfare causes recession…Welfare hinders private business (Hicks and Moore, 1992, p. 390)

A Beka additionally makes the implication that welfare is a result of the loss of biblical standards. "England became a welfare state because people lost their respect for the Bible" (Hicks, 1999, p. 278). Likewise, it affirms that Christians should not believe in social reform programs such as welfare or support a Democratic agenda because these represent a humanistic position. The texts portray Democrats as associated with either socialism or communism. The sixth grade text states explicitly that welfare and Democratic politicians echo the words and leaders of communism (Osborn, 2006). Likewise, it is stated, "Scandinavia's socialism and welfare have caused many problems there" (Hicks, 1999, p. 320).

In contrast, the Republican Party is lauded as having the values necessary in turning America back to God. Specifically, Ronald Reagan, the popular Republican president, is credited with standing for the spiritual restoration of America. As examples:

> Reagan confronted liberalism by cutting welfare and restoring individual financial decisions. (Hicks and Moore, 1992, p. 396)

> Ronald Reagan wanted to return America to her traditional Christian values. (Moore, 1998, p. 302) Traditional values include church, family and free enterprise became known as the Reagan Revolution. (Hicks and Moore, 1992, p. 395)

> President Reagan returned America to her traditional Christian values. (Hicks and Moore, 1992, p. 395) The Supreme Court, under Reagan, began to interpret the United States Constitution more in line with the traditional values of the Founding Fathers. (Moore, 1998, p. 303) Reagan's attempt to restore America became known as the Reagan Revolution. (Moore, 1998, p. 302)

Reagan's successor, George Bush is likewise recognized as being great because of his similar stance on traditional values, and the association is further made between Christianity and private ownership: "Margaret Thatcher restored England's Christian heritage by promoting private ownership of property" (Hicks, 1999, p. 278).

IMPLICATIONS

Some may question whether the values transmitted in the A Beka curriculum contribute to diversity tensions within American society. The creation of a citizenry that may be inclined to anti-Catholic or partisan bias because of its exposure to A Beka is certainly of concern in this regard (Paterson, 2000b). It is commonly the case that partisan bias that drives political affiliation in some neoconservative circles is the result of positions on single issues. The prolific use of A Beka texts indicates a strong fundamentalist position in the United States that remains an expression of tensions among neoconservatives and liberals that often occur within school literature. As Wodak and Meyer (2001) assert

> Texts are often sites of struggle in that they show traces of differing discourses and ideologies contending and struggling for dominance. (p. 11)

From a critical theoretical perspective, because of the connections between power and language, and power and ideology, only when discourse is examined and sociocultural power relationships unveiled can the oppressed be made aware of their situations and the power of the dominant be interrupted (Biesta, 1998). It is the aim of critical pedagogy to transform schools in ways that illuminate hidden meanings, promote awareness of inequities and give students opportunities to question language. Giroux (1994) argues

> [Critical] pedagogy...signals how questions of audience, voice, power, and evaluation actively work to construct particular relations between teachers and students, institutions and society, and classrooms and communities....Pedagogy in the critical sense illuminates the relationship among knowledge, authority, and power. (p. 30)

Of great concern, students immersed in this literature may not be given opportunities to decontextualize information needed to make relevant applications to society. Regardless of sectarian perspectives, children should be provided with opportunities to make critical judgments rather than handed strands of perceived truths. Certainly, to teach within the parameters of a given faith is the right of every private school, but ideological spoon feeding flies in the face of sound pedagogical practice. Speck and Prideaux (1993) comment on the low-level cognitive tasks that emphasize simple association and recall activities of ACE texts, a similar group of fundamentalist texts, and that despite the reviling of B. F. Skinner by the Christian Right, the materials make heavy use of programmed learning, and rewards (Hunter, 1987, cited in Speck and Prideaux, 1993).

It is not the teaching of religious beliefs that may be most alarming but rather the conflation of those beliefs in an environment that stifles critical questioning and evaluation of the texts. Ira Shor (1992) defines critical pedagogy as such

> habits of thought, reading, writing, and speaking which go beneath surface meaning, first impressions, dominant myths, official pronouncements, traditional clichés, received wisdom, and mere opinions, to understand the deep meaning, root causes, social context, ideology, and personal consequences of any action, event, object, process, organization, experience, text, subject matter, policy, mass media, or discourse. (p. 129)

In addition, what is excluded in texts is equally as disconcerting since exclusion can be a powerful mechanism for marginalization. The omission of viewpoints other than those which align with fundamentalist Christianity creates a monovocal narrative to history in these settings. The absence of multiple perspectives suggests room for a marginalizing and deprecating view of others. For example, A Beka texts cover the conservative Supreme Court justice Clarence Thomas in detail while excluding the first African American justice, Thurgood Marshall (Moore 1998). Paterson (2000a) supports the following theme in her findings:

> Inclusion and exclusion of individuals and groups—that is, conservatives are cited and quoted with approval, while liberals are given less coverage, omitted, or treated in a critical fashion.

Because schools are avenues of power for the dominant, socially constructed and accepted truths reflecting a dominant ideology are ultimately reified in curriculum choices as these begin to be viewed as neutral and natural (see Apple, 1995; Darder, 1991; Giroux, 1981; Kanpol, 1999; McLaren, 1998). It is reasonable to question whether hegemonic devices are at play in texts that act out a representation of the consensual dominance of students who are indoctrinated within the culture of the Christian Right.

Conclusion

Critical theorists share a concern that the transmission of knowledge often presents "neutral" fact that is, in reality, charged with political ideologies that support current dominant cultural positions. The A Beka history texts serve as concrete examples of the ways in which such processes are played out in Christian schools in the

United States. Positions taken in the texts are formed in resistance to secular ideology and contribute to political and cultural tensions in the United States. A Beka is deeply entrenched in political dialogue which denigrates Democrats and other groups who differ from Christian fundamentalist ideology. In particular, the writings connect biblical texts with resistance to diversity to create a curriculum steeped in the political values of the Christian Right.

In *Education for Critical Consciousness*, Freire (2005) discusses the importance of raising awareness in order to see oppression in one's life, the ability to view the world from a detached perspective, and to develop a critical consciousness. Implications for teachers involve a conscious effort to build illuminating practices in an effort to raise awareness of power relationships. Given their concerns for their own perceived oppression in contemporary society, it is within the realm of critical consciousness that both the writers and readers of A Beka can set their sights for progress. And in doing so, they may even liberate themselves.

REFERENCES

Apple, M. (1995). *Education and power* (2nd ed). New York: Routledge.

Apple, M. (2001). *Educating the "right" way: Markets, standards, God, and inequality*. New York & London: RoutledgeFalmer.

Apple, M. (2006). *Educating the "right" way: Markets, standards, God, and inequality*, (2nd ed). New York & London: RoutledgeFalmer.

Bartlett, T. (2006, March 24). A college that's strictly different: Secretive Pensacola Christian controls student life with tough regulations and unwritten rules. *The Chronicle of Higher Education*. Retrieved April 10, 2009, from https://netfiles.uiuc.edu/hschein/www/readings/Pensacola Christian.htm.

Biesta, G. J. J. (1998). Say you want a revolution…Suggestions for the impossible future of critical pedagogy. *Educational Theory*, 48 (4), pp. 499–510.

Cremin, L. (1964). *The transformation of the school*. New York: Vintage Press.

Darder, A. (1991). *Culture and power in the classroom: A critical foundation for bicultural education*. Westport, CT: Bergin & Garvey.

Flemming, D. and Hunt, T. (1987).The World as seen by students in accelerated Christian education, *Phi Delta Kappan*, 68, pp. 518–523.

Freire, P. (2005) *Education for critical consciousness*. New York: Continuum International Publishing Group.

Geisler, Norman L. (1983). *Is Man the measure?* Grand Rapids, MI: Baker Book House, pp. 7–8.

Giroux, H. (1981). *Ideology, culture and the process of schooling*. Philadelphia, PA: Temple University Press.

Giroux, H. A. (1994). *Disturbing pleasures: Learning popular culture*. New York: Routledge.

Guinness, O. (1983). *The gravedigger file: Papers on the subversion of the modern church period*. Downers Grove, IL: InterVarsity Press.

Gutek, G. A., (2001). *Historical and philosophical foundations of education: A biographical introduction*, Upper Saddle River, NJ.: Merrill Prentice Hall.

Hicks, L. E. and Moore J. H. (1992). *New world history and geography*. Pensacola, FL: Pensacola

Christian College. [A Beka, *New World History and Geography in Christian Perspective, Grade 6*]

Hicks, L. E. (1999). *Our world: History and geography in Christian perspective.* Pensacola, FL: Pensacola Christian College. [A Beka, *Old World History & Geography in Christian Perspective, Grade 5*]

Howse, B. (2005). *One nation under man? The worldview war between Christians and the secular left.* Nashville, TN: Broadman & Holman Publishers.

Hunter, R. (1987). *Accelerated Christian Education, Inc.: Marching to a different drummer.* Brisbane, Queensland: Brisbane College of Advanced Education, Mt. Gravatt Campus.

Kanpol, B. (1999). *Critical pedagogy: An introduction,* (2nd ed). Westport, CT: Bergin & Garvey.

Koepsell, David R. (n.d.) On the frontlines of the Culture War. *Secular Humanist Bulletin, volume 20, Number 2.* Retrieved from http://www.secularhumanism.org/index.php?page=koepsell_20_2&section=library

McLaren, P. (1998). *Life in schools: An introduction to critical pedagogy in the foundations of education* (3rd ed). New York: Longman.

Menendez, A. J. (1993). *Visions of reality: What fundamentalist schools teach.* Buffalo, NY: Prometheus Books.

Moore, J. H. (1997). *Our American heritage* (3rd ed.). Pensacola, FL: Pensacola Christian College. [A Beka, *Our American heritage, grade 3*]

Moore, J. H. (1998). *The History of our United States,* (3rd. ed.). Pensacola, FL: Pensacola Christian College. [A Beka, *The history of our United States, Grade 4*]

Osborn, D. C. (2006). Resisting "secular humanism": A critical analysis of the A Beka history curriculum, grades K-6. *Unpublished doctoral dissertation,* University of Connecticut, Storrs, CT.

Parsons, P. F. (1987). *Inside America's Christian schools.* Macon, GA: Mercer University Press.

Paterson, F. (2000a). Building a conservative base: Teaching history and civics in voucher supported schools. *Phi Delta Kappan, 82* (2), pp. 150–155.

Paterson, F. (2000b). Teaching intolerance: Anti-Catholic bias in voucher-supported schools. *The Educational Forum, 64,* 139–149.

Paterson, F. (2003). *Democracy and intolerance: Christian school curriculum, school choice, and public policy.* Bloomington, IN: Phi Delta Kappan Educational Foundation.

Peshkin, A. (1986). *God's choice: The total world of a fundamentalist Christian school.* Chicago: The University of Chicago Press.

Rand, L. (2003). Reading as a site of spiritual struggle. In M. Helmers, (ed.), *Intertexts: Reading pedagogy in college writing classrooms* (pp. 51–68). Mahwah, NJ: Lawrence Erlbaum Associates.

Reitman, S. W. (1992). *The educational Messiah Complex: American faith in the culturally redemptive power of schooling.* Sacramento, CA: Caddo Gap Press.

Rose, S. D. (1990). *Keeping them out of the hands of Satan: Evangelical schooling in America.* New York: Routledge.

Shor, I. (1992) *Empowering education: Critical teaching for social change.* Chicago: University of Chicago Press.

Speck, C., & Prideaux, D. (1993). Fundamentalist education and creation science. *Australian Journal of Education, 37,* 279–295.

Spring, J. (2001). *The American school: 1642–2000.* New York: McGraw-Hill.

Thiessen, E. J. (1993). *Teaching for commitment: Liberal education, indoctrination, and Christian nurture.* Montreal, Canada: McGill-Queen's University Press.

Wodak, R. & Meyer, R. (Eds.). (2001). *Methods of critical discourse analysis.* London: Sage.

CHAPTER FOUR

Critical Pedagogy in the Foreign Language Education Context

Teaching Esperanto as a Subversive Activity

TIMOTHY REAGAN

A number of language educators are growing increasingly dissatisfied with the status quo of our profession. The thrust of the "standards movement" does not resonate with them as advancing the cause of language education. Instead, it feels as though language curricula are being "sterilized" and packaged in a way that eliminates much of the creativity and passion that led many of us into this field in the first place. To be sure, nothing in the language standards, including the much heralded "five C's" of foreign language circles, precludes creativity. The impression may stem from a remarkably stark contrast between the direction of curricula and the context in which language education takes place in the United States. To be frank, static curricula are poor shadows when compared to the growing vibrancy of linguistic diversity, which is enriching communities...with increasing frequency. (Osborn, 2006, p. 1)

Critical pedagogy emerged in the 1970s and 1980s in the work of a number of educational scholars as both a theoretical framework for understanding what takes place in schools and, more importantly, as a political and ideological effort to challenge what takes place in schools. Grounded in the writings of Paulo Freire (1970, 2005), and extrapolated in the works of such individuals as Henry Giroux (1981, 1983, 1988), Aronowitz and Giroux (1985), Giroux and McLaren (1986), Giroux and Simon (1988), Peter McLaren (1986, 1987, 1988a, 1988b, 1988c), Joe Kincheloe (2008), Joan Wink (2005), Michael Apple (1982, 1986), and others, critical pedagogy sought to offer a more positive and optimistic view of education than that of earlier reproduction theories (Luke, 1992, p. 26). Essentially, as Carmen Luke has explained,

> Critical pedagogy's positive thesis is based on the assumption that if the "text" and experience of schooling are changed (i.e., elimination of racism, sexism, classism), then students' lives and, hence, civil society will be changed for the better. That is, if students are given (equal) opportunity to articulate their cultural experiences, and if teachers help students discover how they self-construct cultural meanings and identities within and against the ideological frameworks of mass culture, institutional settings, and discourses—then students will have the critical tools with which to act in morally responsible, socially just, and politically conscientious ways against individual and collective oppression. In this view, critical self-determination will lead to a democratic transformation of schooling and society. (1992, pp. 26–27)

Basically, then, critical pedagogy is about empowering both teachers and students, and is therefore not in any way subject-specific in its goals or nature. In spite of this, though, some subject areas have been far more influenced by both the general literature about critical pedagogy and in terms of subject-specific literature. In the case of second language education, there has been an interesting dichotomy with respect to the role played by critical pedagogy. In the areas of bilingual education and the teaching of English as a foreign language overseas, a substantial body of critical literature has developed. This is perhaps understandable, since in these two contexts issues of domination, oppression, and imperialism are fairly obvious. At the same time, foreign language educators in the United States have remained largely, though by no means completely (Alred, Byram and Fleming, 2006; Byram, 1989; Guilherme, 2002; Kumaravadivelu, 2003, 2007; Norton and Toohey, 2004; Ortega, 1999; Osborn, 2000, 2002, 2006; Reagan, 2005, 2009; Reagan and Osborn, 2002), disconnected from discussions and debates about critical pedagogy.[1] As Lourdes Ortega has noted,

> The field of foreign language teaching [has failed] to recognize the fact that both societal attitudes towards languages and power struggles resulting from ownership of a language and culture by particular groups are inextricably embedded in the definition of goals for language education.…Foreign language education and the foreign language teaching profession need to be reconceptualized in light of socio-cultural, political, and professional forces that affect the realities and potentials of foreign language teaching communities. (1999, p. 243)

A large part of the problem has been that, unlike in other fields, the role of the teacher in the foreign language classroom is uniquely powerful. As Barbara Craig has explained,

> Traditionally, the [foreign/second language] teacher's role has been seen as that of an authoritative expert. This view is based on the conception of knowledge as a quantifiable intellec-

tual commodity. The teacher, as an expert in a field of inquiry or as an expert speaker of a language, has more of this knowledge than his or her students have. Because this knowledge has a separate existence outside of its knowers, it can be given, or taught, to the learners by the teacher-expert. (1995, p. 41)

In this chapter, I want to explore the potential role of the teaching of Esperanto in contributing to a more critical approach to foreign language education. The chapter will be organized into four parts: first, an overview of the history and nature of Esperanto itself; second, the use of Esperanto in raising language awareness in general in students; third, the use of Esperanto in raising, specifically, the critical language awareness of students; and fourth, the empirically demonstrated propaedeutic value of Esperanto in promoting further and additional language learning by students.

THE HISTORY AND NATURE OF ESPERANTO

Esperanto is not only an artificially constructed, planned language, but it is the only such language to have achieved much more than a modicum of success. In the U.S. context, foreign language educators have often tended to see Esperanto not merely as amusing, but also as something of a challenge and even an affront. This reaction is due to a number of factors, not the least of which is the "artificialness" of the language. More than this, foreign language educators have been puzzled about why one would choose to learn Esperanto instead of devoting the same time and energy to learning a natural language. The resistance to Esperanto, though, is based more on misinformation and misunderstanding than on any real, well-grounded objection (Fonseca-Greber and Reagan, 2008; Forster, 1982, 1987; Goodman, 1978).

Esperanto is a product of post-Enlightenment thought in a variety of ways. From the seventeenth century, there had been numerous efforts to construct artificial languages—initially, for primarily philosophical rather than linguistic purposes (advocated by no less a figure than René Descartes), and later, as attempts to resolve the social and political barriers created by linguistic diversity (Eco, 1994; Guerard, 1922; Janton, 1993 [1973, 1988], pp. 1–22; Knowlson, 1975). By the 19th century, this second sort of undertaking had become the norm, and by far the most successful of the artificial language projects had been Volapük. Volapük, in spite of its initial successes, failed to survive both its own complexity and the efforts to control its development by its creator, Fr. Johann Martin Schleyer (Golden, 1997; Guerard, 1922, pp. 96–106). Esperanto was created in the wake of the failure of Volapük by a young Polish Jewish ophthalmologist, Lazar Ludwik Zamenhof, in 1887—marked by the publication in Warsaw of a Russian-language pamphlet entitled *La lingvo internacia de Doktoro Esperanto* ("The International Language of

Dr. Hopeful"). Zamenhof had grown up in the town of Bialystok, in Russian-occupied eastern Poland. His childhood experiences in this multilingual, multicultural, multinational, multireligious, and deeply divided city led to his concern for the need to unify humanity (Boulton, 1960).

For Zamenhof, a successful common language for all humanity would have to meet three necessary conditions (Nuessel, 2000, pp. 31–32). Such a language would have to be very easy to learn; it would have to have a logical, simple, and regular structure; and there had to be rewards for individuals to learn the language (Janton, 1993 [1973, 1988], p. 26). The language that he created, originally called simply *la internacia lingvo* ("the international language"), was intended to meet all of these conditions. It is important to note here that Esperanto was never intended to replace any natural language; rather, the goal was for the language to function as a common second, or auxiliary, language for all people. Thus, bilingualism (in one's mother tongue and in Esperanto) would ensure that every human being would both maintain his or her own language and be able to communicate directly with every other human being. Additionally, because virtually everyone would use Esperanto as a second language, a kind of level playing field would be established, since no one would have the advantage in multilingual settings of using their own native language.

The language that Zamenhof created, although by no means succeeding in its broad objective of becoming a shared universal language, nevertheless survived and even, to some extent, thrived over the course of the 20th century—in spite of becoming a target for suspicion and even oppression in many societies (Lins, 1990; Piron, 1989; Sadler and Lins, 1972). Although estimates vary considerably (from tens of millions to the more common figure of 1,000,000) (Richardson, 1988, p. 18), and are exceptionally difficult to evaluate critically, at the start of the 21st century, there are very conservatively at least 120,000 fluent speakers of Esperanto in the world, and hundreds of thousands of others who have at least a passing knowledge of the language (Nuessel, 2000, p. 24); though Glendhill (2000, p. 10) provides an even lower estimate of 40,000 truly fluent speakers. In any event, what is clear is that Esperanto, compared to all other efforts to create artificial or planned languages, has been remarkably successful (Auld, 1988; Forster, 1982; Large, 1985; Okrent, 2006). As Janton has noted,

> "All theoretical argument is beside the point: Esperanto already works," affirmed the well-known linguist Antoine Meillet in 1928. Hundreds of thousands of Esperantists have proved him right. Anonymous students in night classes or scholars of work repute, together they have vitalized the movement through their dedication and idealism. Over the past century, the idea and project of a single idealistic individual, Lazar Ludwik Zamenhof, has extended across the continents as a multifaceted, pluralistic, but united diaspora, a harbinger of that world order of which Zamenhof dreamed. Unlike other planned languages, Esperanto emerged from its intellectual and social birthplace and established itself among

the modest but hardworking and thoughtful elements of society that have defended it obstinately and generously over the years. (Janton, 1993 [1973, 1988], p. 129)

Although it is indeed difficult, if not impossible, to estimate the number of speakers of Esperanto, it is considerably easier to observe its status and use in the contemporary world. As Richardson notes, "Taken worldwide, the Esperanto movement these days is a far-flung but close-knit network of mostly independent bodies. Local, national, and international organizations, as well as specialized societies, book and magazine publishers, and even a few special-interest groups work side-by-side to further the language and its usefulness. Among these disparate bodies there is considerable cooperation, but little hegemony: rarely does one group have any real authority over another" (1988, p. 45). The Esperanto movement is united in part by the *Universala Esperanto-Asocio* ("Universal Esperanto Association") as well as by various local and national organizations. There is a wide array of publications (books, journals, magazines, and newspapers) available in Esperanto, including both translated materials and original publications written in Esperanto (Sutton, 2008). There are annual World Esperanto Congresses, as well as a voluntary travel service, the *Delegita Servo* (actually, more of a system of local representatives), and specialty organizations representing religious groups, sports groups, cultural groups, and so on. In short, there is a well-established and effectively functioning international Esperanto speech community (although perhaps it may be more accurate to call it a "speech network"). Esperanto has also been the focus of a good deal of linguistic and interlinguistic research (Tonkin and Fettes, 1996; Wood, 1982), especially in the area of interlinguistics (Blanke, 2003, 2006; Dulicenko, 1988, 1989; Fettes, 2001, 2003a, 2003b; Fiedler, 2008; Jansen, 2007, 2008; Pool and Fettes, 1998; Schubert, 1989; Sikosek, 2006; Tonkin, 1997).

In terms of its structure, Esperanto is both, and simultaneously, remarkably simple and quite sophisticated (Hana, 1998; Jordan, 1992; Kalocsay, 1963 [1931]; Kalocsay and Waringhien, 1985; Moore, 1980). The core of Esperanto grammar is provided in Zamenhof's "Sixteen Rules," which provide a basic scaffolding for the language (Zamenhof, 1963 [1905]). In a nutshell, the grammar, orthography, and pronunciation of Esperanto are absolutely regular. All nouns in the singular end in *−o*, and all adjectives end in *−a*; the pluralism is formed by adding a *−j*. There is also an objective case for nouns and adjectives, using *−n*, so we have

libro	book, a book (e.g., *La bona libro estas sur la tablo*. "The good book is on the table.")
libron	book, a book (e.g., *Mi havas bonan libron*. "I have a good book.")
libroj	books (e.g., *La bonaj libroj estas sur la tablo*. "The good

	books are on the table.")
librojn	books (e.g., *Vi acetis du bonajn librojn.* "You bought two good books.")

Adverbs end in–*e* (*rapide* "quickly"). Finally, verbs are not conjugated by person and differentiate tense, mood, and so on, as follows:

Mi parolas	I speak, I am speaking
Mi parolis	I spoke, I was speaking
Mi parolos	I will speak
Mi parolus	I would speak
Parolu!	Speak!
Paroli	To speak

Although the "Sixteen Rules" are certainly basic to the language, they provide an incomplete description of the grammar of the language (Nuessel, 2000, p. 24), as Janton has explained, "Fundamental though they may be, these rules alone cannot describe the language adequately. Esperanto cannot be reduced to such a skeletal structure: like all living languages, it has its own complex autonomy. Accordingly, we must apply to it the same methods of investigation as we would use for any living language"(1993 [1973, 1988], p. 44). Perhaps without realizing it himself, Zamenhoff created a skeletal structure for Esperanto which allowed a complex set of morphological processes. Without going into unnecessary detail here, one of the more intriguing aspects of Esperanto is found in its use of affixes. By adding various prefixes and suffixes, a huge vocabulary can be created from a remarkably small lexical base. For instance, using the base word *patro* ("father"), one can construct

gepatroj	parents
patrino	mother
bopatro	father-in-law
bopatrino	mother-in-law
gebopatroj	in-laws
eksbopatro	ex-father-in-law
patraro	a group of fathers

gepatrao   a group of parents

Similarly, from the verb *lerni* ("to learn"), one can create *lernejo* ("school"), *lernulo* ("student"), and so on. Of course, English and many other languages employ the same fundamental process, but in Esperanto the process is fully and completely regularized.

In short, Esperanto constitutes both a relatively easy to learn language with which learners can have an initially positive language learning experience, as well as one that provides both a metalinguistic framework for understanding how language in general works and an exposure to a multilingual, multicultural, and multinational linguistic community.

ESPERANTO AND LANGUAGE AWARENESS

When educators talk about "language awareness," we are actually talking about two quite different things: language awareness *per se* and critical language awareness. The difference is a significant one. Although I will return shortly to the issue of critical language awareness, for now the following quote from Kumaravadivelu makes clear the potentially powerful role of such awareness in the foreign language classroom:

> Language awareness, general as well as critical, should form an integral part of language education as well as content education. Language awareness is essential for the realization of an individual's full potential and, through that, for the realization of a nation's democratic ideals. Fostering general and critical language awareness is one way of connecting the curricular agenda of a teaching program with the learning purpose of an individual learner, and both with contemporary sociopolitical order....While language awareness activities are commonly associated with the development of advanced skills in critical thinking, reading, and writing, they are useful for grammar learning and teaching as well. Clearly, language awareness facilitates the process of noticing or consciousness-raising on the part of the learners. It is then possible that such a process of noticing could activate the learners' intuitive heuristics, ultimately enhancing their state of readiness to internalize the grammatical system of their L2. (2003, p. 175)

Language awareness is a concept that gained increasing popularity in the language education professions in the 1980s and 1990s. The phrase language awareness has all of the characteristics of an educational slogan and thus has been elusive with respect to any clear definition of its exact meaning. However, one reasonable attempt at defining the concept was made by a number of educational linguists in the early 1990s, and their working definition for the concept, which still seems reasonable, was that language awareness involved, "a person's sensitivity to and conscious awareness of the nature of language and its role in human life" (James and Garrett,

1992, p. 8). In other words, one of the objectives for any liberal education ought to be a general awareness of and sensitivity to linguistic issues writ large. This is most clearly seen, perhaps, in the student's mastery of the metalanguage necessary to discuss any language, including his or her own. Such language awareness can be developed in the context of any foreign language course, to be sure, but for a variety of reasons, studying some languages is likely to be more effective than others. As Richardson has suggested with respect to Esperanto, "Then again, Esperanto's potential value to education could prove decisive. We have seen how teaching Esperanto in elementary and high-school classes results in better understanding of how languages work, promotes language skills generally, and can lead to more (and more effective) foreign-language study besides. Schools that cannot afford full-blown foreign language programs can afford to teach Esperanto, and with superior results in the long run" (1988, p. 62).

Among the arguments that can be offered for Esperanto in this context is that the learning of Esperanto has positive benefits for students' knowledge and understanding of their own language as well as of human language in general. The advantage offered by Esperanto with respect to raising students' language awareness is based on the language's absolute regularity. This regularity means that in the context of teaching and learning Esperanto matters of language awareness are especially natural and appropriate to raise in the classroom. As the instructor's materials for the British *Springboard…To Languages!* project explains, "Important aspects of the *Springboard* language awareness programme are discussing with pupils the similarities and differences that exist between languages, and encouraging a positive view of different cultures and lifestyles. The [programme] contain[s] possible activities for raising language awareness and language-links which may be used as a basis for discussing countries, cultures and languages" (Springboard to Languages, 200, p. 1).

Language awareness as laid out here is both desirable and appropriate as an educational goal, but, certainly from the perspective of critical pedagogy, it is also far from sufficient. This is where the concept of *critical* language awareness comes in, and it is to such critical language awareness that we now turn.

Esperanto and Critical Language Awareness

Critical language awareness, like critical pedagogy in general, is in the final analysis concerned with empowerment (Andrews, 2007; Fairclough, 1992, 1995, 2001; Wallace, 1997). Empowerment involves not only helping students to recognize, understand, and question discourse, but also, as Norman Fairclough has pointed out, it "has a substantial 'shock' potential, and it can help people overcome their sense of impotence by showing them that existing orders of discourse are not immutable.

The transformation of orders of discourse is a matter of the systemic destructuring of existing orders and restructuring of new orders" (2001, p. 202). An important facet of this process of empowerment is recognizing that discourse is in fact *negotiated* between and among students and teachers. In short, as Karabel and Halsey observed in the late 1970s, "Teachers and pupils do not come together in a historical vacuum: the weight of precedent conditions the outcome of 'negotiation' over meaning at every turn" (1977, p. 58).

There are, of course, many different ways in which critical language awareness might be developed in the foreign language curriculum. However, changes to the foreign language curriculum have been notoriously difficult to implement at the classroom level. One viable approach to introducing critical language awareness in the foreign language context is to do so via the initial teaching of Esperanto. The common arguments for introducing students to Esperanto prior to teaching them another language combine both practical arguments about language learning and concerns about raising student critical language awareness in general (Fantini and Reagan, 1992). Among the arguments that can be offered for Esperanto in this context are the following:

- Esperanto is easier, and faster to learn than are national/ethnic languages. This claim is most commonly manifested in comparisons of the learning time involved in acquiring competence in Esperanto with that needed for a national/ethnic language.
- The learning of Esperanto offers an effective way of countering ethnocentrism and encouraging an attitude of toleration of cultural and linguistic differences. An important theme in schooling in a growing number of societies, and especially in the United States, during the last two decades has been the concern with the promotion of multicultural education and the concomitant concern with reducing ethnocentrism. These concerns are intrinsic to the study of Esperanto as an international auxiliary language.
- The study of Esperanto helps students to become aware of issues of linguistic inequality and inequity, matters that are especially important for native speakers of English to understand.[2] In addition, the study of the history of Esperanto, and of the Esperanto Movado, raises a number of significant questions about language oppression and discrimination (Lins, 1980).
- The learning of Esperanto facilitates the development of a more global perspective, and provides access to an international cultural community. Especially common in this regard are claims related to the use of international correspondence, pen pals, travel, and so on.

Although issues of critical language awareness can be introduced and discussed in any foreign language classroom, in the context of teaching and learning Esperanto these matters are especially natural and appropriate.

There are additional arguments for using Esperanto to raise critical language awareness in the foreign language classroom as well. Perhaps the most powerful of these have to do with the nature of Esperanto itself and the criticisms that have been lodged against Esperanto. Consider, for instance, Ludwig Wittgenstein's comment about Esperanto: "Esperanto. The feeling of disgust we get if we utter an *invented* word with invented derivative syllables. The word is cold, lacking in associations, and yet it plays at being 'language.' A system of purely written signs would not disgust us so much" (Wittgenstein,[1946] 1980, p. 53). I find this quote fascinating not so much for what it says, as for the incredible emotional and psychological hostility from an individual best known for his commitment to reason and rationality.

Perhaps most common, though, in critiques of Esperanto is what I have elsewhere called the concept of 'linguistic legitimacy': that is, the idea that some languages (and in this context, especially Esperanto) are in some sense better or more "real" than others. Such a position, for linguists, is generally simply unacceptable—though in the case of Esperanto even many linguists seem to lose track of the argument. For instance, when I first raised the concept (using the cases of Esperanto, American Sign Language, and African American English as my examples) as one with which educators should be familiar and concerned, the philosopher of education Donald Vandenberg responded by arguing that

> I find it difficult to imagine any university students majoring in one of the liberal arts ever wanting to fulfill the foreign language requirement by studying Esperanto, ASL, or Black English. It is equally hard to imagine a university giving tertiary school credit for their study…liberal arts programs require foreign languages so that their graduates have access to the culture, i.e., scholarship, "high" culture, that is available in that language. This is not just a matter of words, as it gets to be if one just uses the word "culture" in that sentence. The scholarly reading that I have done with German sources simply cannot be done in Esperanto, ASL, or some dialect of English. They do not really have a "linguistic community" in the strong, robust sense of possessing a body of scholarly literature of their own, the kind to which learning the language can give access. (What is translated into Esperanto is parasitic, and in any case probably available in English.) (1998, pp. 83–84)

For our purposes here, I will ignore Vandenberg's comments about American Sign Language and African American English, though they are also dangerously misinformed, and focus only on his views of Esperanto.

Vandenberg's response involves claims of fact, and he is simply wrong about them. Students at many universities around the country, and around the world, do in fact choose to study Esperanto, and they often *do* receive university credit for doing so (for the case of Esperanto, see Fiedler, 2008; Janton, 1993 [1973], pp. 122–124).

There are a number of other factual errors in Vandenberg's response that can be addressed as well. He argues, for instance, that "there is no equivalent [to Goethe's *Hermann und Dorothea*] in Esperanto...." This is, of course, an aesthetic judgment, but it is not clear how Vandenberg was in a credible position to make such a judgment. If the way in which we distinguish languages worth studying from those not worth studying is to be by comparison to Goethe (an interesting point of departure, in my view: Why not Dante, Mencius, or the *Rg Veda*?), then surely we need to be knowledgeable about what literature is actually available in different languages. The fact that Vandenberg is not familiar with original Esperanto literature in no way means that it does not exist, nor does it address the very real aesthetic merits of such literature (Auld, 1988; Gregor, 1976; Janton, 1993 [1973], pp. 95–111; Richmond, 1993a, 1993b, 1993c; Sutton, 2008). Furthermore, Vandenberg's off-the-cuff dismissal of Esperanto literature as "parasitic" demonstrates yet another problem—one can almost hear the earlier 20th century objections to Esperanto by anti-Semites in such language. As for access to scholarly material, here too Vandenberg is simply not well informed. I have personally attended a number of academic conferences in which the language of scholarly discourse was Esperanto, and have heard papers on many complex and sophisticated academic topics in Esperanto—presentations that often would simply not be available in English. There are also scholarly and academic articles and books on a number of topics that, again, are not available in English. Last, Vandenberg's assertion that Esperanto "do[es] not have a 'linguistic community' in the strong, robust sense of possessing a body of scholarly literature of their own" actually conflates two quite different matters. The presence of a strong linguistic community that utilizes Esperanto, at least as such communities are defined by sociolinguists, is simply beyond any reasonable debate. The restriction or redefinition of such communities to those which possess a "body of scholarly literature" (and one in the western tradition, no less) is in fact something of a red herring in the context of this discussion. First, as I have already argued, such bodies of literature do exist for Esperanto. More significantly, though, if this criterion were to be employed as part of the definition of a "linguistic community" (something that no competent linguist, I think, would consider), then we would also rule out the vast majority of languages spoken around the world.

Vandenberg's response to the position that I have taken regarding the concept of "linguistic legitimacy" is about far more than language, I believe. I suspect that his real (although admittedly unarticulated) concern is with the opening up of academe in recent years to languages, literatures, and perspectives beyond those which have been historically acceptable. In short, his objective is a profoundly conservative one, grounded in a hierarchical view of culture, scholarship, and language that is tied, albeit implicitly, to issues of power and domination. In contrast to the view posited by Vandenberg, I would stress that discourses, as Michel Foucault has suggested, "are about what can be said and thought, but also about who can speak, when, and with what authority. Discourses embody meaning and social relationships; they constitute both subjectivity and power relations" (Ball, 1990, p. 2). What is fundamentally at issue, on Foucault's account, are both the systems by which discourse is controlled, and how discourse can be delimited (1970 [1966], 1972a [1969], 1972b, 1975, 1976, 1984a, 1984b, 1994a, 1994b, 2006 [1972]).

The point that I have tried to make and expand on here is simply that the notion of "linguistic legitimacy" (i.e., that it is possible to make value judgments and comparisons about the relative values of different languages) is in fact wrongheaded. The criteria that are generally employed to make such judgments are in fact irrelevant, and the very notion of an illegitimate language is simply not defensible on linguistic grounds. Finally, I would argue that where such distinctions and judgments are made, they are inevitably grounded in extra-linguistic factors and are tied to social, political, and ideological agendas. What is at stake here is social justice and the way in which we characterize and respond to the Other and to Otherness. It is just such issues that are at the heart and core of any concern for critical language awareness in the classroom.

THE PROPAEDEUTIC VALUE OF ESPERANTO

As an *a priori* language, Esperanto has the advantage of an absolutely regular structure, coupled with a morphological system that makes it, to some extent, an agglutinative language.[3] This, coupled with the fact that its core vocabulary is both relatively small and largely of Romance and Germanic derivation,[4] makes Esperanto easier to learn than natural languages (Fantini and Reagan, 1992). Thus, Esperanto has a number of propaedeutic advantages, among which are

- ~ Esperanto is easier, and faster to learn than are national/ethnic languages. This claim is most commonly manifested in comparisons of the learning time involved in acquiring competence in Esperanto with that needed for a national/ethnic language.
- ~ Esperanto can be taught more efficiently and explicitly than can national/ethnic languages. The basic idea here is that while national/ethnic languages are generally best taught inductively, this is not necessarily the case with Esperanto, and, further, that direct, explicit instruction will make both teaching and learning more efficient. The fundamental idea here is that because Esperanto strives to avoid the irregularities, inconsistencies, and complexities of national/ethnic languages (while at the same time preserving the fullest possible degree of linguistic expression), several

assumptions are commonly made about its learnability. Specifically, it is often argued by advocates of Esperanto that (a) Esperanto is more learnable (i.e., that any given level of proficiency can be achieved in Esperanto with less effort and in shorter time than with any national/ethnic language) and (b) that its superiority in terms of learnability is much greater than any inherent biases in its vocabulary or structure that would favor speakers of some languages (e.g., speakers of Indo-European languages) over others.
~ The learning of Esperanto has propaedeutic effects with respect to the learning of other languages, and perhaps even other subject matter. In other words, the learning of Esperanto will reduce the time needed for the learning of other language (and perhaps other subject matter, such as geography, mathematics, etc.). As an investment, in short, learning Esperanto may have significant benefits unrelated to the acquisition of the international language itself.
~ The learning of Esperanto has a positive effect on students' self-confidence. As a result of successful learning of Esperanto, students will feel more competent and empowered, and this will result in a higher level of self-confidence (which, in turn, can result in improved learning in other areas).
~ Learning Esperanto is especially appropriate for students with special needs (including both gifted/talented students and those with learning disabilities). Although different arguments are used, claims have been made that students at both extremes of the population may have greater interest in and success with Esperanto than with other types of subject matter (Quick, 1989; Wood, 1975).

In short, the regular structure of Esperanto and its ease of learnability make it an ideal choice for developing second language learning skills for students (Maxwell, 1988). Although all language learning is difficult, learning a language like Esperanto, especially as a first foreign language, can promote positive experiences with and attitudes toward additional language learning.

Conclusion

An essential component of the development of a meaningful critical pedagogy in foreign language education settings is the development of critical language awareness (Osborn, 2000; Reagan, 2005, 2009; Reagan and Osborn, 2002), coupled with meaningful success in foreign language learning. As Catherine Wallace has suggested,

> A critical pedagogy presupposes an approach to language education in which learners and teachers aim to achieve some critical distance from language use in a range of spoken and

written texts. Conversely, approaches under the broad umbrella of critical language awareness need to be located within a critical pedagogy if they are to have credibility as educational practice...Critical understanding can be understood at two broad levels: first, in the cognitive sense of "conscious awareness"; secondly...a deeper sense of "critical" as the ability and willingness to critique the ideological bases of language choice and variation. (1997, p. 241)

What I have attempted to argue here is that one potentially powerful way in which this might be achieved is through the teaching of Esperanto in the foreign language context. As Richardson has suggested,

Then again, Esperanto's potential value to education could prove decisive. We have seen how teaching Esperanto in elementary and high-school classes results in better understanding of how languages work, promotes language skills generally, and can lead to more (and more effective) foreign-language study besides. Schools that cannot afford full-blown foreign language programs can afford to teach Esperanto, and with superior results in the long run. (1988, p. 62)

Esperanto, then, could easily be the "nose of the camel in the tent" of foreign language education in our efforts to redirect such efforts to become more critical.

And how does critical foreign language education in general, and the teaching of Esperanto in particular, relate to the theme of this book—resistance in education? Basically, resistance theories in education are concerned with articulating the moral and political potentials of opposition to schooling as it is currently constructed both in American society and in other societies around the world (Abowitz, 2000; Hill and Rosskam, 2009). Resistance theory is thus concerned, ultimately, with challenging oppression: oppression as cultural hegemony, oppression as capitalist accumulation, and oppression as discursive effect (De Lissovoy, 2008). Oppression with respect to language in educational settings occurs in a number of ways, including the failure to recognize the language rights of minority children (Guillorel and Koubi, 1999; Kontra, Phillipson, Skutnabb-Kangas, and Váradt, 1999; May, 2005; Patrick, 2005; Phillipson, 2000; Skutnabb-Kangas, 2000; Skutnabb-Kangas and Phillipson, 1995), the denigration or denial of linguistic legitimacy to particular language varieties (Reagan, 1997), both in terms of the languages offered for study in U.S. public schools and in how those languages are taught (Reagan, 2005, 2009; Reagan and Osborn, 2002), and a host of other ways. The teaching of Esperanto does not solve these problems, of course, but it does provide a setting in which discussion of and teaching about all of these issues can take place (Fonseca-Greber and Reagan, 2008). Thus, what the inclusion of Esperanto really offers is the opportunity to assist students to become more aware of and critical about matters of language, including language oppression, both in the school and in society writ large.

It provides, in short, a potentially powerful challenge to linguistic hegemony, broadly conceived, in the school, and, ultimately, in society.

Notes

1. The phrase "foreign language" has been largely replaced in recent years by well-meaning educators and policy-makers who want to emphasize that many of the languages that we teach in U.S. schools are not really "foreign" at all. Spanish, for instance, is the native language of millions of U.S. citizens, and has been spoken in parts of the territory that now constitutes the United States for centuries—longer, in fact, than there has been a United States. Although I accept this point, I would maintain that when we teach such languages to English-speaking students, they are nevertheless "foreign" to the students themselves—a point that, in turn, has consequences when we talk about "foreign language education" requirements and the case of American Sign Language, for instance. Further, the currently used term for languages taught in our schools—"World Languages"—strikes me, to be honest, as downright silly. English is clearly a "World Language" (perhaps in some sense *the* "World Language"), but is obviously excluded from this category. French and Spanish are "World Languages," of course, but is Japanese? What about Navajo, which is taught as a second language in parts of the country? Esperanto, the focus of this chapter, might well be considered to be the model case of a "World Language," but I very much doubt that my colleagues in foreign language education had it in mind when they adopted the "World Language" label. So, with some hesitation, I am continuing to use the phrase "foreign language."
2. It is interesting to note, however, that in spite of the explicitly articulated concern with matters of linguistic inequality in the Esperanto movement, there is nonetheless a comparable phenomenon within the movement itself. As Jane Edwards has observed, "The fact is, that, given the nature of the Esperanto movement, excellent Esperanto is one of the modes of establishing oneself as a person of importance in the movement....In fact, generally speaking, the qualifications for leadership in the Esperanto movement are good Esperanto, a willingness to work for the propagation of the language, and to have no outward signs of being certifiably insane" (1993, p. 29).
3. The claim that Esperanto is basically an agglutinative language is argued by Wells (1989, pp. 33–34), though others have argued that this is at best an incomplete description. Gledhill, for instance, argues that Esperanto demonstrates a number of important non-agglutinating linguistic aspects, "including the freedom of word derivation and monomorphism that are reminiscent of isolating languages" (2000, p. 40).
4. In fact, the Esperanto lexicon includes words derived from Romance languages (especially French and Latin), Germanic languages (primarily German, Yiddish, and English), Balto-Slavic languages (especially Russian, Serbo-Croatian, and Polish, as well as Lithuanian), Greek, and finally, small numbers of lexical items from Hebrew, Arabic, Japanese, Chinese, and other languages (Gledhill, 2000, pp. 20–26; Janton, 1993 [1973, 1988], p. 46). Estimates of the distribution of the lexicon by source language vary somewhat, but it is reasonable to suggest that between 70% and 75% of the lexical items in Esperanto are Romance in origin, and 10% to 20% are Germanic in origin. For studies of the effect of Jewish languages (specifically, Yiddish and Hebrew) on Esperanto, see Gold (1980, 1982) and Piron (1984); for the effects of Russian on Esperanto, see Kolker (1988).

References

Abowitz, K. (2000). A pragmatist revisioning of resistance theory. *American Educational Research Journal,* 37, 877–907.

Alred, G., Byram, M., & Fleming, M. (Eds.). (2006). *Education for intercultural citizenship: Concepts and comparisons.* Clevedon, UK: Multilingual Matters.

Andrews, S. (2007). *Teacher language awareness.* Cambridge, UK: Cambridge University Press.

Apple, M. (1982). *Cultural and economic reproduction in education.* London: Routledge and Kegan Paul.

Apple, M. (1986). *Teachers and texts.* London: Routledge and Kegan Paul.

Aronowitz, S., & Giroux, H. (1985). *Education under siege.* South Hadley, MA: Bergin & Garvey.

Auld, W. (1988). *La fenomeno Esperanto* [The Esperanto phenomenon]. Rotterdam, Netherlands: Universala Esperanto-Asocio.

Ball, S. (Ed.). (1990). *Foucault and education: Disciplines and knowledge.* London: Routledge.

Blanke, D. (2003). *Interlinguistic und Esperantologie* [Interlinguistics and Esperantology]. (Esperanto-Dokumente 7). Bamberg, Germany: Deutscher Esperanto-Bund e.V., Geschäftsstelle.

Blanke, D. (2006). *Interlinguistische Beiträge: Zum Wesen und zur Funktion internationaler Plansprachen* [Interlinguistic contributions: On the creation and function of international planned languages]. Frankfurt am Main, Germany: Peter Lang.

Boulton, M. (1960). *Zamenhof: Creator of Esperanto.* London: Routledge & Kegan Paul.

Byram, M. (1989). *Cultural studies in foreign language education.* Clevedon, UK: Multilingual Matters.

Craig, B. (1995). Boundary discourse and the authority of language in the second language classroom: A social-constructivist approach. In J. Alatis, C. Straehle, B. Gallenberger, & M. Ronkin (Eds.), *Georgetown University round table on languages and linguistics 1995: Linguistics and the education of language teachers* (pp. 40–54). Washington, DC: Georgetown University Press.

De Lissovoy, N. (2008). Conceptualizing oppression in educational theory: Toward a compound standpoint. *Cultural Studies, Critical Methodologies,* 8, pp. 82–105.

Dulicenko, A. (1988). Projects of international and universal languages. *Interlinguistica Tartuensis,* 5, pp. 126–162.

Dulucenko, A. (1989). Interlinguistics: Essence and problems. *Interlinguistica Tartuensis,* 6, pp. 18–42.

Eco, U. (1994). *La sercado de la perfekta lingvo* [The search for the perfect language]. Pisa, Italy: Edistudio.

Edwards, J. (1993). Esperanto as an international research context. In I. Richmond (Ed.), *Aspects of internationalism: Language and culture* (pp. 21–34). Lanham, MD: University Press of America, in conjunction with the Center for Research and Documentation on World Language Problems.

Fairclough, N. (Ed.). (1992). *Critical language awareness.* London: Longman.

Fairclough, N. (1995). *Critical discourse analysis: The critical study of language.* London: Longman.

Fairclough, N. (2001). *Language and power* (2nd ed.). Harlow, Essex, UK: Longman.

Fantini, A., & Reagan, T. (1992). *Esperanto and education: Toward a research agenda.* Washiington, DC: Esperantic Studies Foundation.

Fettes, M. (2001). Les géostratégies de l'interlingualisme [The geostrategies of interlinguistics]. *Terminogramme,* 99/100, pp. 35–46.

Fettes, M. (2003a). The geostrategies of interlingualism. In J. Maurais & M. Morris (Eds.), *Languages in a globalising world* (pp. 37–46). Cambridge, UK: Cambridge University Press.

Fettes, M. (2003b). Interlingualism: A world-centric approach to language policy and planning. In H. Tonkin & T. Reagan (Eds.), *Language in the twenty-first century* (pp. 47–58). Amsterdam, Netherlands: John Benjamins.

Fiedler, S. (2008) Interlingvistiko/esperantologio kiel fako en universitatuj: Spertoj el Leipzig [Interlinguistics/Esperantologies as a specialty in universities: Experiences from Leipzig]. *Informilo por Interlingvistoj*, 65, pp. 2–25.
Fonseca-Greber, B., & Reagan, T. (2008). Developing K-16 student standards for language learning: A critical examination of the case of Esperanto. *Critical Inquiry in Language Studies*, 5, pp. 44–63.
Forster, P. (1982). *The Esperanto movement*. The Hague, Netherlands: Mouton.
Forster, P. (1987). Some social sources of resistance to Esperanto. In *Serta Gratvlatoria in Honorem Juan Régulo, II (Esperantismo)* (pp. 203–211). La Laguna, Spain: University de La Laguna.
Foucault, M. (1970). *The order of things: An archaeology of the human sciences*. New York: Vintage. Original publication in French 1966.
Foucault, M. (1972a). *The archaeology of knowledge and the discourse on language*. New York: Harper & Row. Original publication in French 1969.
Foucault, M. (1972b). *Naissance de la clinique* [Birth of thte clinic] (2nd ed. rev.) Paris: Presses Universitaires de France.
Foucault, M. (1975). *Surveiller et punir: Naissance de la prison* [To supervise and punish: Birth of the prison]. Paris: Gallimard.
Foucault, M. (1976). *Histoire de la sexualité I* [History of sexuality I]. Paris: Éditions Gallimard.
Foucault, M. (1984a). *Histoire de la sexualité II* [History of sexuality II]. Paris: Éditions Gallimard.
Foucault, M. (1984b). *Histoire de la sexualité III* [History of sexuality III]. Paris: Éditions Gallimard.
Foucault, M. (1994a). *Ethics: Subjectivity and truth*. New York: The New Press.
Foucault, M. (1994b). *Power*. New York: The New Press.
Foucault, M. (2006). *History of madness*. London: Routledge. Original publication in French 1972.
Freire, P. (1970). *Pedagogía del oprimido* [Pedagogy of the oppressed]. Buenos Aires, Argentina: Siglo Veintiuno Editores Argentina.
Freire, P. (2005). *Pedagogia da esperança* [Pedagogy of hope]. São Paulo, Brazil: Paz e Terra.
Giroux, H. (1981). *Ideology, culture, and the process of schooling*. Philadelphia, PA: Temple University Press.
Giroux, H. (1983). *Theory and resistance in education*. London: Heinemann.
Giroux, H. (1988). *Schooling and the struggle for public life*. Minneapolis, MN: University of Minnesota Press.
Giroux, H., & McLaren, P. (1986). Teacher education and the politics of engagement: The case for democratic schooling. *Harvard Education Review*, 56, pp. 213–227.
Giroux, H., & Simon, R. (1988). Critical pedagogy and the politics of popular culture. *Cultural Studies*, 2, pp. 294–320.
Glendhill, C. (2000). *The grammar of Esperanto: A corpus-based description* (2nd ed.). Muenchen, Germany: Lincoln Europa.
Gold, D. (1980). Towards a study of possible Yiddish and Hebrew influence on Esperanto. In I. Szerdahelyi (Ed.), *Miscellanea interlinguistica* (pp. 300–367). Budapest, Hungary: Tankönyvkiadó.
Gold, D. (1982). Pli pri judaj aspektoj de Esperanto [More on the Jewish aspects of Esperanto]. *Planlingvistiko*, 1, pp. 7–14.
Golden, B. (1997). Conservation of the heritage of Volapük. In H. Tonkin (Ed.), *Esperanto, interlinguistics, and planned languages* (pp. 183–189). Lanham, MD: University Press of America.
Goodman, T. (1978). Esperanto: Threat or ally? *Foreign Language Annals*, 11, pp. 201–203.
Gregor, D. (1976). Der kulturelle Welt des Esperanto [The cultural world of Esperanto]. In R. Haupenthal (Ed.), *Plansprachen* [Planned languages] (pp. 297–304). Darmstad, Germany: Wissenschaftliche Buchgesellschaft.
Guerard, A. (1922). *A short history of the international language movement*. London: T. F. Unwin.

Guilherme, M. (2002). *Critical citizens for an intercultural world: Foreign language education as cultural politics*. Clevedon, UK: Multilingual Matters.
Guillorel, H., & Koubi, G. (Eds.). (1999). *Langues du droit, droit des langues* [Languages of right, right of languages]. Brussells: Bruylant.
Hana, J. (1998). *Two-level morphology of Esperanto*. Unpublished M.A. thesis, Charles University, Prague, Czech Republic.
Hill, D., & Rosskam, E. (2009). *The developing world and state éducation: Neoliberal depredation and egalitarian alternatives*. New York: Routledge.
James, C., & Garrett, P. (1992). *Language awareness in the classroom*. London: Longman.
Jansen, W. (2007). *Woordvolgorde in het Esperanto* [Word-order in Esperanto]. Utrecht, Netherlands: Netherlands Graduate School of Linguistics.
Jansen, W. (2008). *Inleiding in de Interlinguïstiek* [Introduction to interlinguistics]. Amsterdam, Netherlands: Universiteit van Amsterdam.
Janton, P. (1993). *Esperanto: Language, literature, and community*. Edited by H. Tonkin, trans. by H. Tonkin, J. Edwards, & K. Weiner-Johnson. Albany: State University of New York. Original publication in French 1973; Esperanto version published in 1988.
Jordan, D. (1992). *Being colloquial in Esperanto: A reference guide for Americans*. Lanham, MD: University Press of America.
Kalocsay, K. (1963 [1931]). *Lingvo, stilo, formo* [Language, style, form]. Budapest, Hungary: Librejo Pirato.
Kalocsay, K., & Waringhien, G. (1985). *Plena analiza gramatiko de Esperanto* [Complete analytic grammar of Esperanto] (5a ed.). Rotterdam, Netherlands: Universala Esperanto-Asocio.
Karabel, J., & Halsey, A. (Eds.). (1977). *Power and ideology in education*. New York: Oxford University Press.
Kincheloe, J. (2008). *Critical pedagogy* (2nd ed.). New York: Peter Lang.
Knowlson, J. (1975). *Universal language schemes in England and France*, pp. 1600–1800. Toronto: University of Toronto Press.
Kolker, B. (1988). ????? ???????? ????? ? ??????? ????????? [The contribution of the Russian language to the lexicon of Esperanto]. *Interlinguistica Tartuensis*, 5, pp. 74–91.
Kontra, M., Phillipson, R., Skutnabb-Kangas, T., & Várady, T. (Eds.). (1999). *Language: A right and a resource*. Budapest: Central European University Press.
Kumaravadivelu, B. (2003). *Beyond methods: Macrostrategies for language teaching*. New Haven, CT: Yale University Press.
Kumaravadivelu, B. (2007). *Cultural globalization and language education*. New Haven, CT: Yale University Press.
Large, A. (1985). *The artificial language movement*. Oxford, UK: Basil Blackwell.
Lins, U. (1980). *La dangera lingvo* [The dangerous language]. Moscow, Russia: Progreso.
Luke, C. (1992). Feminist politics in radical pedagogy. In C. Luke & J. Gore (Eds.), *Feminisms and critical pedagogy* (pp. 25--53). London: Routledge.
Maxwell, D. (1988). On the acquisition of Esperanto. *Studies in Second Language Acquisition*, 10, pp. 51–61.
May, S. (2005). Language rights: Moving the debate forward. *Journal of Sociolinguistics*, 9, pp. 319–347.
McLaren, P. (1986). *Schooling as a ritual performance: Towards a political economy of educational symbols and gestures*. London: Routledge.
McLaren, P. (1987). Education as counter-discourse: Towards a critical pedagogy of hope. *The Review of Education*, 13, pp. 58–68.
McLaren, P. (1988a). Language, social structure, and the production of subjectivity. *Critical Pedagogy*

Networker, 1, pp. 1–10.
McLaren, P. (1988b). Culture or canon? Critical pedagogy and the politics of literacy. *Harvard Education Review,* 58, pp. 213–234.
McLaren, P. (1988c). On ideology and education: Critical pedagogy and the politics of education. *Social Text,* 19/20, pp. 153–185.
Moore, J. (1980). The structure of Esperanto. *Babel: Journal of the Australian Federation of Modern Language Teacher's Association,* 16, pp. 25–27.
Norton, B., & Toohey, K. (Eds.). (2004). *Critical pedagogies and language learning.* Cambridge, UK: Cambridge University Press.
Nuessel, F. (2000). *The Esperanto language.* New York: Legas.
Okrent, A. (2006). A visit to Esperantoland. *The American Scholar,* 75, pp. 93–108.
Ortega, L. (1999). Language and equality: Ideological and structural constraints in foreign language education in the U.S. In T. Huebner & K. Davis (Eds.), *Sociopolitical perspectives on language policy and planning in the USA* (pp. 243–266). Amsterdam, Netherlands: John Benjamins.
Osborn, T. (2000). *Critical reflection and the foreign language classroom.* Westport, CT: Bergin & Garvey.
Osborn, T. (Ed.). (2002). *The future of foreign language education in the United States.* Westport, CT: Bergin & Garvey.
Osborn, T. (2006). *Teaching world languages for social justice: A sourcebook of principles and practices.* Mahwah, NJ: Lawrence Erlbaum Associates.
Patrick, D. (2005). Language rights in indigenous communities: The case of the Inuit of Arctic Québec. *Journal of Sociolinguistics,* 9, pp. 369–389.
Phillipson, R. (Ed.). (2000). *Rights to language: Equity, power, and education.* Mahwah, NJ: Lawrence Erlbaum Associates.
Piron, C. (1984). Contribution à l'étude des apports du yidiche à l'espéranto [Contribution to the study of contributions from Yiddish to Esperanto]. *Jewish Language Review,* 4, pp. 15–29.
Piron, C. (1989). Who are the speakers of Esperanto? In K. Schubert (Ed.), *Interlinguistics: Aspects of the science of planned languages* (pp. 157–172). Berlin, Germany: Mouton de Gruyter.
Pool, J., & Fettes, M. (1998). The challenge of interlingualism: A research initiative. *Esperantic Studies,* 10, pp. 1–3.
Quick, M. (1989, May/June). Does anyone here speak Esperanto? *Gifted Child Today,* pp. 15–16.
Reagan, T. (2005). *Critical questions, critical perspectives: Language and the second language educator.* Greenwich, CT: Information Age Publishing.
Reagan, T. (2009). *Language matters: Reflections on educational linguistics.* Charlotte, NC: Information Age Publishing.
Reagan, T., & Osborn, T. (2002). *The foreign language educator in society: Toward a critical pedagogy.* Mahwah, NJ: Lawrence Erlbaum Associates.
Richardson, D. (1988). *Esperanto: Learning and using the international language.* Eastsound, WA: Esperanto League for North America, in cooperation with Orcas Publishing.
Richmond, I. (1993a). Esperanto and literary research. In I. Richmond (Ed.), *Aspects of internationalism: Language and culture* (pp. 35–39). Lanham, MD: University Press of America, in collaboration with the Center for Research and Documentation on World Language Problems.
Richmond, I. (1993b). Esperanto literature and the international reader. In I. Richmond (Ed.), *Aspects of internationalism: Language and culture* (pp. 103–118). Lanham, MD: University Press of America, in collaboration with the Center for Research and Documentation on World Language Problems.
Richmond, I. (1993c). Internationalism and cultural specificity in Esperanto prose fiction. In I.

Richmond (Ed.), *Aspects of internationalism: Language and culture* (pp. 119–132). Lanham, MD: University Press of America, in collaboration with the Center for Research and Documentation on World Language Problems.

Sadler, V., & Lins, U. (1972). Regardless of frontiers: A case study in linguistic persecution. In S. K. Ghosh (Ed.), *Man, language and society* (pp. 206–215). The Hague, Netherlands: Mouton.

Schubert, K. (Ed.). (1989). *Interlinguistics: Aspects of the science of planned language.* Berlin, Germany: Mouton de Gruyter.

Sikosek, M. (2006). *Die neutrale Sprache: Eine politische Geschiche des Esperanto-Weltbundes* [The neutral language: A political history of the Esperanto world community]. Bydgoszcz, Poland: Skonpres.

Skutnabb-Kangas, T. (2000). *Linguistic genocide in education—Or worldwide diversity and human rights?* Mahwah, NJ: Lawrence Erlbaum Associates.

Skutnabb-Kangas, T., & Phillipson, R. (Eds.). (1995). *Linguistic human rights: Overcoming linguistic discrimination.* Berlin: Mouton de Gruyter.

Springboard to Languages. (2006). *Springboard: Raising language awareness: Teacher's pack.* Barlaston, Stoke-on-Trent, UK: Esperanto UK

Sutton, G. (2008). *Concise encyclopedia of the original literature of Esperanto.* New York: Mondial.

Tonkin, H. (Ed.). (1997). *Esperanto, interlinguistics, and planned languages.* Lanham, MD: University Press of America.

Tonkin, H., & Fettes, M. (1996). *Esperanto studies: An overview.* (Esperanto documents 43-A). Rotterdam, Netherlands: Universala Esperanto-Asocio.

Vandenberg, D. (1998). A response to Reagan. *Educational Foundations,* 12, pp. 83–85

Wallace, C. (1997). The role of language awareness in critical pedagogy. In L. van Lier & D. Corson (Eds.), *Encyclopedia of language and education, Volume 6: Knowledge about language* (pp. 241–249). Dordrecht, Germany: Kluwer.

Wells, J. (1989). *Lingvistikaj aspektoj de Esperanto* [Linguistic aspects of Esperanto]. Rotterdam, Netherlands: Universala Esperanto Asocio.

Wink, J. (2005). *Critical pedagogy: Notes from the real world* (3rd ed.). Boston: Pearson.

Wittgenstein, L. (1980). *Culture and value.* Chicago: University of Chicago Press. Original publication 1946.

Wood, R. (1975). Teaching the interlanguage: Some experiments. *Lektos: Interdisciplinary Working Papers in Language Sciences* (Special Issue: Papers from the Seminar on Interlinguistics, Modern Language Association). Louisville, KY: University of Louisville.

Wood, R. (1982). *Current work in the linguistics of Esperanto* (Esperanto documents 28-A). Rotterdam, Netherlands: Universala Esperanto-Asocio.

Zamenhoff, L. (1963). *Fundamento de Esperanto.* Maramande, France: Esperantaj Francaj Eldonoj. Original publication in Esperanto in 1905.

CHAPTER FIVE

Teaching (and Learning from) the White Rose

DAVID I. SMITH

Should resistance be praised? That seems to depend on the nature of the resistance, and on what is being resisted. Resistance is ethically parasitic—its good (or lack thereof) can only be determined in relation to the realization of other goods. We resist temptation in pursuit of wholeness and at other times resist the promptings of conscience in the interests of ego-satisfaction. We set ourselves to resist deception; we also find ourselves resisting the truth. We resist change, or we resist the status quo—and either may be justifiable or culpable depending on whether the new or the old is more just, more life-giving. We resist impositions, tasks, and ideas laid upon us by others, and in doing so, we may be displaying admirable independence of thought or ill-judged sloth and resentment. The presence or absence of resistance, despite the cachet of inherent rectitude that clings to the term, does not yet tell us a great deal about who is on the side of the angels.

It matters what is being resisted, what the grounds for resistance are, and whether the motivation is more than self-assertion, personal antipathy, or refusal to take full account of another's reality. There are times when capitulation is the right move ("You really should go see the doctor about that, I keep telling you and you don't listen!"), times when the vague nobility of resistance talk may itself be an ideological mask for some form of egocentricity. Resistance is thus normatively tied to discernment, to the tricky task of distinguishing good from evil, the healthful from the diseased, and the destructive from the life-affirming. Sometimes the distinction is mercifully obvious, sometimes it's not so clear exactly what to resist.

Language classrooms enjoy no insulation from this dynamic (Reagan and Osborn, 2002; Smith and Osborn, 2007). They involve people, social and cultural patterns of meaning, institutional structures and forms of power, and all-too-human artifacts, stories, and images. Insofar as the wider world is not the way it is supposed to be, and language classrooms emerge within and partake of that wider world, we should expect discernment-leading-to-resistance to be a needed ingredient in the language classroom (as in any other educational setting). Reflective appropriation of the call to teach implies taking this into account, perhaps finding ways of turning it to account. Resistance may take the form of student non-cooperation with cultural discourses and exercises of teacher and institutional power that are seen as arbitrary, coercive, prejudicial, or simply meaningless (Canagarajah, 1999). My interest here is more in the teacher's contribution and in the possibilities of pedagogical design. Specifically, can the intermediate-level world language classroom be intentionally constructed as a place where discernment-leading-to-resistance can be explored, even learned? How do big-picture concerns such as resisting injustice and alienation become contextualized in the particularities of the meager vocabulary and simple syntax of early language lessons? I will pursue these questions through a particular, concrete example: Teaching about the White Rose.

A First Attempt

A group of fourteen- and fifteen-year-olds, students at an urban, multicultural secondary school in central England, sits waiting for the start of German class. The students are in their third year of German. Some have made impressive progress, some seem to have made little headway and still possess meager ability to understand or produce the new language. On the screen at the front of the classroom an old photograph appears, framed by neither title nor text.[1] It is an outdoor scene—blurred images of trees are visible in the background. In the center, a young woman stands in a knitted jacket, apparently leaning on something. Her brow is deeply furrowed, and with the deep shadows under her eyes and somber set of her mouth she radiates a sense of duress. She is flanked by two young males, at least one of whom is in military uniform (the shoulders of three others are to varying degrees also visible). There is no eye contact between the three of them; both men are staring down, with grim expressions, at something that one of them is writing on a small pad of paper. The girl is flanked by their grim faces, positioned precisely between their darkly shadowed, averted pairs of eyes.

I began to use this photograph in class out of a conscious attempt to resist the consumerism of the language textbooks available to me at that time (Smith, 2007). It was the early 1990s, I had been teaching for just a few years, and the secondary school textbook market was awash with volumes consisting largely of more-or-less communicative exercises built around menus, timetables, advertisements, vacation brochures, and the like. The laudable eagerness to trade structural drilling for actually doing things with words seemed to be accompanied by a willingness to reduce virtually all language use to the parameters of drab consumer transactions and instrumental activities (Cook, 2000). Insofar as people appeared in the texts, they tended to be either stock-photo people, whose purpose for existing was to have pets and siblings, purchase clothes, and prefer beef to chicken, or cartoon people engaging in brief episodes of odd behavior for the sake of some language function or structure. In both cases they were people without stories, beliefs, struggles, or social context. In neither case was it easy to fully believe in their existence—they consistently failed to doubt, suffer, hope, pray, commit, face hard choices, believe, aspire, or die (Smith and Dobson, 1999; Smith, 2003). They existed only as a means to particular linguistic ends, not as ends in themselves, and those linguistic ends for the most part had little contact with the discourse of courage, humility, hospitality, faith, and justice (Purpel and McLaurin, 2004). The assumption seemed to be that at the earlier stages of language learning, limitations on linguistic resources meant that we had to spend most of our time talking about shopping, eating, and hobbies. This photograph offered a more human window into the lives of particular Germans whose lives were rather more complex, and yet seemed approachable with a fairly basic linguistic palette.

Reading the picture requires first a certain kind of acquiescence or submission, a willingness to take time to contemplate, to take in the setting, the clothing, the body language, the expressions, and the mood. Such acquiescence at the same time requires resistance to ingrained habits of hasty and superficial consumption of images. The class begins, and we work our way into the photo through simple questions—How many people? (Three? Really? Oh, four—no, five...six!) What are they wearing? Where are they? How old is the photo? How old are the people? How are they feeling? (Tell me more. Any more words for their feelings?) The questions gradually move from observation to speculation: What just happened? What is going to happen? Why are they feeling this way? Here things become more complex. The students identify the World War II setting, apply their schematic assumptions, and surmise that perhaps she is Jewish, perhaps she is being arrested. While these last two points call for a little help with vocabulary, we are otherwise thus far well within the bounds of the sayable for intermediate language learners. At this point I introduce data that resist this initial interpretation: the names of the three are added to the picture—Sophie Scholl, Hans Scholl, and Christoph Probst. The young woman and the soldier appear to be either married or siblings, and adjustments must be made to our interpretations. New possibilities emerge: Has the woman done something to put her in opposition to her brother? Is her husband going off to war? I continue to inject information: a family tree (Ah, they are siblings), a tombstone (She died in her early twenties? How did that happen?), more photos (He had children? They are all students?), complicating the problem posed by the original photo and inviting students into an ongoing revision of initial perceptions. Layer by layer we refine our first interpretations, and this gradual (and visual) process allows the language to remain simple and accessible to the students, as successive vocabulary domains (age, clothing, facial features, feelings, family relationships, school subjects, and so on) are gradually reviewed or introduced. Eventually, we have discovered that these students were part of a resistance group known as the White Rose, and that they lost their lives resisting the Nazi regime through anti-war leaflets in the early 1940s (Dumbach and Newborn, 2006).

I had been looking for ways of including more ethically and spiritually complex representations of people in my language curriculum, representations of humans who did more than transact and cared about more than their possessions, hobbies, and career choices. In this combination of an evocative photograph, a weighty biographical narrative, and an inductive, problem-posing approach (Osborn, 2006), I gradually came to see significant pedagogical possibilities. I have to confess that the first time I used the White Rose story it was in the form of a short extract from a magazine article accompanied by eight or ten rather dull comprehension questions—teaching, ironically, about a resistance group in a way that offered no resistance to deadening pedagogical norms. It took several tries to begin to find a more fruitful convergence of topic and approach.

There were signs that students shared my resistance to consumer trivia. When I first began using this photograph as a way into the topic, the preceding weeks of slogging through units on youth hostels, hotels, gas stations and ticket offices had been punctuated by the query: "Why do we have to learn this?"—a query that utilitarian assurances had done little to quell. Now, part-way through our perusal of the photograph, a student raised a hand and asked, "Is this true?" "Ja, natürlich ist es wahr, of course it's true," I replied. "Why haven't we learned about this before?" she responded, "This is important." She asked in English, underlining the continuing challenges: How to deal with truly important material in a second language classroom while linguistic resources are still very limited? How to resist postponing complex meaning until advanced classes?

And so we turned from image to words. I prepared various activities designed to get us further into the story (several are contained in Baker et al., 1996). One involved a collection of quotations connected with the eventual executions: a headline from 1942 referring to executions for high treason; another from decades later speaking of murder in the name of the people; a prison guard praising the bravery of the students at the end; Christoph assuring his friends that they would soon see one another in eternity; the Scholls' father declaring that they would go down in history, for in spite of the temporary proclamations of Nazi courts, "there is still a justice"; Sophie's sister, Inge, asking why they have to be to the ones to act, whether it could not be left to others; Sophie insisting that so many have fallen for this regime that it is time for someone to fall in opposition to it. All are linguistically accessible with some vocabulary support. The quotations are initially presented unascribed, and one task for students is to match them with who might have said them, based on their growing knowledge of the story and the people involved. One of the most able students raises a hand: "I can't do this." My teacherly anxieties rise to the surface: perhaps I was too ambitious with the choice of topic after all, perhaps I have designed poorly. I sit with her, and find to my puzzlement that she seems to understand all of the words and phrases needed to complete the activity. I eventually realize that her problem lies elsewhere. She is looking for mechanical clues that will complete the matching exercise for her. Whenever a second language textbook has in the past asked her to match things, it has always been enough to find a first person pronoun and a first person verb ending and put them together, and once the grammatical clue has been located, the meaning of the sentence has been irrelevant. "No," I tell her, "this time you have to think about what is being said and then decide who might have said it." Explicitly freed from the existing horizon of language classroom possibility (freed, ironically, by my present prescriptive insistence on how the activity must be approached), she is immediately able to complete the exercise.

A final activity using the same set of quotations seeks one more time to connect accessible language with the most important challenges: questions for reflection include "Wer hatte Recht, meinst du, Sophie oder Inge? Bist du wie Inge, oder eher wie Sophie?" (Who do you think was right, Sophie or Inge? Are you more like Sophie or more like Inge?) "Welche von den zwei Schlagzeilen ist gerechter?" (Which of the two headlines is more just?) "Zeigen die Zitate Verzweiflung, Angst, oder Hoffnung? Warum?" (Do the quotations show despair, fear or hope? Why?). For the students in this class, the linguistic resources are lacking to conduct lengthy discussions about the source of hope, or the need to approach media constructions of events critically, or the relative merits of active and passive resistance. Stimuli that afford some measure of reflection on these matters can, however, be offered in relatively simple words, and offer the possibility of spending some time in language class worrying about more than the price of a train ticket. At the end of the unit, the ten students in the class are asked on a questionnaire what they have learned. The question is open-ended—they can name information, skills, or linguistic items. Several report that they have learned that not all Germans were Nazis. Two write that they have learned that they should stand up for what they believe in.

A Second Attempt

Time passes, and I am teaching the White Rose story again, this time to undergraduate students in their third semester of German at a Christian liberal arts college in the American Mid-West. Now I am aided by a new resource, one inspired in part by one of the questions noted above: How could these German students display hope in the face of crushing institutional power and the prospect of their own extinction? Marc Rothemund, director of the award-winning 2006 film *Sophie Scholl: Die letzten Tage*, comments in an interview packaged with the U.S. DVD release: "I find this approach to death quite startling: How does such a life-affirming, positive-minded young woman like Sophie Scholl come to terms with the fact that her life is being taken away from her? How does she find meaning in her death? And, of course, as an atheist I ask myself: Is it easier to face death as a believer?" (Zeitgeist Films, 2005; see also screenplay author and co-producer Fred Breinersdorfer's discussion of similar questions in Schuler, 2005, and Regensburger, 2009). His film, focused on the interrogations and trial of Sophie, offers a rich basis for considering the contours of a primarily linguistic resistance to totalitarian authority, and of a pedagogical resistance to the lurking banality of the second language classroom.

The film undermines stereotypical images of World War II resistance movements. Hasenberg (2009) suggests that while Percy Adlon's 1982 White Rose film *Fünf letzte Tage* (Five Last Days) maintained an inward, psychological focus, with Sophie Scholl portrayed as a martyr in a passion story, and Michael Verhoeven's film of the same year, *Die weiße Rose* (The White Rose), offered a sort of "Robin Hood story" with more focus on outward acts of resistance and the growing danger of arrest, the Rothemund/Breinersdorfer film dramatizes the development of Sophie's moral conviction through the process of interrogation. I suggest that a further important theme comes more clearly to the fore in the most recent film: Resistance through Language. Rather than the barbed wire and guns at night common to Hollywood portrayals of the Nazi era, the film is almost exclusively composed of dialogue, dialogue in which the right to name and evaluate social reality is constantly at stake. Accusations and counter-accusations multiply, with the definitions of key terms, or the right to apply them to social reality, often overtly at issue. The film is replete with small examples of symbolic resistance to the Nazi exercise of power—as well as resistance on the part of authority figures to evident prickings of conscience. For present purposes, I will focus on the pedagogical potential of one particular sequence from the end of the film.

While much of the film focuses on the verbal sparring and maneuvering that takes place between Sophie and her interrogator, in the last quarter of the film the linguistic conflict becomes more public and less subtle. The demeaning tirades of

Nazi judge Roland Freisler directly confront, and at times literally attempt to drown out, the protests of the accused students before the Volksgericht ("People's Court"). When Christof Probst seeks to establish grounds for mercy by identifying himself as a father, Freisler denies him the designation: "So ein mieses Vorbild brauchen deutsche Kinder nicht. Sie sind doch unwürdig, Probst" (Breinersdorfer, 2006, p. 277) (Such a rotten role model is not needed by German children. You are unworthy, Probst). When Hans Scholl offers eyewitness testimony to the atrocities of the eastern front, Freisler (floundering somewhat at this point) again denies his interlocutor's status as one morally or rationally competent to speak at all: "Ach, halten Sie den Mund…ach, es ist sowieso…ehrloser Lump…Sie sind doch nichts als ein Dummkopf und ein mieser Verräter" (Breinersdorfer, 2006, p. 284) (Oh, shut your mouth…oh, in any case it's…dishonorable scoundrel….You are nothing but a fool and a rotten traitor). When Sophie refers to the students' "idea," Freisler responds: "Idee? Diesen Dreck hier Idee nennen! Das sieht Vollidioten ähnlich, aber nicht deutschen Studenten" (Breinersdorfer, 2006, p. 286) (Idea? You call this filth here an idea! It smacks more of complete idiots than of German students).

The subject seized by a totalitarian apparatus is, De Certeau (1986, p. 42) argues, "faced not with the value or horror of the system—a ground upon which he would stand strong….The revelation of his own filth, which is what torture tries to produce by degrading him, should be enough to deprive him…of his right to rebel." The state seeks a "confession of putrescence" that reduces the victim to "rottenness" (p. 41). There are clear echoes of this intention in Freisler's repeated attempts to reduce the students to silence by recasting them as "filth," unfit to speak and thus unworthy of a hearing. The right to dissent is denied through the application of labels that deny human worth to the dissenters.

The setting here is, however, the courtroom rather than the torture chamber, and Freisler is unable to suppress completely either the discourse of the leaflets for which the students are on trial or the present responses of the students themselves. He deals with this counter-discourse by assimilating it to his own discursive strategy. Sophie declares that "Wir kämpfen mit dem Wort" (We fight with the word.). Freisler retorts "Etwa mit solchen Beleidigungen?" (What, with insults like these?), quoting from a White Rose leaflet that refers to the Nazi leadership as "teuflisch," "borniert" "Bonzen," "gottlos," "schamlos," "gewissenslos," "blind," and "stupide" (Breinersdorfer, 2006, p. 286) (devilish, bigoted, bigwigs, godless, shameless, without a conscience, blind, stupid). The students too, Freisler charges, have adopted derogatory language, directed at the very party officials who are now returning the favor; he thus seeks to reduce both sides of the exchange to a matter of who can make their insults stick. The earlier interrogations contained significant exchange of arguments, ideas, and attempts to persuade, and this trajectory continues in the brief court speeches of the students, who appeal to personal health, family ties, experience at the front, God, conscience and empathy to justify their positions. (Here students studying the film can be asked to generate a list of grounds appealed to on either side during the court dialogues and consider their validity). Freisler refuses to go beyond a ritual exchange of insults in which his own taunts are presented as possessing a purity backed by the power of state compulsion. At issue is who gets to define whom as subhuman and amoral, and who gets to ascribe morality and reason to their own utterances:

> **Freisler:** Ja, haben Sie denn jeden Funken von Moral und Sitte verloren? Der Führer des deutschen Volkes, Adolf Hitler, hat den Worten Freiheit und Ehre endlich wieder einen Sinn gegeben...Aber das verstehen Sie nicht, Sie können doch nur heimtückisch hetzen.
>
> **Sophie:** Wir hetzen nicht, wir beschreiben die Zustände.
>
> **Freisler**...Schauen Sie sich doch selber mal an, dann sehen Sie den Untermenschen. (Breinersdorfer, 2006, p. 287)
>
> **Freisler:** Well, have you lost every spark of morality and decency? The leader of the German people, Adolf Hitler, has finally given the words freedom and honor a meaning again...but you don't understand that, you can only maliciously spread smears.
>
> **Sophie:** We don't smear, we describe the circumstances.
>
> **Freisler:**...Just look at yourselves, and then you'll see who is the subhuman.)

As his insults are met with resolutely patient argument, Freisler is increasingly reduced to the demand for silence—"Ach, schweigen Sie doch endlich" (Breinersdorfer, 2006, p. 289) (Oh, be silent won't you)—a silence that becomes increasingly ambiguous as his façade of rectitude wears visibly thin. The order to be silent is in the end never complied with until the students are finally silenced by their removal from the court.

Working with these exchanges in a language class, with both the film and extracts from the screenplay on hand, brings to the fore a kind of language commonly either omitted or dealt with in casual or humorous asides—the language of insults and denigration. Some years ago, materials prepared by the British National Curriculum Council for training language teachers in strategies for maximizing target language use in the classroom included the example of a teacher who invented an identical twin sister who only spoke French, pretending to be her during certain classes and adopting a "scathing attitude" towards the English-speaking sister. Remarkably, this was presented as a motivational gambit for emulation—"The kids like the bitching and insults" (National Curriculum Council, 1993, p. 61). The film dialogue discussed above opens the possibility for a more ethically serious engagement with insults. The exchanges portrayed are not a productive negotiation of meaning but rather a fight for meaning; they foreground the exercise of power through naming and the close relationships between speech and selfhood and between insult and physical violence. The Volksgericht scene portrays insults as a form of dehumanization that legitimizes violence rather than as a source of careless humor. It can provide impetus for teacher and students to reflect on the power of language to wound and to heal and not merely to exchange information or get things done. Language learning should not be merely about expanding our ability to say more things; it must also harbor the question of what things we will choose to say and whom we will harm or heal by saying them.

Students can be asked to consider, individually or in groups, each of the following statements from the dialogue in terms of its validity and its relationship to the other statements:

Christof: "Flugblätter sind doch nur Worte!" (But leaflets are only words!)

Sophie: "Wir kämpfen mit dem Wort." (We fight with the word.)

Sophie: "Wir hetzen nicht, wir beschreiben die Zustände." (We don't smear, we describe the circumstances.) (Breinersdorfer, 2006, p.276, 286, 287)

Each statement is spoken by one of the German students to Freisler, yet they do not speak with one voice. They concisely express varying views of language: language as mere inconsequential words, language as the attempted exercise of power, and language as an objective reflection of reality. Language students can be asked to expand each into a short paragraph, unpacking the claims compressed into each utterance, and to consider whether each statement reflects their own view of their own words. Drawing these statements from the film's dialogue, rather than presenting them as abstract positions, invites a further investigation: Why is each statement made by the person who makes it at the specific point in the dialogue where it appears—what *contextual* point is the speaker making and what does he or she hope to achieve? Christoph, for instance, is seeking to obtain clemency for the sake of his wife and young children and so is working to downplay the seriousness of the allegations against him. Each statement intertwines truth-claims and interests.

A further fruitful comparison is suggested by the scenes immediately following the exit from the court room. Silence has already become ambiguous during the court scene—Freisler both demands and fears silence, and the silences that he does achieve reflect moral unease in the courtroom more than submission on the part of the students. After the trial, the students are transported back to the prison, and Sophie is left in a bare cell, where her self-control momentarily gives way to an animal cry of anguish that jarringly evokes the powerlessness and loss of self imposed by the flat denial of a hearing for one's words. There follows a recovery of self, effected by taking up other forms of linguistic expression, no longer directed at the judicial authorities: a letter, a final exchange of words of encouragement with her parents, a brief interaction with her erstwhile interrogator (now silent) in which she reasserts her dignity and humanity, and finally a prayer. Each of these is a reaching out through language for connection, not because these connections can at this point change the outcome, but because they can sustain the self in the face of the verbal assault just sustained (cf. De Certeau, 1986, p. 43).

The prison pastor, a Herr Alt, is in certain respects as ineffectual as Freisler. His age, underlined by his name ("Mr. Old"), his position as a cowed employee of the system that is about to unjustly execute his parishioner, and the compromise to his confession reflected in his non-resistance to evil, place him in contrast to the courage of young Christian students (similar in age and faith to those in my own classroom) who are about to die for their refusal to acquiesce. In the screenplay he is also presented (more strongly than in the final edit of the film) as emotionally weak: he is at a loss for words when he enters Sophie's cell, contrasting with the bold speech of the students in the preceding courtroom scenes. In the screenplay his clumsy efforts at connection come across as labored and stilted in comparison with Sophie's simple directness in both conversation and prayer:

> **Alt:** Ich weiß nicht, wie ich Ihnen in dieser allzu kurz bemessenen Frist nahe kommen und Sie und Ihren Bruder auf Ihren letzten Gang vorbereiten soll.
>
> **Sophie:** Ich möchte beten. Alt ist fast ratlos, ja zitternd, schon jetzt am Rande seiner Nerven. (Breinersdorfer, 2006, p.307)
>
> **Alt:** I don't know how in this all too briefly measured time I can come alongside you and prepare you and your brother for your final journey.
>
> **Sophie:** I would like to pray.)
>
> Alt is almost helpless, even trembling, now already at the limit of his nerves)

The film omits this dialogue (as well as a further request for the Eucharist), and thus opens other readings. Alt enters and introduces himself, and the next thing we hear is Sophie's voice addressing God. Alt follows her lead, lowering his head in prayer after Sophie has already begun to pray—while he is nominally the figure of religious authority, it is Sophie who initiates each move in their interaction. When she has finished praying, he remains silent until she requests a blessing from him, speaking then not with his own words, but with those of the tradition that he is supposed to represent. Set against the preceding court scene, the sequence gives Sophie back her own voice and initiative and presents a male authority figure prepared to listen and affirm rather than berate and deny.

Like Freisler in his role as Nazi judge, Alt is a mouthpiece, channeling a discourse that may or may not represent his personal words. In other words, what saves Alt from complete impotence is that he belongs to a tradition of discourse other and older than that of the Nazi legal system, and it is in becoming the mouthpiece of this tradition that he is able to bring a third element to the discursive combat between the students and the authorities. At Sophie's request, Alt responds with a Trinitarian blessing:

> Alt: Es segne dich Gott der Vater, Der dich nach seinem Ebenbild geschaffen hat. Es segne dich Gott der Sohn, Der dich durch seine Leiden und Sterben erlöst hat. Es segne dich Gott, der heilige Geist, Der dich zu seinem Tempel bereitet und geheiligt hat. Der Pfarrer macht das Kreuzzeichen über Sophies Stirn und fährt fort:
>
> Alt: Der dreieinige Gott…sei dir gnädig im Gericht und bewahre dich zum ewigen Leben.
>
> Beide: Amen.
>
> Alt: Niemand hat größere Liebe, den er sein Leben last für seine Freunde. Gott ist bei dir. (p. 308)
>
> Alt: May God the Father bless you, who has made you in his image. May God the Son bless you, who has redeemed you through his suffering and death. May God the Holy Spirit bless you, who has prepared you as his temple and made you holy. [The pastor makes the sign of the cross over Sophie's forehead and continues.]
>
> Alt: May the triune God be merciful to you at the judgment and keep you for eternal life.
>
> Both: Amen.
>
> Alt: No one has greater love than that he lays down his life for his friends. God is with you.)

These words are, of course, themselves capable of being turned to oppressive use. The biblical "image of God" language was, however, probably originally coined in resistance to oppressive features of Babylonian society, extending a term previously reserved only for rulers to apply to each human being (Middleton, 2005). Here, in Alt's prayer, these words of blessing offer a discursive frame in which language is able to build up and strengthen rather than tear down, and in which the mention of a "Gericht" (court) connotes mercy and the hope of ultimate justice in contrast to the travesty just experienced.

An ongoing challenge in the intermediate language classroom is to find ways of scaffolding interaction with significant ideas so that the demands of discussing them can be brought within the scope of students' linguistic resources. A simple listing exercise can at this point generate concrete grounds for meaningful comparison. Based on the film scenes, students can generate descriptions in German of the appearance, postures, and demeanor of both Freisler and Alt. They can proceed to note similarities and dissimilarities. Following this, students can use the screenplay to identify all of the nouns and adjectives applied to Sophie by Freisler and then those used of her by Alt. This generates a linguistically accessible framework for considering the differences between a language of curse and a language of blessing (and, depending on the students involved, may also bring to the surface complexities and difficulties in the latter).

Cavanaugh (1998), exploring the relationship between totalitarian repression and religious resistance, refers to the social imagination as a "vision which organizes the members into a set of coherent performances, and which is constantly reconstructed by those performances" (p. 12). This formulation enables consideration of the connection between liturgy and social embodiment. Cavanaugh explores (with regard to the Pinochet regime in Chile) the potential of Christian liturgical discourse to be domesticated to the performances of an oppressive social imagination, or to provide the grounds for resisting it and sustaining an alternative social self. In the trial scene, we have witnessed a struggle of social imaginations and an official liturgy of condemnation; in the prayer scene a counter-liturgy is enacted. Alt himself remains a cipher—whether he is supposed to be a man of faith overcome by fear or a spineless puppet of the regime is unclear. What we have are Alt's words, and Sophie's appropriation of those words. Alt's lack of ability to contribute any words of his own, his reciting of authoritative formulae, and his complicity with the state structures present the possibility of reading his discourse as one more form of oppression, another kind of bid to shape a state-determined social imagination. Sophie's request for and appropriation of those words, however, offers a reconfiguration which finds in the theological formulations a language of blessing deeper than the state's discourse of vilification, and draws from them the resources to sustain a self other than and in resistance to that projected by the Nazi court, despite the present impossibility of overthrow of the opposed power. The liturgical blessing is followed by a brief scene in which Sophie, Christof, and Hans are reunited one last time, the three standing in an embrace that gains Trinitarian resonances from what preceded it. "Es war nicht vergebens" (it was not in vain), says Christof. The screenplay responses of Sophie and Hans ("Wir kommen zusammen drüben an," "Ja, zusammen"—We'll arrive together over there. Yes, together.) are replaced in the film by a silent embrace; either way, the scene is suggestive of the potential of faith to sustain a sense of self and a solidarity able to resist the imputation of putrescence.

Cook has argued that the focus of language curricula should be broadened from preoccupation with "the mundane transactional discourse of modern work" to include "the ancient playful discourse concerning intimacy and power" (Cook, 2000, p. 160), including stories, jokes, songs, and prayers—"public discourse which is valued for its personal significance" (Cook, 2000, p. 170). This formulation points to the inadequacy of viewing prayer as a purely inward, personal matter; prayer also functions as public discourse that affects both self and others and may be studied as such. From time to time I remind students in my language classes that their acquisition of competence in a new language is not merely extending their ability to find remunerative employment or navigate needed services while travelling; it is also expanding their ability to either bless or curse speakers of their new language, and thus lays upon them responsibility for the effects of their target language speech. Textbooks rarely consider this aspect of language, rarely even go as far as to balance the occasional rehearsal of consumer complaints with specific practice in culturally appropriate forms of encouragement and praise. A systematic comparison of Alt and Freisler presents discourses of blessing and curse and also contrasts shrill, interruptive, authoritarian discourse with what might charitably be read as a listening, responsive stance (albeit in this case activated by fear, insecurity and impotence) that leaves space for the interlocutor's personal worth. Asking students to read these scenes closely, open to their ambiguities, and to identify and name the similarities and differences between Freisler and Alt, exposes the intersection of speech, ethics, and identity in a linguistically manageable way, provokes awareness of the difference between individual and social voices (Kramsch, 1993), and may challenge both students and teacher to consider when their words act as curse, how their words might instead shelter others, and to what texts, traditions, or communities they might turn in order to appropriate and sustain a language of blessing.

Conclusion

Clearly these suggestions do not exhaust the pedagogical potential of this story; they are presented merely as suggestions. I offer them as illustrations of how various specifically contextualized forms of resistance may intertwine in an intermediate language class. A story of resistance becomes paired with attempts to resist the utilitarianism and dogged secularity of much language classroom discourse, and in turn opens spaces to provoke students to consider what is affirmed and what is resisted in their own learning and speaking. The underlying conviction is that it matters what stories are given space in the language classroom, for "the stories we tell, the narratives that give coherence and meaning to our lives, set the terms within which we are able to formulate the possibilities of existence" (Simon, 1992, p. 60).

At each turn in this account I have attempted to do justice to the complexities and ambiguities of resistance. Resistance enters into the teaching sequences that I have described in three ways. It is the topic under discussion, as we learn about young Germans who found purpose in resisting evil and of necessity had to improvise concrete ways of resisting those who held power over them. As I quickly realized when beginning to work with this material, teaching this topic called for resistance to aspects of the language pedagogies in which I had been trained, which tended to be preoccupied more with information transfer and transactional effectiveness than with the ethical weight of words; it thus fell to me as a teacher to resist aspects of my own professional discourse and inherited practice. In the process, of course, I am hoping that space will be opened up for students to reflect critically on what and how they will resist, and to what they will submit, and what kinds of worlds their words will create for others. In each of these three aspects, resistance is bound up with submission—certain words, convictions, norms must be submitted to in order to resist others, in order to name those others as anti-normative. I see (and desire) no way past the implication that teaching languages requires ethical discernment as well as applied linguistic know-how.

Whether the pedagogical suggestions offered here are to be resisted or affirmed depends on the degree to which they can contribute something to the true flourishing of teachers and students; that lies beyond what can ultimately be decided by this author. I am only the teacher in the foregoing account, and have but tried to tell my side of the story as I seek to uncover what is, or could be, at stake in my classroom and my designs for learning. No doubt I will in future iterations find things to resist in my own practice; perhaps also things to which I have yet to sufficiently submit.

NOTE

1. The picture can be viewed, for instance, at http://www.jewishvirtuallibrary.org/jsource/Holocaust/rose.html (accessed Tuesday, May 12, 2009).

REFERENCES

Baker, D., Brammer, H., Chapman, C., Dobson, S., Heywood, K., & Smith, D. (1996). *Charis deutsch: Einheiten 1–5*. St. Albans: ACT.

Breinersdorfer, Fred (ed). (2006). *Sophie Scholl: Die letzten Tage*. Frankfurt am Main: Fischer.

Canagarajah, A. S. (1999). *Resisting linguistic imperialism in English teaching*. Oxford: Oxford University Press.

Cavanaugh, W. T. (1998). *Torture and eucharist: Theology, politics, and the body of Christ*. Oxford:

Blackwell.
Cook, G. (2000). *Language play, language learning.* Oxford: Oxford University Press.
De Certeau, Michel. (1986). *Heterologies: Discourse on the Other.* Transl. Brian Massumi. Minneapolis: University of Minnesota Press.
Dumbach, A., & Newborn, J. (2006). *Sophie Scholl & the White Rose.* Oxford: Oneworld.
Hasenberg, P. (2009). Heldin auf Augenhöhe: Wahrheitsanspruch und dramaturgische Bearbeitung in der Darstellung der Sophie Scholl im Film. In D. Regensburger & G. Larcher (Eds.), *Paradise Now!? Politik—Religion—Gewalt im Spiegel des Films* (pp. 123–148). Marburg: Schüren.
Kramsch, C. (1993). *Context and culture in language teaching.* Oxford: Oxford University Press.
Middleton, J. R. (2005). *The liberating image: The Imago Dei in Genesis 1.* Grand Rapids: Brazos Press.
National Curriculum Council (1993). Target practice. Developing pupils' use of the target language. York: National Curriculum Council.
Osborn, T. A. (2006). *Teaching world languages for social justice: A sourcebook of principles and practices.* Mahwah, NJ: Lawrence Erlbaum.
Purpel, D. E., & McLaurin, W. M. (2004). *Reflections on the moral & spiritual crisis in education.* New York: Peter Lang.
Reagan, T. G., & Osborn, T. A. (2002). *The foreign language educator in society: Toward a critical pedagogy.* Mahwah, NJ: Lawrence Erlbaum.
Regensburger, D. (2009). *Sophie Scholl—die letzten Tage.* Interview mit Drehbuchautor und Koproduzent Fred Breinersdorfer. In D. Regensburger & G. Larcher (Eds.), *Paradise Now!? Politik—Religion—Gewalt im Spiegel des Films* (pp. 112–122). Marburg: Schüren.
Schuler, U. (2005). "Die einzige deutsche Heldin." Interview mit dem Drehbuchautor Fred Breinersdorfer über "Sophie Scholl—die letzten Tage." *Das Parlament*, 42, 7.
Simon, R. I. (1992). *Teaching against the grain: Texts for a pedagogy of possibility.* Toronto: OISE Press.
Smith, C. (2003). *Moral, believing animals: Human personhood and culture.* Oxford: Oxford University Press.
Smith, D. I. (2007). Moral agency, spirituality, and the language classroom. In D. I. Smith & T. A. Osborn (Eds.), *Spirituality, social justice and language learning* (pp. 33–50). Greenwich, CT: Information Age Publishing.
Smith, D. I., & Dobson, S. (1999). Modern languages. In S. Bigger & E. Brown (Eds.), *Spiritual, moral, social and cultural education: Exploring values in the curriculum* (pp. 98–108). London: David Fulton.
Smith, D. I. & Osborn, T. A. (Eds.), (2007). *Spirituality, social justice and language learning.* Greenwich, CT: Information Age Publishing.
Zeitgeist Films. (2006). *Sophie Scholl—die letzten Tage.*

CHAPTER SIX

Dialogic Resistance in Education

Tsunesaburo Makiguchi, Daisaku Ikeda and Transformative Language Learning

JASON GOULAH

The U.S. education system acts like a closed circuit both charged by and charging neoliberalism and its push for economic and militaristic triumphalism. It consequently fosters in students solipsism and zero-sum competitiveness at the expense of empathy and valuation of ecological interdependence; this vector of influence manifests in what I call a nexus of destruction or the intersecting pressures of increased environmental degradation, climate shock, resource scarcity, population growth, migration, political instability, religious and ethnic division, war, and global income disparity. As a teacher, teacher trainer, and researcher in language and culture education, I have considered the relationship between this nexus of destruction and foreign and second language learning, calling for a transformative approach that places the nexus of destruction at the heart of curriculum and instruction (Goulah, 2006; 2007a, 2007b, 2008, 2009a). In this chapter, I continue my call for transformative language learning as resistance pedagogy against the forces of neoliberal competitiveness in language education under the influence of No Child Left Behind (NCLB, 2001). I break new ground by contextualizing my argument in Tsunesaburo Makiguchi and Daisaku Ikeda's Buddhist-influenced philosophies of value-creation pedagogy, humanitarian competition, human revolution, dependent origination, and dialogue.

Neoliberal Competition, NCLB, and Language Education

Neoliberal ideology embodies NCLB's push for cutthroat competition and market preparation in the form of mandated yet underfunded accountability and standards-based reform designed to undermine the social democratic policies that have largely benefited disenfranchised members of society (Brown, 2006; Eferakorho, 2006). Despite George W. Bush's trumpeting NCLB as a "back to basics" corrective against "discrimination of the soft bigotry of low expectations" (1999, p. 17), it has subreptitiously locked non-dominant students in their minority status while creating advancement avenues for their already advantaged peers. Eferakorho cogently argued,

> In principle, NCLB proposes to be an equity-driven reform because of expressed concerns for equalizing educational opportunities for all, closing the achievement gaps, using education as a vehicle for social mobility, and its close alignment with political impulse to use education to promote responsible citizenry. NCLB is predicated on the logic that the United States does not compare favorably to other advanced industrial nations as measured on international comparative data, and consequently fears losing its coveted dominance in the global economy. In practice, however, in spite of its rhetoric to promote equity-based reform, NCLB is actually a competitiveness-driven reform informed by a neoliberal ideology designed to improve the quality of education through competition. The emphasis on competition underscores the economic purpose of education, and simultaneously belies the espoused commitment to equity. (p. 256)

In critiquing and challenging neoliberalism in education, we must consider more than just its cultivation of economy-based competition. Kirk and Okazawa-Rey (2000) argued that neoliberalism operates on a one-two punch approach of unfettered monetarism and materialism on one hand and militarism on the other. This militaristic aspect is articulated in Section 9528 of NCLB, which provides military recruiters access to schools and students' personal information. At a socioeconomically disadvantaged suburban school where I taught, this manifests in recruiters regularly setting up tables outside the cafeteria to recruit children as young as 13 years old. Recruiters' presence is rarely counterbalanced with university or scholarship representatives soliciting opportunities. Moreover, as that school and many like it conform with NCLB's accountability measures, they routinize test-prep/test-taking to such a degree that neither parents nor students question yearly administration of the Armed Services Vocational Aptitude Battery (ASVAB), a subversive military scouting tool with no bearing on students' academic achievement or graduation. Time is taken from students' normal classes for the test, which the military uses to identify students' military capabilities and to recruit.

Neoliberalism and foreign language education

Neoliberalism's one-two punch also overtly and covertly informs foreign language learning and instruction, both directly in recent "policy" papers and indirectly through implementation of NCLB. First, while scholars have discussed the lack of a national foreign language "policy" and what one should look like (Blake and Kramsch, 2007; Byrnes, 2006; Modern Language Association [MLA], 2007), none considered foreign language learning's relationship to the nexus of destruction, particularly in terms of human-induced climate change or destabilization of environmental and human diversity and sustainability. Instead, most predicated their arguments on the idea that language policy should shift to post-9/11 needs vis-à-vis economic globalization and military efforts. I have responded in depth to the MLA's policy paper (Goulah, 2008), but suffice it say, foreign language and culture study aligned with America's selling and bombing practices cannot cultivate knowledgeable valuation of a language and culture deep enough to transform our ecologically damaged, spiritually, and geopolitically divided world. Contrary to the MLA committee's opinion, the "environment" (read: context) in which they sought to contribute to the policy discussion is not unlike any in the past. Only the languages and countries are different. If we continue to peg language policy and practices on governmental and corporate foci of military and economic crisis shifts, we will forever move from language to language and country to country, remaining at a surface level of cultural understanding and appreciation while developing resentment and dwindling enrollment along the way (Allen, 2007; Blake and Kramsch, 2007; Brecht, 2007; Herman, 2002). Our history of German, Japanese, and Russian as foreign languages exemplifies this; the 126.5% and 51% respective growth in Arabic and Chinese enrollment since 2002 (Furman, Goldberg, and Lusin, 2007) illustrates that the American "policy" of learning, teaching, and funding languages for militaristic and economic reasons has not changed. Arabic was popularized because of its strategically critical label associated with terrorism and the wars in Iraq and Afghanistan. Iraq not coincidentally is rich in oil, which underscores the relationship between energy, pollution, environment, climate change, politics, and language learning vis-à-vis Arabic. Chinese enrollment grew concomitant with China's economic growth, which has created environmental disaster and epic pollution (Kahn and Yardley, 2007).

The same neoliberal ideology of competition influencing foreign language policy discussions more directly but covertly influences foreign language education through implementation of NCLB. First, the objectification of content found in the "back to basics" mentality of NCLB, a longtime approach advanced by positivism, also exists in the objectification of foreign language through a mastery over proficiency model. Reagan (2004) argued, "What we do is engage in the objectification of the construct of 'language,' which then leads us to misunderstand the nature of language and to accept technicist views of the teaching and learning of languages" (p. 41). He continued that such positivist objectification not only objectifies the language, but it also objectifies a number of "other related constructs as well: not only 'grammar' and 'vocabulary,' but also that of 'native speaker,' 'culture,' 'communication,' 'performance,' 'production,' 'literacy,' and so on" (p. 47). While many scholars call for subjectivity and proficiency, examination of classroom practices and pre- and in-service teachers' anecdotal experiences indicates a strong focus on objectified mastery. Second, NCLB's mandated accountability and standards-based reform have caused schools to spend more time and money instructing "back-to-basics," "drill and test" skills in subjects tested under NCLB's purview: math, reading, science, and social studies. Increased time in these "core" courses means decreased time in foreign language(s). Third and exacerbating this is a market-induced decrease in school funding because local, state, and federal agencies reduce revenue by giving tax breaks to retain corporations (Brown, 2006). In middle and low socioeconomic districts this process means reduced presence of foreign language(s) at non-mandated levels or "streamlining" all students into one foreign language, usually Spanish (Goulah, 2003; Kubota and Catlett, 2008). In extreme cases foreign language is cut entirely.

Neoliberalism, second language education, and immigration

The U.S. government's politically divided, unsuccessful attempts to reform immigration policies in 2006 and 2007 happened concurrently with less publicized but no less divisive maneuverings to legislate English as the national (possibly official) language (Pear and Hulse, 2007; U.S. English, 2007). Both actions indicate an official current of exclusion and oppression under the guise of homeland security and national heritage (Pear, 2007b; U.S. English, 2007), and both smack of neoliberal ideology (Holborow, 2006) in their successful attempt simultaneously to globalize English as the lingua franca of free-market capitalism while limiting the flow of non-dominant people into the dominant society. Despite legislators' comments of non-discriminatory applicability, their actions occurred in seeming response to increased Latino immigration and Spanish prevalence.

Twenty-five states have legislated English as the official language through voter initiatives, constitutional amendments, or statutes (Crawford, 2007). This year, Oregon voters determined whether to set time limits for access to English second language (ESL) classes for the state's 64,000 English language learners (the majority of whom are native Spanish speakers). The ballot proposal sought to limit ESL instruction to two years, despite abundant language acquisition research indicating that basic proficiency takes at least three years while academic proficiency takes as many as five to seven, if not more (Cummins, 1981). NCLB stipulates that English language learners must pass standardized tests in English within three years. In language reminiscent of Bush's NCLB rhetoric, Bill Sizemore, sponsor of the Oregon measure and an anti-tax activist who was the Republican gubernatorial nominee in 1998, said, "The measure was intended to help immigrants, not sideline them. He said schools warehouse their students in ESL courses longer than necessary to keep federal and state money flowing" (Silverman, 2008). Sizemore's comments echo the "sameness as fairness" (Gutierrez, 2008) mentality that frames proponents' support of NCLB's competitiveness. Gutierrez rejected this mentality as the United States is not the same culturally, linguistically, racially, or socioeconomically. She argued that non-native English speaking students must be allowed to use their entire language tool kit to realize their full potential. Moreover, Sizemore's tax-based rationale evidences the broader neoliberal market ideology undergirding the push to change English education law. Tienda (2008) argued in her American Educational Research Association Presidential Invited Address, "English Mastery and Academic Achievement," that non-native English speaking students should master English before continuing Spanish so they can compete academically to compete economically in a globalized world. This line of thinking from an authoritative, bilingual sociologist is indicative of neoliberal ideology's powerful persuasion in education.

Whether legally binding or foreboding, the above policies and politicking, have broad implications on second language/bilingual education vis-à-vis equity, access, and social justice, and they illustrate an American schizophrenia toward language education: While neoliberalism pushes most native English speaking students toward Spanish as a foreign language, it forces all native Spanish speaking students to master English. Finally, the above policies and politicking also manifest the militarism of neoliberal competitiveness: The U.S. government is considering erecting a wall (portions of which already exist) reminiscent of the Berlin wall along the U.S.-Mexico border to stop immigration, and non-military Americans have organized an armed minuteman movement to keep undocumented immigrants from entering the country.

The combined result of the abovementioned forces of a neoliberal worldview in education is a myopic limitation of global, cultural, and linguistic views for non-dominant native English speakers and an inability of large numbers of non-dominant, non-native English speakers to compete in NCLB-guided education for neoliberal free-market preparation. Consequently, the majority of non-dominant students fail to compete with their advantaged peers for lofty and lucrative jobs the system tricks them into thinking they can obtain, and in the process of futile "competition" they remain non-dominant and the global nexus of destruction strengthens and expands. Exacerbating this gap is a pervasive reality that non-dominant students unable to compete academically find their hopes assuaged by a false sense of "militarism as patriotism" by the government and recruiters in their schools. Moreover, such micro-level aspects of neoliberal competitiveness spread to the macro level as our educational system of economic and militaristic competitiveness fed by and feeding globalization is itself globalized. China, India, and Russia, among others, are rapidly educating their students to compete in the global free-market vision, and each is militarizing with similar rapidity. With both developments, more of the world's population is unintentionally complicit in strengthening the nexus of destruction. O'Sullivan (1999) argued,

> Globalization of educational goals does not lead to a consciousness of a wider and diverse world. This is the incredible irony of the globalization process. What appears to happen in the advance toward globalization is the simultaneous development of monoculture. What is surely needed, in our present historical moment, is an education that counters the focus of the monoculture and opens all of us to the richer planetary culture of diversity. (p. 252)

Like the gap between the rhetoric and reality of NCLB, O'Sullivan (1999) has argued, "…there is a widening disparity between what the globalization process says it is doing and the realities of our current situation. These contradictions leave contemporary educators confused as to their loyalties and their work. This is where transformative education becomes relevant to the situation" (p. 34). Next, I consider transformative world language education in the context of Makiguchi and Ikeda's "Soka education" as a resistance ideology against the abovementioned demoralizing and destructive system.

Transformative World Language Learning, Makiguchi, and Ikeda

Transformative learning and Buddhism

The transformative education to which O'Sullivan refers involves,

> experiencing a deep structural shift in basic premises of thought, feelings and actions. It is a shift of consciousness that dramatically and permanently alters our way of being in the world. Such a shift involves our understanding of ourselves and our self-locations; our relationships with other humans and with the natural world; our understanding of relations of power in interlocking structures of class, race, and gender; our body-awareness; our visions of alternative approaches to living; and our sense of possibilities for social justice and peace and personal joy. (O'Sullivan, 2002, p. 3)

Transformative learning resists neoliberal free-market ideology as a guiding principle for education, instead operating on and encouraging a planetary consciousness "that locates our lives in a cosmological context much more breathtaking than the market vision" (O'Sullivan, 2002a, p. 7). Such an approach cultivates an ethic of interconnected empathy with humanity, the environment, the planet, and the universe in response to the nexus of destruction. It is a path to understanding the value of all human, linguistic, cultural, and environmental diversity as necessary expressions of the unfurling of the universe. O'Sullivan (1999) has contextualized development of such a planetary consciousness in curricular consideration of four constituent elements: a new cosmology, ecological selfhood, quality of life, and spirituality. Elsewhere I have explicated this planetary consciousness and applied its constituent elements to foreign and second language and culture learning (Goulah, 2005, 2006, 2007a, 2007b, 2008, 2009a); I do not reiterate those discussions here. Rather, I break new ground in my application—what I have called transformative world language learning—by locating it in the philosophies of Japanese Buddhist resistance pedagogues Tsunesaburo Makiguchi (1871–1944) and Daisaku Ikeda (1928–). Specifically, I consider their collective development of value-creation pedagogy, humanitarian competition, human revolution, dependent origination, and dialogue as those elements anticipate O'Sullivan's new cosmology, ecological selfhood, quality of life, and spirituality, and are part and parcel of a planetary consciousness; more importantly, they provide an alternative guiding ideology to (language) education than the neoliberal one currently in place.

Buddhism and Buddhists have been referenced in literature concerning transformative learning (Hart, 2004; O'Sullivan, 1999; Riley-Taylor, 2002) and, more specifically, cosmology (Brown, 1994; Lydon, 1995), spirituality (Miller, 2000; Moffett, 1994), and education (Goodman, 2003; Kumashiro, 2004; Miller, 2002). However, few scholars have considered transformative learning or its constituent elements in conjunction with Makiguchi or Ikeda. Inclusion of Buddhist elements provides the non-Buddhist reader opportunities to see the rich resources Buddhism offers the world, particularly with regard to transformative learning, language education, and resistance pedagogy. My inclusion here in the context of foreign and second language and culture education aims to complement extant considerations of various Christian approaches to foreign and second language learning toward social justice (Smith and Carvill, 2000; Smith and Osborn, 2007).

Tsunesaburo Makiguchi and Daisaku Ikeda in context

Tsunesaburo Makiguchi lived his life during Japan's staunch militaristic policy of expansion into Asia. Guided by the slogan "national wealth and military strength," this policy promulgated a pedagogical practice of militarism and drill and practice teaching that prepared impressionable children to be obedient subjects of the State rather than critical, contributive members of society. A schoolteacher and principal, Makiguchi spent his private and professional life trying to rectify this educational system, which he deemed entirely misguided and miseducative (Kumagai, 2000). He was "troubled by the domination of education by examinations...and by the emphasis of teachers on memorization of facts" (Bullough, 1989, p. xvi); he opposed the militaristic raison d'être of Japanese pedagogy and was imprisoned in 1943 as a thought criminal because he opposed State Shintoism. He died in prison from malnutrition at the age of 73.

In 1928, Makiguchi embraced Nichiren Buddhism and two years later became founding president of the Soka Kyoiku Gakkai (the Society for Value Creating Pedagogy), a lay Buddhist organization dedicated to applying Buddhist humanistic principles and value creation to education and members' daily lives. The Soka Kyoiku Gakkai later became the Soka Gakkai (Value Creation Society), and Daisaku Ikeda, never having met Makiguchi but influenced and mentored by Makiguchi's direct disciple, Josei Toda, the organization's second president, became its third president in 1960. Ikeda soon internationalized the Soka Gakkai and, as the foremost interpreter of Makiguchi's ideas, realized them in the creation of secular Soka schools, which include colleges and universities in Japan and the United States' K-12 schools in Japan, a kindergarten and elementary school in Brazil, and kindergartens in Hong Kong, Malaysia, Singapore, and South Korea (Ikeda, 2001b, 2006). In addition, membership in the Soka Gakkai International spans 192 countries and territories, and thousands of its members who are educators are applying Soka education principles in their respective cultural contexts (Gebert and Joffee, 2007; Miller, 2002). Now 81 years old, Ikeda has been recognized with over 250 honorary doctorates and professorships from major world universities for his constant, consistent, and comprehensive actions for peace, culture, and education as president of the Soka Gakkai International and its more than 12 million members worldwide (Touyou Testugaku Kenkyuujyo, 2007).

Makiguchi and Ikeda's educational philosophies

Whereas a solipsistic and competitive neoliberal ideology governs today's education system, Makiguchi and Ikeda have argued that the underlying ethos of education should be the cultivation of students' happiness. Happiness here is not a shallow or self-serving hedonism; it is a more substantial process of personal growth that benefits the self and society. According to Bethel (1989),

> The idea that for Makiguchi happiness is more than a preoccupation with one's own immediate satisfaction becomes clear when he stresses that a prerequisite for happiness is the devel-

opment within each person of a social consciousness that enables understanding and appreciation of the extent to which all humans are indebted to the society in which they live, "not just for their basic needs and security, but for *everything* that constitutes happiness." The tragedy of education in modern Japan, according to Makiguchi, was precisely that it had failed in the development of social consciousness within students, its most important and most basic task, and had succeeded, rather, in creating exactly the opposite, a happiness-destroying preoccupation with immediate personal and material satisfaction. (p. 5)

Makiguchi argued that deep, absolute happiness resides in students' ability to create value, an idea grounded in his philosophy of value (1981–1988; see also Makiguchi, 1964), which emerged in part as a critique of the Kantian perspective of value pervasive at the time. Whereas Kant theorized value as truth, good, and beauty, Makiguchi substituted gain for truth, and made clear "the definition of value as the relationship between subject and object" (Ikeda, 1964). Makiguchi argued that humans cannot create matter, but they can create value. The creation of value exists in people's subjective response to truth/reality, not the mere existence of truth/reality itself. Makiguchi's philosophy of value and value creation pedagogy is, therefore, a call for individuals to create "beauty," "gain," and "good" where beauty is a measure of partial, sensory response within an individual, gain is the measure of a relationship that extends and expands the total vital experience of the individual, and good is to the social collective what gain is to the life of the individual (Gebert and Joffee, 2007). Makiguchi contended, "(i)n each case, it is not so much anything inherent in the nature of the object evaluated as it is the criteria of the evaluating subject that dictate the level of relevance recognized between them" (cf. Bethel, 1989, p. 75). The goal in this understanding, then, is that education cultivates in students the ability to create value, with the ultimate aim of thereby creating absolute happiness for the individual and society.

In one sense, value creation can be viewed as a continuation and refinement of Makiguchi's early concept of "humanitarian competition" (also translated as "humanistic competition") evident in his philosophy of human geography, a precursor to O'Sullivan's ecological selfhood (1903/1981–1988; cf. Bethel, 2002). To be sure, Makiguchi's ideas of value creation and humanitarian competition are distinct and separate from each other in his writing. He introduced the latter in 1903 without ever discussing it again. Yet in the context of transformative learning, the two educational ideas can be viewed on a continuum in Makiguchi's lifetime work, wherein humanitarian competition is expressed as the social "good" in value-creation. Moreover, Makiguchi espoused such a value-creating humanitarian competition in light of ecological interconnectedness as an alternative educational vision to that of militarism and materialism present at the time. According to Gebert and Joffee (2007), Makiguchi, held that education based on awareness of the connections between human life and the natural and social environment could help develop the moral character of students. He hoped that people educated this way would construct an interdependent and harmonious world wherein military and economic competition between nations would be supplanted by "humanitarian competition" based on a recognition of mutual interests and benefit. (pp. 68–69)

Humanitarian competition in the above sense was rooted in Makiguchi's understanding that individuals' identities are present at local, national, global and even universal levels, and span human and non-human phenomena in a dialogic relationship (Goulah, 2009b). Humanitarian competition spans these levels whereby as the individual grows, the sphere of the effect grows from the local to the universal and, at the same time, "contributions to global humanity on a planetary level reverberate back to the national and local levels" (Ikeda, 2005, pp. x–xi). According to Ikeda,

> Makiguchi argued that the ultimate purpose of the state [in the concept of humanitarian competition] is, therefore, the pursuit of prosperity of human civilization and the advancement of human reason. To this end, states should shift from competition in the military, political, and economic spheres to what he termed a "humanitarian competition" of contributions to human happiness. (p. xi)

Makiguchi espoused humanitarian competition among cultures and civilizations whereby "engaging in dialogue with one another could carry out a kind of friendly and humanistic competition among themselves. In this way, he believed, they could open up a brighter future for the human race, one that promoted mutual harmony and prosperity for all" (Ikeda, 2002, p. xxxiii). Ikeda most recently contextualized humanitarian competition in light of the abovementioned nexus of destruction.

> Humanitarian competition was a vision of an international order in which the world's diverse states strive to positively influence each other, to coexist and flourish together rather than pursuing narrowly defined national interests at each other's expense. I feel that the work of solving the global environmental crisis provides a unique opportunity to move toward such a world. (2008, p. 31)

The totality of Makiguchi's philosophies from human geography in 1903 to community studies in 1912 to value creation in 1930 evidence an approach to education whereby value creation happens in the context of a geosocial consciousness (Goulah and Gebert, 2009). In practice, and indeed in line with O'Sullivan's transformative learning, Makiguchi extended such a value-creating, humanistically competitive relationship in eco-cosmological terms from the local to the universal, arguing in 1903: "Every aspect of the entire universe can be found in the small, limited area of one's home community" (2002, p. 22). He continued in 1912, without the concept of [the sun and moon], the foundations for all order and regularity on Earth would be emptied of content. This is why one can say that these are the most distant and at the same time proximate phenomena. I believe of all the various phenomena within the local community, they are the first that we should observe. (1981–1988, Vol. 3, p. 188)

In 1930, Makiguchi argued in *System for Value Creation Pedagogy* that the subject of human life includes the entire universe (*shinrabanshyou*), which can be classified into two categories: natural and human phenomena. He continued that in general anyone can interact or communicate with Nature, but they will not achieve a life of happiness if they do not harmonize their lives with it. After categorizing astronomical, land, aquatic, atmospheric, biological, inorganic, and human phenomena as natural phenomena and means of living, means of grouping, social groups, social classes, division of labor in society, and political, economic, educational and cultural phenomena as human phenomena, Makiguchi argued,

> These are just general divisions, but they can be infinitely subdivided, which is beyond the scope of this work. I have addressed the particulars in *Jinsei chirigaku* [*The Geography of Human Life*, 1903/1981–1988; cf. Bethel, 2002] and *Kyoujyu no to go chuushin toshite no Kyodoka Kenkyu* [*Research into Community Studies as the Integrating Focus of Instruction*, 1912/1981–1988]. These works teach students how to harmonize their lives with the natural and human worlds, that is they provide instruction for how to create value from all aspects of phenomena; they are ultimately nothing more than plans for students to create value in their lives. (1981–1988, Vol. 6, p. 364).

The above continuum in Makiguchi's educational philosophy from the local community to universal phenomena anticipates O'Sullivan's idea of a new cosmology and ecological selfhood. Ikeda expanded and refined Makiguchi's idea of cosmological awareness as a site for learning by identifying it part and parcel with human potential for inner transformation in a process he has termed "human revolution" (*ningen kakumei*). In language reminiscent of O'Sullivan's, Ikeda (Krieger and Ikeda, 2002) stated that "(w)hereas science begins with a reformation of the external world, Buddhism starts with reforming the inner human world—what we call the human revolution—and moves on to society" (p. 107). He continued elsewhere,

> any lasting global solutions to sufferings resulting from biotechnological and environmental problems and the proliferation of weapons of mass destruction must begin with what might be called individual human revolution. This means that instead of being absorbed in the minor self or the ego, each individual must recognize his or her own connection with all life in the cosmos. (Henderson and Ikeda, 2004, p. 1)

This concept matches with the tenets of transformative learning. For example, as O'Sullivan (1999) advocated rectifying education by advancing a new cosmological approach, Ikeda (2001a) considered such a notion in light of identity: "What interests me as a Buddhist is how we should address the problem of identity. This is because I believe the correct identity base for a true citizen of the world must be one of a global—even cosmic—awareness" (p. 78). Echoing O'Sullivan (1999) and encompassing this idea of a cosmological identity, Ikeda added, "I suggest, rather, that for the sake of overcoming the identity crises undermining the health of modern humanity we must attempt to discover a new cosmology" (2001a, p. 164).

Makiguchi's human geography and humanitarian competition toward value creation in combination with and refined by Ikeda's human revolution in cosmological terms find reason in the Buddhist concept of "dependent origination," the idea that the individual is connected to and, in a Bakhtinian sense, formed in the sentient and insentient Other. At this time marked by a "yawning sense of spiritual emptiness" (Ikeda, 2007a, p. vii) and fundamentalist deterministic worldviews, Buddhist spirituality offers dependent origination, which,

> holds that all beings and phenomena exist or occur in relation to other beings or phenomena. Everything is linked in an intricate web of causation and connection and nothing—whether in the realm of human affairs or of natural phenomena—can exist or occur solely of its own accord. In this view, a greater emphasis is placed on the interdependent relationships between individuals than on the individual in isolation. (Ikeda, 1991)

In other words, "(e)ach individual being functions to create the environment that sustains all other existences. All things are mutually supporting and interrelated, forming a living cosmos" (Nagashima, 2004, p. 21). This concept provides a spiritual foundation for O'Sullivan's ecological selfhood from the local to the universal.

The totality of Makiguchi and Ikeda's ideas posits that value creation and humanitarian competition cannot happen, given the doctrine of dependent origination, at the economic or militaristic expense of the Other. This is a fundamentally different ideology for education than neoliberal competitiveness currently in place. One should not read this chapter as my advocating Buddhist proselytization by the teacher. Rather, it shows the presence of the consciousnesses contributing to transformative learning: ecological selfhood and cosmological citizenship through human revolution based on value creation and humanitarian competition in line with dependent origination. It spans the local to the global and extends from the individual to dominant and non-dominant human, environmental, cultural, and linguistic spheres. Under this concept, the power of the individual is important. As each individual undergoes a transformation, or human revolution, and encourages others to cultivate their greater selves, exponential results are realized. Such exponential results can lay the foundation for a peaceful and sustainable planet. As Ikeda (Henderson and Ikeda, 2004) stated, "Consequently, it is the duty of each of us to participate as members of the life community in the evolution of the universe. We can do this by guarding earth's ecological system" (p. 124).

Soka education, dialogue and transformative world language learning

For ease of terminology, I henceforth label Makiguchi and Ikeda's above-mentioned ideas collectively as "Soka education." The question becomes, then, how does Soka education inform transformative world language learning? Juxtaposing Soka education with neoliberalism begins to answer this question. In line with transformative learning, Osborn (2006) argued that, "...we reject the supremacy of the marketplace, and with it the nation-state, as the primary force determining how [language] curriculum is established and evaluated" (p. 17). It warrants stating that Makiguchi did not, per se, share this view, although Bethel (1989) periodically casts him in such a light. Consider again Bethel's following quote: "Makiguchi's main objection to the educational system of his day was that it failed in the development of social consciousness and, in fact, created unhappiness by systematically encouraging a preoccupation with personal and material gain" (p. 5; see also Jaffe, 1993, p. 102). Similarly, Bethel provides the following as a passage from Makiguchi's *System for Value Creation Pedagogy*:

> No single element is so disruptive and damaging to the happiness of individuals and to the well-being of the society as a whole as that of wealth and the uses people make of it....Alfred Nobel put it well when he insisted that although it is possible to inherit property, it is impossible to inherit happiness. This is one of the most important lessons we can hope to learn in this age of ruthless competition and materialistic obsession. (p. 25)

However, scrutiny of the original Japanese reveals that Makiguchi did not include the first sentence before this often-quoted reference to Nobel. Rather, Makiguchi writes, "In general there is nothing more detrimental than confusing [the relation between true happiness to wealth]" (1981–1983, Vol. 5, p. 131).[1] Moreover, with regard to Bethel's (and Jaffe's) interpretation, it is difficult to read Makiguchi as opposed *entirely* to personal and material gain in light of happiness given his inclusion of individual "gain" as a component part of his philosophy of value (1981–1988, Vol. 5/1964), which he addresses pedagogically as a "teaching material of economic valuation of life" (1981–1988, Vol. 6, p. 365). That said, while Soka education indeed incorporates students' personal and material gain as a constituent element, it assuredly transcends neoliberal education for the marketplace in the grand scheme, particularly when considering value-creation's elements of "beauty" and "good." The essence of Soka education lies in Ikeda's (2003, 2007b) refinement and application of it in an ethic and practice of dialogue, whereby the role of subjectivity and identity are crucial for intercultural understanding, sustainable ecological interconnectedness, and social justice. This of course means dialogue in the traditional sense in language education, but it also means two-way interaction with the Other in a non-authoritarian vector of influence in a Bakhtinian sense (Makiguchi,

1981–1988; Bethel, 2002; Goulah, 2009b). I have argued that such interaction can happen in the language classroom through a transformative world language learning approach to culture in a Vygotskian notion of sense in language (2006, 2007a), as well as through socio-dialogic construction of students' understanding and target language articulation of environmental and political elements vis-à-vis the target culture (2007b, 2009a).

Makiguchi made few references to foreign language education. To be fair, he argued that in the context of meaningful and useful education for the daily lives of students like children of tenent farmers or daughters of working class merchants, it is "some kind of disaster that foreign language courses…are not discarded" (1981–1988, Vol. 6, p. 362; cf. Bethel, 1989, p. 188). Such comments are limited in his 10-volume complete works, and one should read them not as his advocating subjugation of female students or drawing class lines; in fact, much of his educational ideas reveals the opposite. Rather, one must remember that he espoused his pedagogy during the first third of the 1900s, a time marked by limited rights and clear class distinctions in Japan and comparatively limited worldwide cultural, economic, social, or technological integration. While Makiguchi stressed the role of language both epistemologically and curricularly (much of his work considers Japanese national language education), he argued that foreign language study was superfluous in his vision of education grounded in Japanese children's local environment. Nevertheless, Ikeda (2001b) argued the importance of foreign language study in the context of value-creation pedagogy, stating, "Globalization means that linguistic proficiency is becoming an indispensable ability. Language skills can help to bring the world together" (p. 93). He continued, "The most important thing is to educate people so that they are broadly cultivated and have a mastery of languages" (ibid, p. 135). The first degree offering at Soka University of America was graduate training in second and foreign language education, and Bliss (1992), Goulah (2005, 2009a), Hatano (2009) and Heinesen (1995) have shown language learning to be a constituent element of applications of value creation pedagogy, particularly in an American context and in light of current geopolitical and social circumstances.

In particular, application of Soka education fits the aim of a transformative world language approach, which includes theoretical and practical examination of cosmology, ecological selfhood, quality of life, and spirituality through dialogue. Epistemologically, this reliance on dialogue is integral. Vygotskian and Bakhtinian sociocultural theory places dialogue at the center of human development. While Vygotsky did not express it in terms of violent versus just, it is no overgeneralization to compare the "technization." Makiguchi (1983–1988) and Reagan (2004) rejected as violence against the student's learning and development. The cosmological perspective articulated by Makiguchi, Ikeda, and O'Sullivan seeks to identify with other cultures and languages as part of our planetary-based ecological selfhood. For in dialoging with the Other in a Makiguchi-Bakhtinian sense (Goulah, 2009a; Holquist, 2002), we understand something akin to Buddhist dependent origination, our existence because of our dependence on the Other:

> The whole world depends on mutual interdependence. Nothing exists in isolation. Modern cosmology, the results of ecological study and the Buddhist doctrine of dependent origination all teach us this: We live in a system of interrelations with other humans, nations, societies and the natural world. Human spiritual poverty spews forth in war and environmental pollution, which disrupt these relations. (Ikeda in Krieger and Ikeda, 2002, p. 111)

Such dialogism will not happen, as it has not happened (Herman, 2002), via historical rationales popularizing foreign and second language study in the United States. A spiritually divided, post-9/11 world cannot sustain a policy of language study for militarism (Allen, 2007; Brecht, 2007) or monetarism/materialism (Blake and Kramsch, 2007), all of which cause climate change and its attendant nexus of destruction. Like Freire after him, Makiguchi argued that,

> the aim of education is not to transfer knowledge; it is to guide the learning process, to equip the learner with the methods of research. It is not the piecemeal merchandizing of information; it is to enable the acquisition of the methods for learning on one's own; it is the provision of keys to unlock the vault of knowledge. Rather than encouraging students to appropriate the intellectual treasures uncovered by others, we should enable them to undertake on their own the process of discovery and invention. (1981–1988, Vol. 6, p. 285; cf. Bethel, 1989, p. 168)

Thus, true education in Makiguchi's (and Ikeda's) terms—dialogism toward value creation for self and other—is inherently subjective and inherently taps students' subjectivities in identity reformation. Norton (2000) illuminated the role an individual's multiple and non-static subjectivities play in identity formation through language development. Riley-Taylor (2002) similarly argued that we have "multiple subjectivities that are constituted through language" (p. 41) and which are always in a state of "becoming." It is this "becoming" that allows us to change our focus and approach education in order to give a planetary vision precedence. She stated that this will allow the individual (the student) to find a relational experience with the environment and the universe as well as to reconnect the mind with the body, which has been neglected in today's education.

Combining Norton and Riley-Taylor's notions in light of Ikeda's dependence on dialogue, we understand that it is our subjective aspect that "becomes" through dialogue. In other words, engaging in dialogue fosters "knowledge-in-action" (Applebee, 1996), whereby we discover emerging meanings—identities—within ourselves (Nystrand, 1997) as we negotiate new knowledge about issues under discussion (such as transformative learning's constituent elements).

It is this aspect of the language learner with which I am concerned here. As students' subjectivities are challenged through dialogue, knowledge-in-action occurs, as does a subsequent transformation of attitudes, opinions, and actions. With transformative world language learning in light of Soka education, we attempt to raise issues of eco-spirituality, cosmological citizenship, and ecological interconnectedness so as to place them at the forefront of students' minds in the language classroom. Dialogic consideration of such issues will affect perceptions of identity in a cosmological or planetary context.

This notion of subjectivities is important from a Buddhist perspective, which teaches that all people possess all potentials, or subjectivities. This philosophy is akin to the issue Smagorinsky and O'Donnell-Allen (2000) raised concerning what constitutes an "ideal" student. They stated that scholars argue the ideal student is: "caring, subversive, thoughtful, culturally literate, civic-minded, imaginative, democratic, joyous, virtuous, politically liberated, personally liberated, self-motivated, scientific, skeptical, reflective, free, domestic, inquiring and compassionate" (pp. 166–167). While the concept of an "ideal" or "perfect" person in the completed sense is antithetical to Buddhism, Buddhism considers these and, indeed, a host of other positive and negative subjectivities as natural characteristics in everyone. Each student has such subjectivities, which may manifest themselves at any time. Epistemologically these subjectivities are challenged, realized, eschewed, and shaped through dialogue. Teachers must foster dialogically this "educational human revolution," or becoming, through content-based approaches to the constituent elements of O'Sullivan's planetary consciousness, what Ikeda has termed a "consciousness of global citizenship" (2007a). Within a social constructivist framework, students tap and understand implicitly and explicitly these subjectivities in themselves throughout the course of student-student/teacher-student/student-nature dialogue. The goal is that through dialogue and teacher scaffolding, students begin to understand global issues vis-à-vis their own subjectivities and, thereby, begin to develop a deep cultural planetary literacy necessary for the development of a global cultural consciousness.

Conclusion

This chapter challenges the second and foreign language educators to resist neoliberal influences of competitive militarism and monetarism, which negatively impact humanity and the environment and shape the purpose and practice of language education. It also challenges educators to foster students who resist such trends. It provides a new current, based on Makiguchi and Ikeda's educational philosophies, for second and foreign language educators to cultivate students' community-based, inner development in individually and culturally relevant ways toward a globally transformed humanity. The way to achieve this is through a transformative world language learning approach of value-creating humanitarian competition grounded in dependent origination, which Ikeda has argued happens at the interface of dialogue. The ultimate resistance, then, for scholars, educators and students is a persistent practice of such dialogue. It is this worldview of dialogic resistance that must undergird foreign and second language education if we, as transformative language educators, aim to challenge and resist the neoliberal competitiveness causing the nexus of destruction.

NOTE

1. My critique of Bethel and Jaffe's work is not meant disparagingly. Rather, it is a small response to Bethel's hope that "a new generation of bilingual scholars and researchers will further examine and analyze Makiguchi's writings and their implications for educational policy and practice" (1989, p. 13).

REFERENCES

Allen, R. (2007). Flavor of the moment: Whence, why, and how? *The Modern Language Journal*, 91, 258–261.
Applebee, A. N. (1996). *Curriculum as conversation: Transforming traditions of teaching and learning*. Chicago, IL: Chicago University Press.
Bethel, D. M. (Ed.). (1989). *Education for creative living:Ideas and proposals of Tsunesaburo Makiguchi*. Ames, IA: Iowa State University Press.
Bethel, D. M. (Ed.). (2002). *A geography of human life (English edition)*. San Francisco, CA: Caddo Gap Press.
Blake, R. & Kramsch, C. (Eds.). (2007). The issue: National language educational policy. *The Modern Language Journal*, 91, 247–283.
Bliss, H. C. (1992). Creating value in the Hoikuen. *Holistic Education Review*, 5, 52–57.
Brecht, R. (2007). National language educational policy in the nation's interest: Why? How? Who is responsible for what? *The Modern Language Journal*, 91, 264–265.
Brown, B. (1994). Toward a Buddhist ecological cosmology, In M.E. Tucker & J.A.Grim (Eds.), *Worldviews and ecology: Religion, philosophy, and the environment* (pp. 124–37). Maryknoll, NY: Orbis Books.
Brown, F. (2006). Educational equity, globalization and the No Child Left Behind Act. In F. Brown & R. C. Hunter (Eds.), *No Child Left Behind and other federal programs for urban school districts* (pp. 309–319). The Netherlands: JAI Press.
Bullough, R. V. (1989). Foreword. In. D. M. Bethel (Ed.), *Education for creative living:Ideas and proposals of Tsunesaburo Makiguchi* (pp. xiii–xvii). Ames, IA: Iowa State University Press.
Bush, G. W. (1999). Education: No Child Left Behind. In *Renewing America's Purpose: Policy addresses of George W. Bush, July 1999–July 2000* (pp. 13–30). U.S.A.: Republican National Committee

and Bush for President, Inc.

Byrnes, H. (2006). The power of language: U.S. language policy five years after 9/11 Plenary session panel at ACTFL 2006. Retrieved October 1, 2007, from http:www1.georgetown.edu/departments/german/faculty/byrnes/lecturesandpresentations/Byrnes.ACTFL.11-06.pdf.

Crawford, J. (2007, April 3). *Issues in U.S, language policy*. Retrieved September 24, 2007 from http: ourworld.compuserve.com/homepages/JCRAWFORD/langleg.htm#State.

Cummins, J. (1981). Age on arrival and immigrant second language learning in Canada. A reassessment. *Applied Linguistics*, 2, 132-149.

Eferakorho, J. (2006). Public education in an era of neoliberal globalization: The broken promise of No Child Left Behind. In F. Brown & R. C. Hunter (Eds.), *No Child Left Behind and other federal programs for urban school districts* (pp. 249-262). The Netherlands: JAI Press.

Furman, N., Goldberg, D., & Lusin, N. (2007). *Enrollments in languages other than English in United States institutions of higher education, fall 2006*. Modern Language Association.

Gebert, A. & Joffee, M. (2007). Value creation as the aim of education: Tsunesaburo Makiguchi and Soka education. In D. T. Hansen (Ed.). *Ethical visions of education: Philosophies in practice* (pp. 65-82). New York, NY: Teachers College Press.

Goodman, A. (2003). *Now what? Developing our future*. New York, NY: Peter Lang.

Goulah, J. (2003). No to "Spanish first." *Language Association Journal, New York State Association of Foreign Language Teachers*, 58(2), 11-12.

Goulah, J. (2005). *Transformative second and foreign language learning: Cultivating a deep culture of global citizenship and global literacy for the 21st century*. Unpublished doctoral dissertation. University at Buffalo, NY.

Goulah, J. (2006). Transformative second and foreign language learning for the 21st century. *Critical Inquiry in Language Studies*, 3, 201-221.

Goulah, J. (2007a). Toward *pax terra-humana:* Cultural transformative learning and a planetary literacy in the foreign language classroom. *Journal of Transformative Education*, 5, 163-176.

Goulah, J. (2007b). Village voices, global visions: Digital video as a transformative foreign language learning tool. *Foreign Language Annals*, 40(1), 62-78.

Goulah, J. (2008). Transformative world language learning: An approach for environmental and cultural sustainability and economic and political security. *Journal of Language and Literacy Education* [Online], 4(1), 6-23. Available: http://www.coe.uga.edu/jolle /FLIssue/transformative.pdf.

Goulah, J. (2009a). Makiguchi in the 'fractured future': Value-creating and transformative world language learning. *Educational Studies*, 45(2), 193-213.

Goulah, J. (2009b). Tsunesaburo Makiguchi and Mikhail Bakhtin in dialogue: Pedagogy for ecological selfhood and spatial literacy. *Journal of Asian-Pacific Education*, 29(2), 265-279.

Goulah, J. & Gebert, A. (Eds.). (2009). Tsunesaburo Makiguchi's educational philosophies [special issue]. *Educational Studies*, 45(2), 109-229.

Gutierrez, K. D. (2008). Developing a sociocritical literacy in the third space. *Reading Research Quarterly*, 43(2), 148-164.

Hart, T. (2004). Opening the contemplative mind in the classroom. *Journal of Transformative Education*, 2(1), 28-46.

Hatano, K. (2009). Voice in EFL education in a Japanese context: Makiguchi's perspectives in the concept of "voice." *Educational Studies*, 45(2), 165-180.

Heinesen, N. (1995). *Soka education: Value-creating pedagogy as applied to language education*. Unpublished master's thesis. Soka University of America Graduate School.

Henderson, H. & Ikeda, D. (2004). *Planetary citizenship: Your values, beliefs and actions* can *shape a sus-*

tainable world. Santa Monica, CA: Middleway Press.

Herman, D. M. (2002). "Our patriotic duty": Insights from professional history, 1890–1920. In T. A. Osborn (Ed.), *The future of foreign language education in the United States* (pp. 1–29). Westport, CT: Bergin & Garvey.

Holborow, M. (2006). *Ideology and language: The interconnections between neo-liberalism and English*. Retrieved September 1, 2008 from http://firgoa.usc.es/drupal/node/29985.

Holquist, M. (2002). *Dialogism: Bakhtin and his world*. New York, NY: Routledge.

Ikeda, D. (1964). Preface to English edition. In T. Makiguchi, *Philosophy of value* (pp. i–iii). Tokyo, Japan: Seikyo Press.

Ikeda, D. (1991, September 26). *The age of "soft power" and inner-motivated philosophy*. Paper delivered at Harvard University, Boston, MA. Retrieved October 5, 2008 from http://www.daisakuikeda.org/index.php?mid=resources&sub=works&sub2=lect&quid=10.

Ikeda, D. (2001a). *For the sake of peace: Seven paths to global harmony, a Buddhist perspective*. Santa Monica, CA: Middleway Press.

Ikeda, D. (2001b). *Soka education: A Buddhist vision for teachers, students and parents*. Santa Monica, CA: Middleway Press.

Ikeda, D. (2002). Foreword. In T. Makiguchi, *A geography of human life (English edition)*, D. M. Bethel (Ed.). San Francisco, CA: Caddo Gap Press.

Ikeda, D. (2003). A global ethic of coexistence: Toward a "life-sized" paradigm of our age. *Living Buddhism: Journal for Peace, Culture and Education*, April, 4–25.

Ikeda, D. (2005). Foreword. In N. Noddings (Ed.), *Educating citizens for global awareness* (pp. ix–xi). New York, NY: Teachers College Press.

Ikeda, D. (2006, May 19). Respect and greet everyone as Buddhas. *World Tribune*, 2–3.

Ikeda, D. (2007a). Foreword. In D. T. Hansen (Ed.), *Ethical visions of education: Philosophies in practice* (pp. vii–ix). New York, NY: Teachers College Press.

Ikeda, D. (2007b). *Restoring the human connection: The first steps to global peace: 2007 peace proposal*. Tokyo, Japan: Soka Gakkai.

Ikeda, D. (2008). *Humanizing religion, creating peace: 2008 peace proposal*. Tokyo, Japan: Soka Gakkai.

Jaffe, C. (1993). Tsunesaburo Makiguchi: Teacher, philosopher, value creator. *Teaching Education*, 5(2), 101–105.

Kahn, J. & Yardley, J. (2007, August 26). As China roars, pollution reaches deadly extremes. *The New York Times*. Retrieved August 26, 2007, from http://www.NYTimes.com.

Kirk, G. & Okazawa-Rey, M. (Eds.) (2000). Neoliberalism, militarism, and armed conflict. *Social Justice*, 27(4), 1–17.

Krieger, D. & Ikeda, D. (2002). *Choose hope: Your role in waging peace in a nuclear age*. Santa Monica, CA: Middleway Press.

Kubota, R. & Catlett, S. (2008). Spanish only for foreign language in the elementary school (FLES): Competing discourses in local language policy. *Foreign Language Annals*, 41(1), 102–118.

Kumagai, K. (2000). Value-creating pedagogy and Japanese education in the modern era. *The Journal of Oriental Studies*, 10, 29–45.

Kumashiro, K. K. (2004). *Against common sense: Teaching and learning toward social justice*. New York, NY: RoutledgeFalmer.

Lydon, A. (1995). An ecozoic cosmology of curriculum and spirituality. *Journal of Curriculum Theorizing: An Interdisciplinary Journal of Curriculum Studies*, 11(2), 67–86.

Makiguchi, T. (1964). *Philosophy of value*. Tokyo, Japan: Seikyo Press.

Makiguchi, T. (1981–1988). *Makiguchi Tsunesaburo zenshu [The complete works of Tsunesaburo Makiguchi].* Tokyo, Japan: Daisan Bunmeisha.
Miller, G. D. (2002). *Peace, value, and wisdom: The educational philosophy of Daisaku Ikeda.* Amsterdam: Rodopi.
Miller, J. P. (2000). *Education and the soul: Toward a spiritual curriculum.* Albany: State University of New York Press.
Modern Language Association. (2007). *Foreign languages and higher education: New structures for a changed world.* Retrieved October 1, 2007, from http://www.mla.org/flreport.
Moffett, J. (1994). *The universal schoolhouse: Spiritual awakening through education.* San Francisco, CA: Jossey-Bass.
Nagashima, A. (2004). The American Renaissance and the Lotus Sutra: A perspective on dependent origination. *Living Buddhism: Journal for Peace, Culture and Education,* Oct, 20–25.
No Child Left Behind Act of 2001, Pub. L. No. 107–110, 115 Stat. 1425 (2001).
Norton, B. (2000). *Identity and language learning: Gender, ethnicity and educational change.* Essex, UK: Pearson Education Limited.
Nystrand, M. (1997). *Opening dialogue: Understanding the dynamics of language and learning in the English classroom.* New York: Teachers College Press.
Osborn, T. A. (2006). *Teaching world languages for social justice: A sourcebook of principles and practices.* Mahwah, NJ: Lawrence Erlbaum.
O'Sullivan, E. (1999). *Transformative learning: Educational vision for the 21st century.* New York, NY: Zed Books Ltd.
O'Sullivan, E. (2002a). The project and vision of transformative education: Integral transformative learning, In E.V. O'Sullivan, A. Morrel, & M. O'Connor (Eds.), *Expanding the boundaries of transformative learning: Essays on theory and praxis* (pp. 1–12). New York: Palgrave.
O'Sullivan, E. (2002b). Transformative learning and holistic learning. *Wholistic Education: Special Interest Group Newsletter,* fall, 3.
Pear, R. (2007b, June 14). Security is focus of revised effort on immigration. *The New York Times.* Retrieved June 14, 2007 from http://www.nytimes.com.
Pear, R. & Hulse, C. (2007, June 29). Immigration bill dies in Senate; Defeat for Bush. *The New York Times.* Retrieved June 29, 2007 from http://www.nytimes.com.
Reagan, T. (2004). Objectification, positivism and language studies: A reconsideration. *Critical Inquiry in Language Studies: An International Journal,* 1(1), 41–60.
Riley-Taylor, E. (2002). *Ecology, spirituality, & education: Curriculum for relational knowing.* New York: Peter Lang Publishing.
Silverman, J. (2008, September 4). States ponder ESL limits in schools. *Associated Press* Retrieved September 4, 2008 from http://www2.ljworld.com/news/2008/sep/04/states_ponder_esl_limits_schools/.
Smagorinsky, P., & O'Donnell-Allen, C. (2000). Idiocultural diversity in small groups: The role of the relational framework in collaborative learning. In C.D. Lee & P. Smagorinsky (Eds.), *Vygotskian perspectives on literacy research: Constructing meaning through collaborative inquiry*(pp. 165–190). New York: Cambridge University Press
Smith, D. I. & Carvill, B. (2000). *The gift of the stranger: Faith, hospitality, and foreign language learning.* Grand Rapids, MI: William B. Eerdmans.
Smith, D. I. & Osborn, T. A. (Eds.). (2007). *Spirituality, social justice, and language learning.* Charlotte, NC: Information Age Publishing.
Tienda, M. (2008). *English mastery and academic achievement.* Presidential invited address. Research on

Schools, Neighborhoods, and Communities: Toward Civic Responsibility, 2008 AERA Annual Meeting and Exhibition, New York, NY.
Touyou Tetsugaku Kenkyuujyo. (2007). *Sekai ga mita Ikeda Daisaku: 200 wo koeta meiyou gakujyutsu shyougou [The world recognizes Daisaku Ikeda: Surpassing 200 honorary degrees]*. Tokyo, Japan: Daisan Bunmeisha.
U.S. English, Inc.: Toward a united America (2007, September 30). Retrieved September 30, 2007 from http://www.us-english.org/inc/default.asp.

CHAPTER SEVEN

Resisting Mandated Literacy Curricula in Urban Middle Schools

MARSHALL A. GEORGE

In a 2000 editorial in *The Nation* focusing on the problems facing American education at the turn of the century, the writer suggested that, "Testing has precise, limited utility in identifying troubled schools, but high-stakes testing is now such a fetish that real teaching is being replaced by 'teaching to the test,' particularly in poor and minority schools." (http://www.thenation.com/doc/20000605/editors, Retrieved January 15, 2010). One wonders if the editors knew that months after that statement was made, a new legislation, passed in the name of sweeping educational reform, would exacerbate the teaching-to-the-test issue that they criticized. Indeed, the first decade of the 21st century has seen the development of an unprecedented emphasis on the testing of American's school children. One major cause of this rise in testing (and thereby teaching to the test) is clear: the passage and implementation of the No Child Left Behind (NCLB) legislation of 2001. The impact of so much testing on curriculum and pedagogy has been astounding. Data from interviews, observations, and curricular materials collected over a four-year period have provided me with great insight into the experiences of teachers of English language arts in New York City middle and high schools since the implementation of NCLB. This chapter is informed by these data along with informal conversations I have had with pre-service and in-service teachers in my role as university English teacher educator for the past twelve years.

No Child Left Behind and Adolescent Literacy

Though noble in its intent to raise student achievement of all American students by closing the achievement gaps that exist among racially and linguistically diverse groups, as well as between students of low and high socioeconomic status, NCLB was a seriously flawed legislation. According to Tom Loveless, a senior fellow at the Brookings Institute, the major criticisms of No Child Left Behind can be summed up in three words: funding, accountability, and testing. (http://www.brookings.edu/opinions/2004/0108education_loveless.aspx). In this chapter, I am going to focus on the impact of this testing and accountability movement on the language arts (a.k.a. literacy) curriculum in New York City and the way that numerous teachers have managed to resist the school level curricular mandates that resulted from NCLB and that prevented them from engaging in creative, thoughtful teaching.

Perhaps the most notable component of NCLB was the mandate of yearly testing in grades three through eight as a means of determining if all students were making adequate yearly progress toward standards in literacy (reading, writing, listening) and mathematics. Acerbically referred to by many teachers as "No Child Left Untested," NCLB included punitive sanctions for schools whose students failed to make adequate progress on standardized tests. More than ever before, the term *high-stakes testing* took on new meaning, causing district and school administrators to make sweeping directives to teachers to raise the test scores of the children in their classrooms.

Part of the strategy employed by many in their scramble to raise test scores has been to assess students' progress throughout the year. Like the high-stakes official tests, these "frequent formative assessments" often take two to three days to administer. Many principals want to simulate the official testing conditions as "trial runs"; therefore, regular schedules are altered to add as many as 12 additional school days each year to further assess students under high-stakes testing conditions (and this is just in literacy—the same holds true for math). One eighth-grade teacher I spoke with recorded 22 days of additional formative/practice testing that occurred in her school on top of the eight actual days utilized for the official state assessments in English language arts, mathematics, science, and social studies. In other words, she and her students lost a full month to testing in her principal's desperate attempt to make adequate yearly progress. No wonder she and her colleagues began to refer to the legislation as No Child Left Untested!

It is important to note that recursive assessments are very important for teachers and learners. The National Council of Teachers of English (NCTE) states that teachers need to be "knowledgeable about many forms of assessment and to be able to use these data-collection tools in order to articulate what students have learned and their growth in using strategies for further learning" (http://www.ncte.org/governance/Assessment). Indeed, all assessment is not bad. However, since even before the onset of this testing craze, scholars and researchers have criticized an overreliance on standardized testing to measure student learning for a myriad of reasons. In one important study, Nichols, Glass, and Berliner (2006) found that despite an enormous amount of pressure created by high-stakes testing, the yearly assessments "had almost no important influence on student academic performance" (p. i). Others have cited the negative impacts testing has, such as the containment of students' engagement with literature (Anagnostopoulos, 2003) or the negative impact it has on the teaching of writing (Hillocks, 2002). Yet students in traditionally underserved public schools in urban areas are being subjected to more and more standardized tests as the expectations for teachers become more and more rigid.

Assessments, both formative and summative, are not the only tactic utilized by desperate school leaders to meet the demands of NCLB. Mandated curricula, often scripted (so that they are "teacher proof"), have found their way into schools all across the nation. While scripted curricula have been utilized in elementary schools for years (Milosovic, 2007), the first decade of the 21st century widely spread to middle and high schools for the first time, often with deleterious effects (Costigan and Crocco, 2006; Crocco and Costigan, 2007; Shippen et al., 2006). According to Valli and Buese (2007), "high-stakes policy directives promote an environment in which teachers are asked to relate to their students differently, enact pedagogies that are often at odds with their vision of best practice, and experience high levels of stress. The summative effect of too many policy demands coming too fast often resulted in teacher discouragement, role ambiguity, and superficial responses to administrative goals (p. 520).

What has been especially tricky for many teachers in New York City, is that literacy mandates are framed by the philosophical orientations of balanced literacy and differentiated instruction, both of which, like ongoing formative assessment, are solidly supported by research and should allow for significant pedagogical creativity and teacher autonomy. This, however, has not been the case in many mandated literacy assessments and instructional programs, where adherence to rigid curriculum maps and specific instructional strategies is expected. Perhaps the best example is the balanced literacy model widely adopted and closely monitored by many administrators across New York City.

Balanced Literacy Instruction

Balanced literacy, a term which originated in California in 1996 (California Department of Education, 1996), is an approach to reading and writing instruction that combines explicit skills and strategies instruction with a meaning based approach emphasizing comprehension and enrichment (Frey et al., 2005). At its inception, it was a model of literacy instruction for young learners in grades K-3, and was a compromise in the reading wars of skills instruction versus whole language. With the publication of *Guiding Readers and Writers, Grades 3–6: Teaching Comprehension, Genre, and Content Literacy* by Fountas and Pinnell in 2001, balanced literacy widely found its way into the upper elementary grades as well. Soon after, New York City joined other urban districts (Tucson, Austin, Los Angeles) in adopting balanced literacy as its preferred approach to reading and writing instruction through grade eight, and even for high school programs focusing on struggling adolescent readers.

Frey and his colleagues suggest that balanced literacy is "a philosophical orientation that assumes that reading and writing achievement are developed through instruction and support in multiple environments by using various approaches that differ by level of teacher support and child control" (2005, p. 272). It is important to understand that balanced literacy is *a philosophical orientation* rather than a *program*, and that it is a solid, well-grounded approach to literacy instruction. Nevertheless, the first decade of the 21st century has seen the emergence of many balanced literacy *programs* for adolescent readers. Though called by various names (Teachers College Model; Ramp Up for Advanced Literacy; Workshop Model; Fountas and Pinnell Literacy Blocks), most middle schools in New York City adopted a balanced literacy program in their scramble to improve test scores when NCLB was implemented. For many, this was a welcome decision, as balanced literacy should allow for much flexibility and teacher creativity. Hand-in-hand with a balanced literacy approach, differentiated instruction became a mantra across New York City and other urban areas around the country.

DIFFERENTIATED INSTRUCTION

According to Carol Ann Tomlinson (1999), the scholar who has most studied and advocated for differentiated instruction (DI), "Differentiated instruction is not an instructional strategy or a teaching model. It's a way of thinking about teaching and learning that advocates beginning where individuals are rather than with a prescribed plan of action, which ignores student readiness, interest, and learning profile" (p. 108). To reiterate her main point, differentiation *is* a way of thinking, *not* a prescribed model. Yet many of the teachers I spoke with report that their administrators, staff developers, literacy coaches, and department chairs placed pressure on them to "do differentiation" or to follow the "differentiated instruction model." For those teachers, Tomlinson (2001) provides further insight into how they might go about this problematic mandate: "In a differentiated classroom, the teacher proactively plans and carries out varied approaches to content, process, and product in anticipation of and response to student differences in readiness, interest, and learning needs" (p. 7). The heart of DI lies with assessment—authentic assessment.

Yet, again, numerous teachers report that administrators have corrupted the ideals of a good model, wanting them to differentiate solely on readiness and deeming learning styles and student interest differentiation to be "nice, but not what we need to get those scores up." When one second-year teacher asked her principal what the difference between total differentiation for readiness and tracking was, the administrator replied, "one [DI] allows you to keep your job, the other [tracking] does not." Likewise, many teachers reported that administrators wanted them only to differentiate on content and process but never product. "We are holding all students to the same standards; therefore, all kids should do the same assignments," one principal told her staff when the question of differentiated products (assessments) came up during professional development. These are not isolated scenarios. I hear them over and over from my graduate students as well as from the teachers I spoke to for this study. Administrators and supervisors have distorted the ideals of differentiation and balanced literacy to become de facto tracking and inflexible, scripted curricula.

It appears that NCLB and its emphasis on standardized assessments have made a profound change in the way that many schools at all developmental levels operate, especially those serving students from low socioeconomic communities. Because principals are so afraid of the draconian measures that would befall their schools if they fail to meet AYP, many, especially those in middle schools where all students in all grades are tested, are resorting to curricular mandates that are not pedagogically sound. Indeed, many have taken the solid ideas of balanced literacy and differentiated instruction and turned them into teacher-proof scripted curricula. Of course, the degree to which a specific program is mandated varies from school to school, and many schools are fortunate to have leaders who are well grounded in the principles of curriculum, assessment, and pedagogy, and fully understand balanced literacy and differentiated instruction. However, many are not so fortunate. I have spoken with numerous teachers who are in untenable situations and only survive by engaging in subversive acts of resistance.

A decade before NCLB was enacted Apple and Jungck (1992) cautioned that when curriculum becomes increasingly controlled, standardized, and systematized and when standardized tests are be-all-end-all, teaching and learning suffers. They suggested that, "instead of professional teachers who care greatly about what they do and why they do it, we may have alienated executors of someone else's plans" (p. 24). Luckily, the teachers whose stories I shall explore *do* care greatly about what they do *despite* being "alienated executors of someone else's plans."

Creative Resistance

As you read the following vignettes, there are several things you need to know. All names are pseudonyms and details of setting have been altered so that no school or teacher can be identified. Data sources for this project include interviews with teachers, observations of classrooms, and examination of curriculum and professional development materials from the schools where the women teach. Each of the teachers works in New York City middle or high schools where a balanced literacy model is mandated, and teachers are expected to teach from a differentiated perspective. In New York City, each school is allowed to make its own curriculum choices—there are no city or district mandates. Having spoken with teachers from different schools that ascribe to the same literacy program, I have come to realize that problems often do not lie with the programs themselves; rather, with the way a given school administration implements the program. The degree to which there is flexibility for these four teachers varies; however, in each case the school administration expects fairly close adherence to "the model."

Jill (grade 6)

Jill, a New York City Teaching Fellow (NYCTF), had been teaching English language arts for three years when I interviewed her. Her first teaching assignment was in a "school at risk," meaning that because it had not met annual yearly progress (AYP), it was being closely monitored by the State to determine if it would remain open. When describing her one-year experience at that school (she subsequently transferred to a much different school), she emphatically stated, "Of all of the accomplishments of my twenty-six years on this earth, surviving [that school] is truly the most amazing. I never imagined I would make it through that year." When asked what made the year so difficult, she responded with a litany of issues that had plagued her and her colleagues in the school; however, the themes that emerged most frequently and with most veracity were mandated course content and instructional delivery. Her principal and literacy coach had strong expectations that she follow a rigidly scripted lesson plan format each day and that she keep pace with a prescribed curriculum map, which designated specific literary and writing genres and reading and writing skills to be "mastered" each month. Her school espoused the Teachers College model of literacy instruction and had professional development support from Columbia University's Teachers College.

When she began her first year of teaching as a New York City Teaching Fellow, Jill had completed nine credits of foundational coursework in a teacher certification program. Part of that training included experience in developing thematic-based, multi-genre literature unit of study. She was excited to implement that introductory theme unit focusing on the theme of *change* during the first month of school, as she believed that the transition from fifth grade to sixth could be daunting for her students and she wanted to support their adjustment period. However, the day before school started, she received a curriculum map and pacing guide which informed her that for the first month she would be required to teach a unit based on a single genre, the memoir, and that she would have to focus her attention on making predictions when reading a memoir. The writing component of the unit was to be a student memoir. Her literacy coach was puzzled when Jill asked if she could begin the year with a two-week multi-genre unit focusing on the themes of change and transition, responding, "of course not; then you will be way behind one year and your kids may not know an important skill that they will be tested on." (Note: neither memoir nor prediction has been included in the NYS sixth grade ELA assessment since its inception in 2005.)

Chagrined, Jill complied and taught "prediction in memoir" during the initial weeks of the school year, shelving her unit on transitions and change. (The following year in a different school where the TC program was less rigidly regulated, Jill was experienced enough to combine her memoir genre study with her thematic unit on transitions and explored the changes faced by the subjects of the memoirs she and her students read and focusing their own memoir-writing assignment on a life-changing event.) While the rigid genre-based curriculum showed no flexibility, Jill did. As she became more confident as a teacher and increasingly questioned the curriculum approach mandated in her school, Jill began to make adjustments in her instruction.

In November of that year, Jill began to utilize the required "Do Now" (a brief activity for students to complete when they enter the classroom, intending to focus their attention on the day's lesson, often by copying an objective from the chalkboard) as an opportunity to introduce her students to poetic language (although poetry was not to be taught until April, National Poetry Month) and to "play with" language. For several weeks, Jill's sixth graders would often enter the classroom to find on the whiteboard a line, a couplet, or a stanza of poetry which they were expected to read and respond to. These snippets of poetry were thematically linked to the genre under study and served to scaffold the skill or strategy lesson mandated by the curriculum map. According to Jill, "when I started with the poetry Do-Nows, I suddenly had 32 sixth graders actively engaged within 30 seconds of entering the classroom, as opposed to the chaos that had been [the norm] for the first part of the year. They loved the poetry!" At first, her principal was concerned about this "out-of-sequence poetry study; however, when Jill pointed out that the formative assessments indicated that her students were missing all of the questions related to poetry, the principal acquiesced.

Not only was Jill's teaching creativity initially impeded by her school's single-genre approach to curriculum, she was also expected to strictly follow a balanced literacy lesson plan format. Framed by the gradual release model of instruction (Pearson and Gallagher, 1983), this literacy model includes a mini lesson and modeled shared reading, followed by guided reading practice and independent reading. The lesson begins with a brief highly focused mini lesson, followed by a shared reading in which the teacher models a reading strategy using a text that all students can see (an enlarged text is most common). For example, during the first weeks of the school year, Jill read aloud excerpts from memoirs, stopping to "think aloud" where a reader might make a prediction about what would happen next. Students are then asked to practice the strategy with a partner before moving on to independent reading, where they are expected to utilize the strategy. During independent reading, the teacher works with small groups (usually homogeneous) to assess and/or provide additional support as they practice previously modeled strategies.

Jill was fairly comfortable with the mini lesson and shared reading portion of the balanced literacy model. What bothered her was that the topic for the mini lessons had been predetermined for the months of September-December, and she was expected to stick to the prescribed schedule of mini lessons. With one of her sixth grade classes, she found that many of the students already knew the strategy being modeled and used it regularly in authentic reading experiences. Therefore, she went "off script" with that one class and moved to more advanced reading strategies. When her principal discovered this, she insisted that Jill return to the pacing calendar and "cover each of the strategies" it listed.

As a creative compromise, Jill's sixth graders had two mini lessons each day—one from the pacing calendar and one based on the students' areas of weakness on the most recent formative assessment. She came up with the idea of having a student teacher for some of the "review" mini lessons. These student teachers were not from the local university; rather, they were students in the class who modeled the strategy in the shared reading portion of the review lesson. This way, students who needed a refresher got it. The second mini lesson was an enrichment lesson, often given during guided reading groups. The principal liked the idea and later mandated it across the sixth grade.

During her first year, Jill found numerous ways of resisting the obdurate curricular and pedagogical demands imposed on her. When questioned, the principal of Jill's school told colleagues that her pedagogical decisions were "scientifically based" and were intended to ensure that students did well on the state assessment so that the school would make adequate yearly progress. At the end of that first year, Jill was able to find a position in another middle school in the city—a school which also asked teachers to base their instruction on balanced literacy, but which, in Jill's words, "understood the theory behind the model and understood the importance of each teacher bringing her own understandings to planning and teaching." Jill's acts of resistance, however small, enabled her to survive her first year of teaching and, more importantly, provided her students with improved learning experiences. She later found out that her students were among the top achievers on the state ELA assessment. Resistance pays.

Catherine (grade 7)

Catherine taught high school English for three years in a small city before moving to New York City to take a job in a small middle school. The school administration in her new school had not adopted a singular curriculum model; rather, the principal had blended a number of models, including Balanced Literacy, Accelerate Reader, 100 Books Challenge, and Read-180. She had expectations that the teachers in her school would utilize components of each of these programs to differentiate instruction in the daily 90-minute literacy block. Catherine's first two years in the middle school were difficult as she was accustomed to a more traditional approach to teaching high school English and was unfamiliar with any of the "programs" her principal expected her to teach. While all aspects of teaching that year were daunting, Catherine found it particularly difficult to teach a curriculum that had very specific timed components and did not allow for much flexibility in timing. Previously trained in differentiated instruction, she was further frustrated by a staff developer who only cared for differentiation based on readiness and was not supportive of Catherine's efforts to build on student interests or learning styles as a means of differentiating for motivation. Likewise, the administration was not keen on differentiation of product. In the name of "Standardization," they wanted all students given the same assessments rather than having choices as to how to demonstrate their knowledge and skills.

Her supervisors were adamant that Catherine and her colleagues spend five to twelve minutes on each mini lesson each day (one for reading; another for writing), which had to include a teacher "think aloud," modeling specific strategies. Catherine recalls her first informal observation, when her assistant principal (AP) informed her that her mini lesson had extended to sixteen minutes and cautioned her, saying "if you exceed the mini lesson allowance by five minutes daily for 180 school days, your children will fail the ELA assessment and you will have to go to summer school. Do you want that?" What the AP refused to acknowledge was that Catherine had combined the reading and writing mini lessons for the day, thereby "saving" eight minutes of instructional time (never mind making explicit connections between reading and writing). The AP (who had a mathematics background) provided no feedback on the content of the lesson, just on the timing and adherence to the prescribed format. Catherine indicated to me that this was the case of all of her observations during the school year.

After that tense informal observation (along with the realization that the administration was more concerned with the logistics of the lesson rather than the content), Catherine bought a digital timer that she kept by her side in the event that she had an unannounced observation. Never again (when supervisors were in the room) did this smart young teacher ever exceed the allowed time parameters for the various components of her lesson. Another frustration related to timing was the expectation that students would engage in silent sustained reading for forty minutes of each ninety-minute block. In the 100-Book-Challenge model, this independent reading occurs during a single block, with the entire class reading. In contrast, the expectation for independent reading in the balanced literacy model (also in place in the school) was that it occurs simultaneously with small teacher-guided reading groups, allowing students to have independent reading time daily but not necessarily uninterrupted silent sustained reading. When asked about the apparent contradictions in the two approaches, the AP downplayed the issue, suggesting that "it's really all the same." More important in his mind was that students spend forty minutes reading independently in class each day.

Catherine and her colleagues were stymied by the administrator's expectations but found ways to make adjustments. Early in the year they realized that their students did not have the stamina to read silently for forty minutes uninterrupted. They felt that it was better to use the balanced literacy approach, where the independent reading occurred in shorter blocks. As the year progressed and students' reading endurance increased, Catherine often provided time for whole class silent sustained reading. Eventually, she decided to alternate the approaches, depending on the rest of her lesson and on the behavior of her students on any given day. However, she had to be careful that in her written lesson plans she was explicit about which approach she was utilizing on any given day, as the administration wanted to ensure that "all literacy programs are being utilized and done correctly."

Like it is in many schools, differentiated instruction was highly valued by Catherine's supervisors. They expected differentiation to occur in each class period, a fairly reasonable expectation in a balanced literacy classroom as independent reading and guided reading are, by definition, individualized. However, her staff developer became highly critical of one of Catherine's lessons when she found students in guided reading groups with materials differentiated by interest, rather than by ability (a.k.a. readiness). Catherine had retrieved each of the texts from different Internet sources and had reformatted them in the same font type and size, leading the staff developer to believe that the texts were not differentiated by difficulty.

The lesson in question occurred when students were working on the reading strategy known as *questioning the author*, a process designed to help students "consider meaning, to develop and grapple with ideas, and to try construct meaning" (Beck et al., 1997, p. 6) from texts. The idea behind the selection of the particular texts in the lesson was that students had a great deal of prior knowledge, even expertise, about the content addressed in the texts (review of a new video game; review of a new music release; review of a new sci-fi movie; and review of new laptop computer) and could work within their reading groups to consider authors' purpose and not just retrieve information (Beck et al., 1997), a skill Catherine had found from her analysis of formative assessments that her students struggled with.

Despite the staff developer's concerns, the lesson went extremely well and Catherine was pleased. Rather than disputing the allegation that she was not using different levels of text, she found an effective, if somewhat subversive, way to stem future criticisms from her supervisors. Anytime she utilized net-based texts for lessons, she made use of her word processor's varied font styles and sizes to "differentiate" the text, keeping her supervisors at bay. According to Catherine, "I often do differentiate on readiness, but sometimes there is good reason to use interests or talents for grouping. I was so mad at [the staff developer] for refusing to acknowledge that this was OK, I did not feel guilty at duping her with the altered font trick."

Similarly, when Catherine created a unit project that had a menu of choices the administration was not pleased (though her students were delighted!). At the end of a unit on historical fiction, in which students had read different books set in different countries, Catherine provided them with options as to how they would demonstrate their knowledge of the book itself along with their knowledge of the country in which the book was set. (Catherine had collaborated with the sixth grade social studies teacher on this interdisciplinary unit.) Her assignment sheet for the project had the objectives for the assessment at the top, and a rubric for assessment on the back. The objectives for all students were the same as was the rubric. Students could demonstrate their knowledge by writing a short dramatization from their novel and performing it for the class; they could film a video documentary of the life of one of the major characters in their book and share it with the class; or they could write a musical ballad about the character's life, record it, and play it for the class. The administration liked each of these assignments but asked that Catherine choose one of them for the entire class to do—again, in the name of "Standardization."

Catherine was devastated and her students were angry (although they had not seen the assignment sheet, the students had heard about the creative assignment regularly from Catherine in class, in an attempt to motivate them to read the books carefully). In this case, the act of resistance came not from the teacher directly, but from one of the parents. The mother of a girl in Catherine's class called her after school on the day that the students had found out that the assignment has been changed to one option—writing a dramatization. Her daughter, who was painfully shy, had been so excited about the musical ballad, as she planned to do a dance along with the musical ballad she was to write. According to the mother, this was the first time that the young girl had gotten excited about a school assignment. Slyly, Catherine told the parent that she had not had any luck changing the principal's mind, but that parents usually had more influence. The mother went to the principal to demand that the three-option assignment be reinstated. The principal gave in. According to Catherine, the presentations far exceeded any other project that her students did all year—so much so that the staff developer and principal both admitted to her that differentiation of product might be acceptable on "rare occasions."

It is hard to understand why administrators and staff developers such as the ones in Catherine's school have such strong beliefs about teaching and learning and why they impose such rigid expectations on their teachers. Whatever the cause, Catherine's ongoing acts of resistance, however small or large, were important for her and for her students. Catherine has aspirations of becoming a school administrator herself, and she swears that she will never become the rigid micromanager that she has worked for and with over the years.

Stephanie (grade 8)

A first year teacher of English, Stephanie was hired in her large middle school because of her fairly extensive training in balanced literacy during the teacher education program from which she had recently graduated. She began the school year excited to implement the innovative assessments she had honed during her student teaching the prior year and hoped to integrate several works of adolescent literature into the eighth grade curriculum by making connections between those novels and works of classic fiction as she had learned to do from her professors at the university (Herz and Gallo, 2005). Being a very talented writer, Stephanie also looked forward to implementing a writer's workshop, in which her students would learn to write in multiple genres. In her first professional development session, she was distressed to discover that no whole class novels were allowed in the school, and that all students were expected to write five-paragraph essays each month during the school year. When she questioned her literacy coach, she was told that she would have to "unlearn" the notions she had picked up in her certification program, but that there would be much support in her efforts to do so. On Day 1 Stephanie's prior experiences in graduate school and as a successful writer were being ignored and she was being told that she would need to unlearn her basic tenets for teaching English language arts.

Stephanie was especially discouraged that she was not going to be allowed to read works of literature with her whole class. According to her literacy coach, given the various reading levels of her students and the school's belief in differentiated instruction, teaching a single novel to the entire class was incongruous with the school's philosophy. "How could you find a book that would be appropriate for all of the students in the class? Any title would be too difficult for some students, and too challenging for others." In addition, the school's administration wanted eighth grade students to read mostly classic works of literature, in an effort to "raise the bar" for all students and to get them ready for high school. Funding was not available to purchase works of adolescent literature, and classroom libraries could have no more than five copies of any single title. Stephanie pointed out that many high school curricula include works of adolescent literature (she had taught the young adult novel *Speak* to her tenth graders the previous year as a student teacher) and that students in ninth grade mostly studied novels together as a whole class, but her logic fell on deaf ears.

Stephanie had several literature-related problems to solve, and she knew she would have to do so in creative and imperceptible ways. She wanted to build her classroom library to include works of middle grade, young adult, and classic literature. To do so she spent her weekends "cruising" stoop sales in the city and yard/garage sales in the suburbs, as well as used book shops in an effort to purchase as many appropriate works of literature as possible. She said that when she told people they were for her classroom library, most people gave her the books free. Rather quickly, her classroom library grew. In order to avoid tipping off those who were opposed to the types of books she wanted in her classroom, she created a library filing system that was color coded and filed alphabetically, so that the works of young adult literature did not stick out. Even if she was not allowed to teach a whole class novel, she could make a wider range of literature available for her students for independent reading.

During the winter of her first year teaching, Stephanie went to a local book store to attend a reading of one of her favorite young adult authors. Because the gathering was small, she was able to spend a few minutes talking with the author, who was distressed to hear that Stephanie wanted to teach one of her novels to her eighth grade class but was forbidden from doing so by school policy. After getting Stephanie's school contact, the author later called the principal, offered to speak to all of the eighth graders in the school and to donate 150 copies of her book to the school. The only payment she would ask for was in the form of feedback from teachers and students about the book. The principal quickly agreed, never thinking that this agreement was in conflict with his own rule. The eighth grade teachers got to teach the novel to their entire classes and the results were outstanding. Never had the school seen such engagement in literature study and such outstanding written essays about a book of study. After this enormously successfull event, school policy was altered to allow one core novel per grade each year.

Regarding the (over)emphasis placed on the five-paragraph essay, Stephanie was perplexed. Having worked in the university writing center as a tutor, she knew that college professors expected student essays to go beyond the traditional five-paragraph essay. In fact, the writing center encouraged college writers to move beyond this "unsophisticated" model. Turner discusses the problems with five-paragraph essays in this book in chapter eight citing the works of Emig, Hillocks, and others. The rule at Stephanie's school was that students were to produce one five-paragraph essay per instructional unit. She was unable to get the administration to modify this rule but did get them to agree that as long as this requirement was met, students could develop other pieces of writing as well. Therefore, Stephanie looked for a way of resisting this inane mandate. Ironically, it was at a workshop entitled Teaching Writing Mathematically that she found her inspiration.

At this workshop, the presenters introduced teachers to a model for making formal writing formulaic. They provided a formula for the number of sentences in a paragraph, the number of supporting details, and the number of paragraphs (five, of course) that would make student writing "more consistent and more academic in nature." Part of the process they described was taking pieces of writing written in non-formulaic ways and "translating" them to the perfect five-paragraph essay. Stephanie recalled, "While I was disgusted by the entire workshop, it did give me an idea. I could turn the activity on its heels and have students to create alternative versions to the five-paragraph essays once they have written them."

So for several of the school-required writing assignments for the year, students quickly wrote their formulaic essays, and spent most of their writing time on writing projects that included movie scripts, graphic texts, newspaper articles, three-paragraph essays, eight-paragraph essays, etc. Stephanie taught her students that the form and length of a piece of writing was dependant on its purpose, audience, and complexity of the content about which they write. The students still produced the requisite five-paragraph essays but learned far more about writing both as process and product (Tompkins, 2007).

In addition to her two eighth-grade English classes, Stephanie was assigned to teach an Academic Intervention Services (AIS) class for a small group of students who were below grade level in their reading assessments, but who had not been classified with any learning disability. When her principal informed her of the assignment of this class, he told her not to worry as it "only involved going through test preparation workbooks." No particular instructional model was expected for this course; in fact, the literacy coach who met with Stephanie a few times during the year informed her that the AIS period was the opportunity for these kids to practice their test taking skills over and over so that when the actual testing day comes, they will be ready. Stephanie was appalled at this approach. In her mind, "these kids" needed much more focused instruction and active learning opportunities that would help them bolster their reading and writing skills.

Stephanie took matters into her own hands. The students had the workbooks on their desks each day (in case someone came into the classroom) but she used the time to work with them in guided reading groups, mostly using materials from popular culture magazines and websites that were of high interest to them, and coaching them on how to engage in active reading. She spent at least half of the time with them on creative writing strategies that were fun but that would improve their writing fluency. Stephanie reflected, "Most kids hate their AIS class. More fights break out during that period than the rest of the school day. My kids loved coming to this class. We had fun. We read. We wrote. We talked. We did practice test taking once a week using the workbooks, but the focus of my class was the students—not the workbooks." In the end, Stephanie's students made progress on the state assessments, but more importantly, their attitudes toward reading and writing improved. According to Stephanie, "Sometimes, the act of resistance is as simple as closing the door to your classroom and doing what you know is the right thing."

Brooke (grade 9)

While many of her colleague teaching fellows were hired in middle schools, Brooke, who had spent a few years working in media advertising, was pleased that she had landed a job in a high school. When she was hired, she was told she would be teaching American literature to eleventh graders—just what she had hoped for. However, when she arrived at the school on the first day of the school year, she discovered that a new program, Ramp-Up Literacy, had been mandated for all ninth graders in the district and that because veteran teachers did not wish to learn the new program, she was being moved to ninth grade so that a senior faculty member could teach the American literature course. Her Department Chair admitted that she herself had just received training from Ramp-Up and that they would all be learning together. The program came with very specific curriculum materials, including a classroom library. According to the Ramp-Up web site, the program provides "Well-crafted instructional materials, including daily lesson plans, homework assignments, and effective ways to illustrate key concepts." (http://www.ncee. org/acsd/literacy/310.jsp accessed August 24, 2009).

According to Brooke and numerous others who have taught in the Ramp-Up program in New York City high schools, these well-crafted materials are actually scripted lessons, with little room for modification. During the initial year of its implementation at Brooke's school, the problems with the inflexible program were exacerbated by the six-month late arrival of classroom libraries and other instructional materials. Brooke described weekly book swaps, where kids brought in their own copies of literature from home and swapped with classmates. Once the books and materials did arrive, teachers and administrators were pleased with the wide selection of works of fiction that made up the classroom libraries. Brooke and her colleagues were most discouraged by the non-fiction selections that they were expected to teach to their ninth grade students.

Brooke described the non-fiction texts as "random batches of books on arbitrary topics, completely unrelated to ninth grade curriculum or ninth graders' interests." She recalled one student who brought a small paperback book about frogs to her desk with a look of disbelief on his face. He informed her that the text was similar to one he used in elementary school and that he was not going to be treated like a third grader. In thinking about this incident, Brooke stated, "True, Ramp-Uup is intended for students who read two or more years below grade level, but [the student] had a point. The book was ridiculous. No high school student can be motivated by this level [of materials]." Brooke and her colleagues spent a great deal of their preparation time looking for alternative non-fiction texts, mostly relying on the Internet for resources. Luckily, her department chair agreed that the texts were inappropriate and supported the teachers' efforts to find alternate texts.

The mandated ninth grade curriculum also did not include any study of the works of William Shakespeare (nor did the program for tenth grade). This was a major issue for Brooke and her colleagues who felt strongly that high school students should experience the pleasure of reading and performing *Romeo and Juliet.* When the school had adopted Ramp-Up, the books in its bookroom had been given to another school in a neighboring district. Thanks to the generosity of a colleague in that district, Brooke was able to borrow back a set of 25 copies of *Romeo and Juliet* and worked a class reading of the classic drama in, despite the absence of room for additional units of study in the mandated curriculum. Again, the support of her department chair made this easier to accomplish. However, other NYCTF colleagues reported less success with modifying the highly scripted Ramp-Up program adopted in their schools. Interestingly, the program was abandoned by many high schools after a year or two of use.

One last area that Brooke identified as being absent from the mandated curriculum, which echoed a complaint of numerous other teachers at other grade levels, was the lack of attention placed on media and digital literacy. None of the mandated curricula had a place for media or digital literacy, both of which are proving crucial in the 21st century (Burke, 2007). Brooke managed to integrate media literacy into her curriculum with the use of short video and audio clips from documentaries, news shows, movies, television, radio talk shows, and Internet web sites. She and her students engaged in critical literacy practices as they attempted to understand the sociocultural elements that guided mass media. Because her students were so interested in media and digital literacy and there were so few opportunities to bring these new literacies into the classroom with the Ramp-Up program, Brooke began an after school media club, which attracted as many as 40 students, becoming the largest extracurricular activity in her small high school. She also provided opportunities for her students to do "alternative book reports" on their independent reading, including podcasts, video trailers, interviews with book characters or authors, and PowerPoint presentations. When asked about her persistence in bringing digital and media literacy to her ninth graders, Brooke responded, "If my kids have any hope of getting out of the hopeless environment in which many of them live, I know it will take more than traditional reading and writing skills. Success in the near future will be equally dependent on the ability to use media and technology critically and intelligently. I don't care what the curriculum map says; I am not going to ignore the realities of today's world to the detriment of my students." Her fervor and dedication are typical of the teachers I have spoken with.

In a time when it is difficult to find qualified teachers interested in entering the profession, the pressure created by high-stakes testing is causing experienced and novice teachers to leave the public school classroom, particularly in urban settings. According to Crocco and Costigan (2007), who have studied the impact of recent curricular mandates on New York City teachers, "Under the curricular and pedagogical impositions of scripted lessons and mandated curriculum, patterns associated nationwide with high-stakes testing, the No Child Left Behind Act of 2001, and the phenomenon known as the "narrowing of curriculum," new teachers in New York City (NYC) find their personal and professional identity thwarted, creativity and autonomy undermined, and ability to forge relationships with students diminished" (p. 512).

While one would hope the governmental and school policies would support their noble efforts, this has not been the case. Indeed, as of this writing, though the NCLB act has not yet been reauthorized, it appears that the emphasis on testing is only growing stronger as we enter the second decade of the 21st century. More than ever, systematic and coordinated acts of resistance are the only hope we have of making a change in American education. The responsibility for resistance to mandated and scripted literacy curricula lies at multiple levels, beginning, but certainly not ending with the English language arts teacher. In the individual classroom, at grade level or departmental meetings, even at school and district wide meetings teachers must take a stand against curricular and instructional mandates that they do not believe to be the best for the students they teach. Likewise, department chairs, curriculum coordinators, literacy coaches—teacher leaders of all kinds are obligated to resist when testing and test preparation become the center of all teaching and learning. Moving up the ladder, school building and district administrators have told me that although they do not necessarily "buy in" to curricular mandates, they bow to the pressure of higher ups. In order to make a real change, our administrative leadership must become involved in the resistance movement.

It is also imperative that parents of school-aged children become involved in the cause. A few years back, parents in the affluent New York City suburb of Scarsdale, NY organized a boycott of state English language arts assessments in protest of the notion that a single assessment can be used to measure progress for all students (Zerkine, 2001). Looking at past incidents of parental involvement in New York City Schools, de Forest (2008) has affirmed "the rights of all parents to oppose a school system that [is] judged inimical to the well being of their children" (p. 39).

Finally, while professional educational organizations such as the National Council of Teachers of English and the International Reading Association have come a long way toward providing support for educators at all levels as they attempt to resist unacceptable curricular mandates, they must continue to advocate for best practice in literacy instruction. Indeed, in an effort to impact legislation related to literacy education, NCTE has established an office in Washington, D.C. and has recently been successful at affecting change "on the Hill."

While I have only shared vignettes of four specific teachers in New York City, I have heard stories from teachers across America who had similar experiences. These young teachers are dedicated to making a difference in our world through their work with young adolescents. Acts of resistance related to mandated or scripted literacy curricula can and must occur at all levels from the individual classroom, at the local, district, and state levels, and even in the national arena. The education of our nation's youth is too important an enterprise for us to allow instructional mandates that we know are not in the best interest of the students in our schools.

REFERENCES

Anagnostopoulos, D. (2003). Testing and student engagement with literature in urban classrooms: A multi-layered perspective. *Research in the Teaching of English* 38(2), 177–212.

Apple, M. W., & Jungck, S. (1992). You don't have to be a teacher to teach this unit: Teaching, technology and control in the classroom. In A. Hargreaves & M. Fullan (Eds.), *Understanding teacher development* (pp. 20–42). New York: Teachers College Press.

Beck, I. L., McKeown, M. G., Hamilton, R. L., & Kucan, L. (1997). *Questioning the author: An approach for enhancing student engagement with text.* Newark, DE: International Reading Association.

Brighton, C. (2002). Straddling the fence: Implementing best practices in an age of accountability. *Gifted Child Today*, 25(3), 30–33.

Burke, J (2007). *The English teacher's companion*, 3rd ed. Portsmouth, NH: Heinemann.

California Department of Education. (1996). *Teaching reading: A balanced comprehensive approach to teaching reading in prekindergarten through grade three.* Sacramento, CA: California Department of Education.

Costigan, A. T., & Crocco, M. S. (2006). *Learning to teach in an age of accountability.* Mahwah, NJ: Lawrence Erlbaum.

Crocco, M. S. & Costigan, A. T. (2007). The narrowing of curriculum and pedagogy in the age of accountability. *Urban Education*, 42(6), 512–535.

de Forest, J. (2008). The 1958 Harlem school boycott: Parental activism and the struggle for educational equity in New York City. *Urban Review: Issues and Ideas in Public Education*, 40(1), 21–41.

Frey, B., Lee, S., Tollefson, N., Pass, L., & Massengill, D. (2005). Balanced literacy in an urban school district. *Journal of Educational Research*, 98(5), 272.

Herz, S.K., & Gallo, D.R. (2005) *From Hinton to Hamlet: Building bridges between young adult literature and the classics*, 2nd ed. Westport, CT: Greenwood.

Hillocks, G. (2002). *The testing trap: How state writing assessments control learning.* New York: Teachers College Press.

Langer, J., & National Council of Teachers of English. (2002). *Effective literacy instruction: Building successful reading and writing programs.* Urbana, IL: NCTE.

McTighe, J., & Brown, J. (2005). Differentiated instruction and educational standards: Is detente possible? *Theory into Practice*, 44(3), 234–244.

Milosovic, S.(2007). Building a case against scripted reading programs. *The Education Digest*, 73(1), 27–30.

Munoz, M. (2007). Improving of reading in high schools: Outcomes of Ramp-Up to Advanced Literacy in a large urban district. *Planning and Changing*, 38, 89–107. (ERIC Document Reproduction Service No. EJ785729). Retrieved July 18, 2009, from ERIC database.

Nichols, S. L., Glass, G. V, & Berliner, D. C. (2006). High-stakes testing and student achievement: Does accountability pressure increase student learning? *Education Policy Analysis Archives*, 14(1). Retrieved April 1, 2008 from *http://epaa.asu.edu/epaa/v14n1/*

Pearson, P. D., & Gallagher, M. (1983). The instruction of reading comprehension. *Contemporary Educational Psychology*, 8, 317–44.

Shippen, M., Houchins, D., Calhoon, M., Furlow, C., & Sartor, D. (2006). The effects of comprehensive school reform models in reading for urban middle school students with disabilities. *Remedial and Special Education*, 27, 322–328.

Shippen, M. E., Houchins, D. E., Steventon, C., & Sartor, D. L. (2005). A comparison of two direct instruction reading programs for urban middle school students. *Remedial and Special Education*, 26, 175–182.

Tomlinson, C. A. (1999). *The differentiated classroom: Responding to the needs of all learners.* Alexandria, VA: Association for Supervision and Curriculum Development.

Tomlinson, C. A. (2001). *How to differentiate instruction in mixed-ability classrooms* (2nd ed.). Alexandria, VA: Association for Supervision and Curriculum Development.

Tompkins, G. E. (2007). *Teaching writing: Balancing process and product* 5th ed. New York: Prentice Hall.

Valli, L., & Buese, D. (2007). The changing roles of teachers in an era of high-stakes accountability. *American Educational Research Journal*, 44(3), 519–558.

Zerkine, K. (2001, May 4). Scarsdale mothers succeed at first boycott of 8th-grade test. *New York Times*. Retrieved November 28, 2009 from www.nytimes.com/2001/05/04/nyregion.

CHAPTER EIGHT

Fighting the Fear of Failure

Resisting the Effects of THE TEST in a Thinking-Based Writing Class

KRISTEN HAWLEY TURNER

Schools, rightfully so, fear failure on standardized tests. In a climate of accountability that is measured primarily by test scores, administrators feel pressure to make Adequate Yearly Progress, and teachers feel pressure to "teach to the test." With high-stakes accountability, it is also no surprise that state tests are referred to in conversation with clear capital letters. THE TEST is the outcome that matters most. The fear of being labeled a "failing school" permeates the culture of many buildings, and it is no surprise that this fear affects instruction.

As a teacher of high school English, I encountered the demands of high-stakes testing. Though I had a passion for teaching writing, I shied away from volunteering for the test preparation classes that focused solely on writing instruction. My fear of the possibility of being assigned to teach one of these classes stemmed from the transparent accountability; if the students in my class were to fail the state test, everyone would know my failure as a teacher of writing. Even as a teacher of freshmen, who would not take the state exam until their junior year, the pressure to teach to the test affected me. I did not want my students to be flagged for the remedial classes. I wanted them to succeed on the practice tests. In response to the pressure I felt, I dutifully drilled the five-paragraph essay that was part of the "instructional norm" (Johnson, Smagorinsky, Thompson, and Fry, 2003, p. 164) among teachers of writing in my district. I listened to colleagues who supported this kind of teaching as effective test preparation, and I convinced myself that my practice was also helping my students become better writers. What I did not realize at that time is that I was dividing the *form* of the writing from the *thinking* that would make it effective.

My experience is not unique. In their study of a novice teacher who adapted her instruction in order to prepare students for standardized assessment of writing skills, Johnson et al. (2003) identified "pressure" and "stress" (p. 164) as two dominant effects of high-stakes testing. As Johnson et al. (2003) report, this teacher said,

> I have all these other things I want to do as far as writing, but up until they take this test, I don't feel like I can do anything else....I'm just trying to get them ready for this test. (p. 165)

The sentiment expressed by this young teacher is one I currently encounter from teachers of all experience levels. Inservice workshops that I conduct often follow the same pattern; teachers praise strategies of effective writing instruction that I share with them, yet they proclaim that they cannot implement them because they must prepare students for THE TEST. Many of them have reduced their teaching to test preparation and their understanding of teaching writing to the forms that will help their students succeed on the test. As Langer (1999) discusses, with this perspective test preparation becomes about raising test scores rather than about "raising both test scores and student learning" (p. 20).

Hillocks (2002) claims that state mandated assessments of writing influence classroom practice in a way that "goes well beyond that commonly known fact that if writing is assessed, writing is taught" (p. vii). In his study that examined several state tests and what teachers do as a result of these mandated assessments, he found that classrooms across the nation are focused entirely on the features of the test without paying attention to the qualities of effective writing instruction that are supported by educational research. Hillocks's analysis brings into question the effects of standardized assessment of writing as well as the nature of the tests themselves. For example, Hillocks found that most states in his study "call only for elaboration of ideas, which may simply mean the restatement of the same idea in nearly the same language" (p. 20), rather than for warranted evidence to support claims. In his analysis of the Illinois state test, he found that "the Illinois 'format' [that encourages five-paragraph themes] does not support the higher level thinking skills....It teaches students that any reasons they propose in support of a proposition need not be examined for consistency, evidentiary force, or even relevance. Nearly anything goes" (p. 136). The effects of this test, then, are to focus classroom instruction on form rather than content, a situation that often eliminates the connection between thinking and writing.

Unfortunately, teachers of all content areas receive very little training in the teaching of writing (Smagorinsky, in press; Tremmel, 2001). They have not had the opportunity to consider what writing is, what makes a piece effective, or how to teach the knowledge and skills necessary to produce a quality essay. In short, few teachers enter the classroom with a "theory of writing" (Hillocks, 2002, p. 19), or a rationale for "what is important, how the types [of writing] relate to each other, what the process of writing is, and so forth" (p. 19). Instead, they rely on their own experiences as students (Smagorinsky, in press), or, as Hillocks (2002) points out, "when teachers have little knowledge of writing, the testing system tends to become the knowledge base for teaching writing" (p. 102). In effect, by selecting the specific kinds of writing tested and by developing criteria for how that writing will be assessed, states assert a theory of writing. When this theory encourages practice that does not mesh with what writers actually do and how students learn to write effectively, the effects are dangerous. In order to resist these ill effects of the test, educators must consider the implicit theory underlying the standardized assessments in light of research in writing instruction.

A Framework for Thinking about Writing Instruction

Developing a teaching stance

Hillocks (2002), a leader in the field of composition research in education, discusses three *rhetorical stances* taken by teachers of writing. *Current traditional rhetoric* assumes that knowledge "may be apprehended directly through observation of the world and our experience in it" (p. 21). According to Hillocks, classrooms that are based in current traditional rhetoric are dominated by lecture, and teachers assume that "once students see what [a given type of essay] should contain, they will be able to write one" (pp. 23–24). Hillocks contrasts this stance with two constructivist rhetorics that put students at the center of the learning process by asking them to construct knowledge for themselves, rather than it being transmitted to them. In the *expressivist rhetoric*, the focus is on "personal insight and the ability to allow writing to grow organically from the writer's own ideas" (p.24). In the *epistemic rhetoric* (Berlin, 1982, as cited in Hillocks, 2002, p. 24), "truth must be argued through dialectical processes" (p. 24). The focus in epistemic classrooms is on problem solving through collaboration, argument, and inquiry.

Earlier work by Hillocks (1986a) delineates three modes of teaching that evolve from these rhetorical stances. The *presentational mode* is teacher-centered, and the teacher explains "certain characteristics he expects [the] writing to display or…processes [the students] might or should use" (Hillocks, 1986a, p. 117). Knowledge is "conveyed directly" (p. 118) by examining models and articulating formal characteristics and rules to be followed. On the other hand, the *natural process mode* places the individual writers at the center of the curriculum. Peers act as readers and responders; students have choice over their topics and forms; and "the teacher's role should be reactive" (p. 121) to students' writing. Finally, in the *environmental mode* teachers "structure activities" (p. 122) that allow students to work collaboratively to meet "clear and specific objectives" (p. 122). Through "concrete tasks," (p. 122) students work toward independence in their writing.

The meta-analysis conducted by Hillocks (1986a) found that teaching that takes a constructivist approach (natural process and environmental) has positive effects on student writing, whereas teaching that follows from a current traditional rhetoric (presentational) produces weak results. His findings indicate that the most effective teaching draws from the epistemic rhetoric (environmental). This research examined only experimental studies from the two decades of writing research prior to its publication. This limitation may spur debate over the conclusions or the relevance of the findings more than two decades after the analysis. However, in the recent meta-analysis conducted by Graham and Perin (2007), the elements of environmental teaching prove still to be effective components of writing instruction. The findings of their *Writing Next* report identify "Eleven Elements of Effective Adolescent Writing Instruction" (p. 4). The authors of the report make it clear that these elements do not comprise a scripted curriculum. Instead, they are tested methods of teaching writing, and the practices can be used in combination to create effective instruction. Though the eleven elements expand upon the findings of Hillocks, the criteria of environmental teaching, including instruction in writing strategies, collaboration, clear product goals, and inquiry, can be seen in this report. Environmental teaching, then, remains at the center of effective writing instruction.

Considering the knowledge writers need

Environmental teaching supports the development of the kinds of knowledge that effective writers need. Borrowing from the work of cognitive psychologists, Hillocks (1986b) delineates between declarative and procedural knowledge. Declarative knowledge is "the knowledge of *what*, a kind of knowledge that can be spoken" (Smith and Wilhelm, 2006, p. 123), while procedural knowledge is "the knowledge of *how*, a kind of knowledge that has to be performed" (p. 123). According to Hillocks (1986b), writers need both of these types of knowledge, and they also need knowledge of form "from sentence to genre" (Smith and Wilhelm, 2006, p. 123) and knowledge of substance, the content of their writing. Influenced by Hillocks's work, Smith and Wilhelm (2006) provide a table that helps teachers think about these four kinds of knowledge as they plan instruction, and they argue that considering declarative knowledge of substance and form, as well as procedural knowledge in both areas, is essential to effective instruction. Their discussion focuses on the ineffectiveness of an "assign-and-assess" (p. 122) tradition. The assign-and-assess mode may include instruction in *what* students need to know about writing in a given genre, but this kind of teaching does not provide students with strategies for generating the content or for producing the written product. In other words, this traditional form of instruction does not teach students *how* to generate the writing.

Seeing writing as high literacy

The distinction between knowledge of *what* and *how* is part of the key to effective writing instruction. Hillocks (2002) found that the majority of teachers "focus on the study of models and teaching the structure of various kinds of writing so that their students learn what goes where in a comparison-contrast paper or in a five-paragraph theme, but not on the production strategies necessary to thinking through the problems" (pp. 200–201). Few teachers ask students to think deeply; they are satisfied that students can provide *reasons* for why their opinion is justified and do not require that writers defend claims with warranted evidence. As Hillocks (2002) notes, some high-stakes assessments encourage "this truncated thinking as good writing" (p. 201) through their tasks, criteria, and benchmark essays. In essence, these tests do not support the teaching of strategies for students to produce content that demonstrates real thinking.

Samgorinsky (in press) suggests that teachers are "too complicit for comfort in going along with the dubious teaching and learning promoted by [standardized] assessments" (p. 45). Likewise, Hillocks (2002) asserts, "We need to recognize [these effects] and call for thoughtful writing" (p. 203). Typical test preparation that includes repeated practice with five-paragraph essays may allow students to gain procedural knowledge of form. They know *what* they need to write (an essay with an introduction, three-body paragraphs, and a conclusion) and they certainly learn *how* to write this form. However, what this type of instruction often lacks is focus on procedural knowledge of content, or what Hillocks (1995) calls *inquiry*. It is through inquiry, or the development of strategies to access content, that students will develop the *thinking* that leads to quality writing.

Focusing on thinking as a key to literacy in the writing class helps to make the distinction between "high literacy" (Bereiter and Scardamalia, 1987, as cited in Langer, 1999) and "the more popular notion of literacy as a set of 'basic' reading and writing skills" (Langer, 1999, p. 1). According to Langer (1999), high literacy "includes the ability to use language, content, and reasoning in ways that are appropriate for particular situations and disciplines" (p. 1). It represents a "deeper knowledge" that "belongs at the heart of teaching" (p. 1). In her study of schools that "beat the odds" by outperforming comparable schools on statewide exams, Langer discovered that these higher performing schools focus instruction "to provide the students with ways to read, understand, and write in order to gain abilities that are marks of high literacy, not merely test-passing skills" (p. 24). Through "cognitive collaborations" (p. 44), where students engage in social activity as compared to "individual thinking" (p. 42), instruction and subsequent learning centers on the skills and knowledge being tested, rather than the tests themselves. Langer argues that "revisioning of both curriculum and instruction requires a careful rethinking of the skills and knowledge that need to be learned" (p. 47).

Langer (1999) points out that schools in her study that beat the odds successfully deconstructed and analyzed tests in order to gain a "deeper understanding of the skills, strategies, and knowledge needed for students to achieve various levels of performance" (p. 22), and they built the curriculum from this work. Though Langer claims these schools developed higher literacy than their counterparts, in many ways instruction was still influenced heavily by the tests themselves. Similarly, Gere, Christenbury, and Sassi (2005) look for "continuities between teaching and testing" (p. 5). These authors resist the temptation to simply denigrate high-stakes tests, an approach that they note is common in the field; instead, they embrace the test, and suggest a solution to "integrate writing on demand into a plan for teaching based on best practices" (p. 5). Considering the test and carefully thinking about the knowledge and skills that are being tested are important in a culture of writing on demand. Certainly this approach is more effective than simply focusing on the test and teaching only to improve scores. However, Hillocks (2002) points out that in many cases, the tests themselves are flawed. The theory of writing that dominates the test does not, in fact, mesh with best practices for teaching writing, and it often leads to reductive teaching that separates content from form, taking the *thinking* out of the writing.

Understanding the importance of talk

Researchers like Donald Graves (1983, 1994), Lucy Calkins (1986), and Nancie Atwell (1998) revolutionized the teaching of writing for elementary and middle schools by promoting process-oriented classrooms that place student interests at the heart of writing. Writing workshop approaches, which these authors champion, allow students to compose multiple drafts and to receive feedback from peers and teachers. For all of these authors, a component of writing workshop is conferencing. Murray (2004) articulates the importance of talk for college writers, and he outlines a workshop approach that engages students in peer conferencing that focuses on a writer's needs. Researchers agree; in process classrooms, talk is important as students conference with others about their writing.

On the surface the place of talk in the writing classroom focuses solely on the dialogue between reader and responder. However, the connection between talk and writing is deeper, and it is one that must be considered in order to focus instruction on the thinking that creates an effective piece. Vygotsky (1986), a leading theorist in the fields of language and education, explores the connection between thought and speech. He asserts, "The structure of speech does not simply mirror the structure of thought....Thought undergoes many changes as it turns into speech. It does not merely find expression in speech; it finds its reality and form" (p. 219). Vygotsky's work suggests that through vocal expression, individuals understand what they know *and* what they think.

This metacognitive nature of oral speech can be harnessed in the writing classroom by incorporating activities that ask students to talk at all stages of writing. Dean (2006) encourages teachers to use talk "as an inquiry strategy" (p. 30) in both informal and formal ways. By structuring activities that focus on talk, "students know enough...to write more knowledgably" (p. 31). Talk, then, can help students develop the content of their writing by helping them to think about what they want to say.

Engaging students in the work

Engagement is a key component to learning, and teachers strive to implement lessons that retain students' attention. In developing literacy in the classroom setting, much can be learned from out-of-school practices. In their study of the literacy activity of adolescent boys, Smith and Wilhelm (2002) draw upon the work of Csikszentmihalyi, who studies *flow*, "the state in which people are so involved in an activity that nothing else seems to matter" (Csikszentmihalyi, 1990, as cited in Smith and Wilhelm, 2002, p. 28). The authors articulate four principles of a *flow* experience that resonate in the data they collected: (1) a sense of control and competence, (2) a challenge that requires an appropriate level of skill, (3) clear goals and feedback, and (4) a focus on the immediate experience (pp. 28–29). In addition to these characteristics, Smith and Wilhelm identify the "importance of the social" (p. 42) as a fifth key component to the adolescents' activity outside of school.

Smith and Wilhelm (2002) argue that the results of their analysis "fundamentally challenge the starting point" (p. 50) of planning instruction. Rather than asking "What am I preparing my students for?" (p. 50), educators must consider how to engage students in a way that can "bring something of the passion to [their] classes that they bring to the activities they engage outside of school" (p. 50). This shift in thinking makes teachers "more immediately accountable for [their] curricular and instructional decisions" (p. 50), and it may encourage educators to resist the pressure of the test and to focus instead on student learning.

A Thinking-based Writing Class

Based on the features of environmental teaching (Hillocks, 1986a), the qualities of epistemic classrooms (Hillocks, 2002), the characteristics of the kinds of flow experiences that lead to engagement (Smith and Wilhelm, 2002), and the importance of talk, I have developed the following key elements to a *thinking-based* writing class, one that focuses on students' learning how to engage in inquiry and how to develop the content of their writing.

- Talk is a key feature of the classroom, and student talk far exceeds teacher talk.
- Talk prepares students for writing by helping them understand what they want to say.
- Students engage in problem-solving activities that are designed to elicit multiple points of view and to provide an appropriate challenge for the skill level.
- Students work collaboratively with peers and have the opportunity to receive immediate feedback on their thinking.
- Students understand the goals of the tasks they are assigned.
- Teachers carefully sequence instruction to encourage the development of students' thinking and writing and to scaffold students to independent practice.

Instructional practice that considers these attributes will not only support the development of students' thinking and lead them to higher levels of literacy, it will also resist the negative effects of standardized assessments whose implicit theories do not encourage effective writing instruction.

Traditional test preparation, which includes drilling the five-paragraph theme, a form of writing useful only in the academic setting, encompasses little student talk, virtually no collaboration or problem solving, and few of the other characteristics of a thinking-based classroom. However, if the five-paragraph essay is reconceptualized as an argument, lessons can focus on the thinking involved in argumentation, rather than a form of writing acceptable only in the school setting. Educators can then begin to address Hillocks's call for thoughtful writing. In doing so, teachers will develop writers who know how to access and use content effectively. They will prepare students who succeed on the test. And they will foster individuals of high literacy who are better thinkers (and better writers) outside of the testing atmosphere.

The thinking behind an argument

In order to resist reductive teaching and at the same time reconceptualize the five-paragraph essay as an argument, educators must consider the following questions:

1. What is an argument?
2. How do students learn to argue effectively?

According to Toulmin (1958), an argument begins with a claim, an arguable position. This opinion, Toulmin says, may be challenged by an opponent who might ask, "What have you got to go on?" (Toulmin, 1958, p. 13). It is this potential conversation that requires individuals to support their assertions with "whatever data, facts, or other backing we consider to be relevant and sufficient to make good the initial claim" (p. 13). Thus, any claim must be supported by data, or evidence, which must be connected to the claim by a warrant, or "the general principle that enables [a writer] to move from the reason to the specific claim" (Lunsford and Ruszkiewicz, 1999, p. 84).

Toulmin discusses other aspects of argumentation, including rebuttal, qualifier, and backing. However, the three main elements of claim, evidence, and warrant provide the basis of argumentative thinking and the starting point for instruction in argument. Teaching students *what* the Toulmin model encompasses—a claim that is supported by warranted evidence—is an easier task than teaching them *how* to generate an effective argument. Both Smith and Wilhelm (2006) and Hillocks (1995) suggest "gateway activities" (Hillocks, 1995, p. 150) that focus on the "features and strategies" (p. 150) of argumentation and that gradually lead students to independence in creating arguments. Through action research that I conducted in my high school English classrooms (Turner, 2004, 2005b), I found that in addition to some of the activities suggested by these authors, the practice of debate is particularly effective in building students' argumentative thinking skills and improving their written arguments. Debate asks students to support claims with warranted evidence, but it also requires them to present a case to a real audience. This face-to-face conversation necessitates both careful attention to the use of evidence and a consideration of the opposing view, two aspects of argumentative thinking that students often find difficult.

Toulmin (1958) suggests that some elements of argumentation are "field-dependent" (p. 15), meaning that they vary according to discipline or community. In later publications (Toulmin, Rieke, and Janik, 1984) the author explores the nature of claims, evidence and warrants, and through his discussion it becomes clear that what counts as evidence varies by context. Furthermore, students often fall into the trap of believing that quantity of evidence outweighs quality. Unfortunately for these novice writers, they do not realize that "having twice as many pieces of inferior evidence does little to constitute superior proof" (Branham, 1991, p. 91). Thus, it is important for students to evaluate evidence in light of both the claims they are making and through the perception of the audience with whom they are arguing. Policy debates allow students to use a variety of evidence to support their positions.

In order to scaffold students to independent evaluation of evidence, I provide debate teams with a *hierarchy of evidence*.[1] This outline helps students to consider the quality of evidence they uncover by analyzing information according to the following scale, listed in descending order of significance:

~ Scientific law
~ Statistical data
~ Expert opinion
~ Opinion of noted individuals
~ Anecdotal evidence

I provide teams with graphic organizers that allow them to collect evidence and rank it in each of these categories as they develop their arguments. I have found that after this process, students attend to issues of quantity and quality as they deliver their arguments in the debate, and this attention carries into their writing. In my experience, essays that were once a series of claims with little or primarily anecdotal evidence, include, after the experience of debate, a previously unseen mixture of sound evidence with high concentrations of statistical data and expert opinion. More importantly, students *think* about the kinds of evidence they are choosing to include as they develop their arguments. They develop the ability to evaluate evidence and include that which will effectively make a case to the intended audience.

Just as considering evidence is essential for "winning" a debate, the process of debate also asks students to consider counterarguments and address them through rebuttals. My classroom research (Turner, 2004) discovered that debate asks students to envision an opponent as they develop their arguments and to see, literally, that opponent, who is sitting across from them during the argument. I found that this recognition of the counterargument played an important role in the process of the small groups as they prepared for the debate and in the processes of individuals as they composed their own written essays after the debate. Thus, this practice helped my students to consider counterclaims and to attend to them through rebuttals, an aspect of argumentative writing that requires abstract thought and one that is rarely addressed in high school. As Hillocks (1995) notes, "Even college students find writing from another point of view difficult without preparation" (p. 148). However, both Hillocks and authors Lunsford and Ruszkiewicz (1999) contend that addressing the counterargument is essential to effective argumentation. In fact, Hillocks (1995) asserts, "To write well, one must become a reader, to divide oneself from the text" (p. 22). What better way to introduce students to this division than by having them face their opposition in a debate? In fact, in the steps Branham (1991) outlines for researching a debate, the author lists brainstorming arguments for both sides as a key component. He explains,

> Before you debate against an opponent, you should debate against yourself. Adopt the viewpoint of your opponent and think strategically from the opponent's perspective. Examine your position from the critical perspective of your adversary. It is only by coming to know the strongest arguments and strategies that your opponent *might* make...that you will truly be prepared to debate. (p. 96)

Thus, debate allows students to think from alternative points of view. This type of thoughtful inquiry develops important skills of argumentation that enable the production of richer written texts.

Debate, if planned carefully, meets the criteria for a thinking-based writing class. When students enter into a debate, they are fully aware of the primary goal and objective: to win. It is easy for them to understand that in order to overcome their opponents, they must present strong arguments with warranted evidence to support their claims. Debate also asks students to work with peers to solve problems, to think critically, and to create effective arguments while the teacher acts only as a coach. The formal structure of debate allows students to assume specific tasks, such as laying out the argument, questioning the counterargument, or rebutting the opposition, and to work collaboratively to achieve a goal. Perhaps the most important aspect of debate for student learning, however, is the immediate feedback it offers. From their opponents students see the strengths and weaknesses of their arguments, and ultimately the judges of the debate offer concrete assessment of their overall thought processes. Finally, the talk that takes place during the preparation and delivery of a debate prepares students for writing their own arguments.

Table 8.1 Debate in a Thinking-Based Classroom

Criteria for a Thinking-Based Classroom	Activity of Debate
Talk is a key feature of the classroom, and student talk far exceeds teacher talk.	Debate is an oral activity. Small groups prepare for debate. Students execute debate. Teacher talk is minimal.
Talk prepares students for writing by helping them understand what they want to say.	Small group work and execution of the debate itself will help students to articulate their arguments. This process will aid their writing.
Students engage in problem-solving activities that are designed to elicit multiple points of view and to provide an appropriate challenge for the skill level.	Students work in small groups to develop and refine their arguments. They must consider the opponent's point of view. The teacher, acting as coach, is able to scaffold the work from small group discussion to individual writing.
Students work collaboratively with peers and have the opportunity to receive immediate feedback on their thinking.	Teams develop and refine arguments. The debate itself provides students feedback from opponents as they point out weaknesses in the arguments. Final analysis of the debate also provides feedback.
Students understand the goals and objectives of the tasks they are assigned.	The purpose of the assignment is to win the debate. Students easily understand this goal and that to achieve it they must develop strong arguments and rebut the opposition.
Teachers carefully sequence instruction to encourage the development of students' thinking and writing and to scaffold students to independent practice.	Scaffolding the practice of debate will support students as they develop the ability to construct an effective argument.

Sequencing the activities of argumentative thinking

Though students, fueled by the atmosphere of competition, are often immediately engaged in the activity of debate, in order to fully develop the thinking behind an argument, it is important for teachers to sequence lessons that build on students' understanding over time. I have found the following sequence effective for helping students learn how to develop effective arguments.

1. *Ping pong debates*

    In order to introduce students to verbal argument and to prepare them for sharing opinions with an audience who will provide immediate feedback, I conduct informal, "ping pong" debates early in the year. In this activity students work in teams to discuss two sides to a given argument and to prepare to debate the opposing side. It is the team's job to develop reasons that their position represents the stronger side of the debate. The teacher provides no instruction on the structure of argument, including the use of evidence to support a claim. It is the teacher's role only to moderate the debate, which proceeds in a back and forth fashion. Each student is expected to speak, responding to the previous speaker or offering new reasons or evidence for his/her team. At the conclusion of the debate, all students discuss the strengths and weaknesses of the arguments presented. Ping pong debates work for nearly any debatable topic. I have used them successfully both with open-ended literature, such as "The Lady or the Tiger" (Stockton, 1890), and with policy issues, such as "Should English be the official language of the United States?"

2. *One v. one debates focused on claims and sub claims*

Written arguments typically require that students defend major propositions with sub claims. In other words, arguments are nested within other arguments. The thinking involved in creating nested arguments is complicated, and it is important for students to practice developing sub claims to support major claims. An activity I have used with this goal in mind is a one-on-one debate, where students argue in pairs and receive feedback on their reasoning from their peer partners. In this activity students select topics to argue and pair with a classmate. They read background information on the topic and together create a defensible, arguable claim (Smith and Wilhelm, 2006). They select opposing sides of the claim and individually prepare sub claims to support their positions. Finally, they present their claims to each other in the form of a one-on-one debate. Students are permitted to create arguments with evidence, but it is more important for them to focus on creating quality claims. After the debate, it is the partner's job to evaluate the sub claims that make up the nested argument and to provide feedback to the peer on the thinking that is represented by these claims. The pair reports what they learned to the class or to the teacher.

3. *Working the Toulmin model*

After my students have practiced arguing in front of and with their peers and after they have experienced writing claims and sub claims, I explain to them the structure of an argument by defining claim, evidence, and warrant and by offering effective and ineffective examples of simple arguments. I use several of the gateway activities described by Hillocks (1995) and Smith and Wilhelm (2006) to help them understand the model and the logic behind it. For example, as these authors suggest, we examine artwork, such as *A Voluptuary Under the Horrors of Digestion*, and use details from the image to make generalizations about the character, ability, or nature of the individual who is featured. In addition, we practice argumentative thinking using "minute mysteries" (Smith and Wilhelm, p. 139), which include brief summaries of a crime with an accompanying picture. Students must develop a "persuasive solution" (p. 139) to the mystery by clearly linking evidence to the claims they make. (See both Hillocks and Smith and Wilhelm for additional detail about both of these activities.) I have also used moral dilemmas (Johannessen, 2001) in order to make arguing relevant to students' lives. In all of these cases, I scaffold students from whole-class to peer-supported to independent work. Students find these activities fun, and I often hear requests to do more of them, but more importantly, they are engaged in argument, and they are developing thinking tools that will be necessary both in and out of school.

4. *Analyzing arguments*

An important aspect of argumentative thinking is the ability to analyze and deconstruct another person's argument. My students have found great satisfaction in analyzing letters to the editor of their local newspapers. More often than not, in the letters they find thinking that includes faulty logic, and they are excited to realize that by looking closely at the writing, they can identify poorly constructed claims and unwarranted evidence. They are appalled when writers do not clearly state a position or include no evidence at all. I ask students to find examples of effective and ineffective arguments in the newspaper, to deconstruct them, and to share their analyses with their classmates. This process further develops their understanding of argument and their ability to think critically.

5. *Structured policy debate*

By the time they are ready to take on the challenge of structured policy debate students have worked with the structure of argument by linking evidence to claims, and they are ready to complicate their thinking by evaluating evidence and considering counterarguments. In another publication I outline steps for a unit on policy debate that effectively replaces the traditional research paper and encourages thoughtful writing (Turner, 2005a). This unit is based on formal policy debate; however, the complicated roles of the *affirmative* and *negative*, which are standard practice in formal, policy debate, and the official vocabulary of *status quo* and *resolve* are not overly accessible, and I have adapted the structure to one that allows my students to engage in an argument in meaningful ways. Using the basic structure of formal debate, competition in my classroom centers on Pro/Con issues of policy, where students simply offer two sides of a debatable question. They work in small groups to develop claims, to find evidence (based on the hierarchy I provide to them), and to consider possible counterarguments. They debate in a timed format in front of peer judges, and they complete the unit by writing papers that defend their individual positions on the topic.

Participating in the unit on policy debate, which solidified my students' knowledge of *what* is an argument and *how* they can effectively construct one, drastically improved their academic writing (Turner, 2005b). They more effectively used evidence to support their claims; they often addressed the counterargument; and their use of sub claims to support claims demonstrated clear, logical thought. In effect, the activity, one that focused on inquiry, developed their argumentative thinking. It helped them understand how to generate an argument, and they were able to apply this procedural knowledge to their writing.

RESISTING REDUCTIVE TEACHING

The sequence of activities presented here represents my shift in teaching writing. As I researched effective writing instruction, I came to realize that I needed to move away from focusing on the form of a five-paragraph essay, a structure that was supported by the theory of writing imposed by the state assessment and one that existed in the culture of my school. By studying the work of Hillocks (1995), I understood that writers need knowledge of form and substance; I recognized that asking my students to produce five-paragraph themes on topics that do not allow for true inquiry was not, in fact, teaching them how to write, even if they were able to produce pieces acceptable for passing the state test. Because I wanted to teach students to *think*, not just to replicate form, I developed a thinking-based writing class. Now I ask students to talk, and to talk a lot, before they write. I ask them to solve problems. I ask them to work collaboratively and to provide feedback to each other. And I carefully structure activities so that they understand the objectives and so that they can succeed independently as thinkers and as writers. In short, I help them learn how to develop content that will lead to thoughtful writing, and I worry less about teaching the form of the test.

Hillocks (2002) states, "We know that testing programs tend to restrict the curriculum to the kinds of knowledge and skills tested" (p.12). In the case of writing, tests often impose a theory of writing that limits teaching to issues of form, and this type of instruction does little to develop the thinking skills that lead to quality writing. Teachers and administrators can resist the effects of THE TEST, however, by creating *thinking-based* writing classes. By teaching students how to develop the content of their writing, by engaging them in inquiry, by inspiring their "cognitive collaborations" (Langer, 1999, p. 44), teachers of writing can develop high literacy. From this instruction, students will develop as thoughtful writers both in and out of school.

It is understandable in this era of high-stakes accountability that teachers and administrators fear failure on standardized assessments. Scores determine funding, and scores stand as the primary means of public evaluation of schools. When students do not pass tests, schools, including the teachers and administrators within them, are deemed "failing." However, it is the responsibility of the educators who are closest to the classrooms where students learn to stand against the negative effects of standardized assessments. In many cases the tests do not promote the development of students who can think critically. Rather, they encourage reductive teaching that focuses more on test scores than actual learning. By fighting the fear of failure that can dominate a school culture, teachers and administrators can resist these effects of THE TEST and promote effective teaching within their classrooms. They can become leaders of a resistance to test-driven instruction that does little to encourage real thinking. They can talk about the test without capital letters punctuating the conversation. Ultimately, they can reap the rewards of educating students who succeed on the test and individuals who become thoughtful learners.

NOTE

1. This hierarchy was originally provided to me at a staff development workshop at the high school where I taught. No source citation was included, and the original author remains unknown to me. I have since adapted it to the information that is provided here.

REFERENCES

Atwell, N. (1998). *In the middle: New understandings about writing, reading, and learning*, (2nd ed.). Portsmouth, NH: Boynton Cook.
Bereiter, C, & Scardamalia, M. (1987). An attainable version of high literacy: Approaches to teaching higher order skills in reading and writing. *Curriculum Inquiry*, 17(1), 10–30
Berlin, J. A. (1982). Contemporary composition: The major pedagogical theories. *College English*, 44(8), 765–777.
Branham, R. J. (1991). *Debate and critical analysis: The harmony of conflict*. Hillsdale, NJ: Lawrence Erlbaum.
Calkins, L. (1986/1994) *The art of teaching writing*. Portsmouth, NH: Heinemann.
Csikszentmihalyi, M. (1990). *Flow: The psychology of optimal experience*. NY: Harper & Row.
Dean, D. (2006). *Strategic writing: The writing process and beyond in the secondary English classroom*. Urbana, IL: NCTE.
Gere, A. R., Christenbury, L., and Sassi, K. (2005). *Writing on demand: Best practices and strategies for success*. Portsmouth, NH: Heinemann.
Graham, S. and Perin, D. (2007). *Writing next: Effective strategies to improve writing of adolescents in middle and high schools*. NY: Alliance for Excellent Education. Retrieved August 28, 2009 from http://www.all4ed.org/files/WritingNext.pdf.
Graves, D. (1983). *Writing: Teachers and children at work*. Portsmouth, NH: Heinemann.
Graves, D. (1994). *A fresh look at writing*. Portsmouth, NH: Heinemann.
Hillocks, G., Jr. (1986a). *Research on written composition:* New directions for teaching. Urbana, IL: ERIC and National Conference for Research in English.

Hillocks, G., Jr. (1986b). The writer's knowledge: Theory, research, and implications for practice. In A. Petrosky & D. Bartholomae (Eds.). *The teaching of writing: Eighty-fifth yearbook of the National Society for the Study of Education*. Chicago: NSSE and University of Chicago Press. pp. 71–94.

Hillocks, G., Jr. (1995). *Teaching writing as reflective practice*. NY: Teachers College Press.

Hillocks, G., Jr. (2002). *The testing trap: How state writing assessments control learning*. NY: Teachers College Press.

Hillocks, G., Jr. (2009). A response to Peter Smagorinsky: Some practices and approaches are clearly better than others and we had better not ignore the differences. *English Journal*, 98(6), 23–29.

Johannessen, L. R. (2001). Teaching thinking and writing for a new century. *English Journal*, 90, 38–46.

Johnson, T. S., Smagorinsky, P., Thompson, L. & Fry, P. G. (2003). Learning to teach the five-paragraph theme. *Research in the Teaching of English*, 38(2), 136–176.

Langer, J. A. (1999). *Beating the odds: Teaching middle and high school students to read and write well*. Washington, DC: Office of Educational Research and Improvement. Retrieved July 3, 2009 from ERIC.

Lunsford, A. A. & Ruszkiewicz, J. J. (1999). *Everything's an argument*. New York: Bedford/St. Martin's.

Murray, D. (2004). *A writer teaches writing*, (2nd ed.). Boston: Heinle.

Smagorinsky, P. (2009). Is it time to abandon the idea of "best practices" in the teaching of English? *English Journal*, 98(6), 15–22.

Smagorinsky, P. (in press). Teaching writing in the age of accountability: Reflections from the academy. In G. Troia, R. Shankland, & A. Heintz (Eds.), *Writing research in classroom practice: Applications for teacher professional development*. New York: Guilford.

Smith, M. W. & Wilhelm, J. (2002). *Reading don't fix no Chevys: Literacy in the lives of young men*. Portsmouth, NH: Heinemann.

Smith, M. W. & Wilhelm, J. (2006). *Going with the flow: How to engage boys [and girls] in their literacy learning*. Portsmouth, NH: Heinemann.

Stockton, F. R. (1890). The lady, or the tiger? In *The lady or the tiger? And other stories*. NY: Scribner. Retrieved August 28, 2009 from http://books.google.com

Toulmin, S. (1958). *The uses of argument*. New York: Cambridge University Press.

Toulmin, S., Rieke, R. & Janik, A. (1984). *An introduction to reasoning*, (2nd ed.). New York: Macmillan.

Tremmel, R. (2001). Seeking a balanced discipline: Writing teacher education in first-year composition and English education. *English Education*, 34, 6–30.

Turner, K. H. (2004, April). There's nothing like a good argument. Paper presented at the meeting of the American Educational Research Association, San Diego, CA.

Turner, K. H. (2005a). The one-stop shop: Addressing all five strands of language arts literacy with the practice of debate. *New Jersey English Journal*, 35–45.

Turner, K. H. (2005b). Toulmin and transfer: The impact of instruction in argument on students' writing across disciplines (Doctoral dissertation, Cornell University, 1990). *Dissertation Abstracts International*, 66, 1682.

Vygotsky, L. S. (1986). *Thought and language*. (A. Kozulin, Trans.). Cambridge, MA: The Massachusetts Institute of Technology.

CHAPTER NINE

"A Small Group of Thoughtful, Committed Citizens"

Social Studies Classrooms as Communities of Practice That Enable Social Action

THOMAS H. LEVINE

> Never doubt that a small group of thoughtful, committed citizens can change the world. Indeed, it's the only thing that ever has.
> MARGARET MEAD (LUTKEHAUS, 2009, P. 34)

Many have wondered about whether schools can—or should—reform society rather than just reproducing existing patterns of power, belief, and behavior. Social studies has been a particularly contentious field in this regard. In the United States, the nature and purposes of social studies teaching have varied considerably across classrooms, schools, and eras.

Some social studies teaching and citizenship education programs aim to socialize future citizens to respect authority and acquire "common convictions and beliefs about what is important or of value" (Sunal and Haas, 2008; see also Anderson, Avery, Pederson, Smith, and Sullivan, 1997; Hertzberg, 1981; Westheimer and Kahne, 2004). Social studies may be doing an important service to students when it helps young people acquire the "values, habits, and beliefs that permit youth to find a niche in adult society" (Marker and Mehlinger, 1992); moreover, promoting common values like fairness, tolerance, or respect for authority may produce the social coherence required for a functioning society and polity. When these outcomes are not at least balanced by teaching that develops critical thinking and independent judgment, however, social studies teaching can be viewed as social control or indoctrination (Hertzberg, 1981). Such teaching may undercut a healthy democracy's need for individual citizens who can think for themselves about what is right and who are willing and able to engage in social and political action.

This chapter offers the following assertion: If social studies is to promote students' agency as social and political actors, schools must build communities of practice in classrooms that foster specific skills and dispositions. In such communities, teachers and students engage together in kinds of thinking and acting that look quite different from traditional, didactic social studies. Teachers guide students into having experiences and gaining repeated practice to develop critical thinking skills, empathy, and the ability to consider and talk about controversial issues. Students experience their time in school as modeling the kinds of collaboration, compromise, and thoughtful decision-making about social engagement that get things done in the world. The aim of such communities is not to socialize students into any specific political beliefs, but to give citizens the tools with which to think for themselves about the social world, and to decide when and how they seek to change it.

This chapter opens by arguing that at present, much social studies instruction may actually inhibit future citizens' capacity to engage in social action. I then consider how social studies instruction in a community of practice could help future citizens acquire the knowledge, skills, and dispositions to thoughtfully decide when and how to engage in social action. The chapter closes presenting four specific approaches to social studies education. Such approaches enacted within communities of practice could model—and foster—the work of small groups of thoughtful, committed citizens seeking to accomplish change.

How Social Studies can Inhibit Social Action

How might typical social studies teaching limit students' acquisition of the understandings, skills, and dispositions to engage in social action? There are several common patterns in social studies education that blunt students' ability to think about or actively engage with the social world.

1. History is comprised of conclusions already reached. First, there is the question of what is included, and how it is presented, in the social studies curriculum. History, as the discipline at the core of the social studies, is a contentious and interpretive exercise, full of opportunities to decide what to leave out, what to emphasize, and what the past means for the present. History textbooks for K-12 students, however, are not usually written by top historians or professionals seeking to create access to the current con-

troversies in the field. Committees write most history texts to address the state standards of the most populous states (American Textbook Council, 1994; Ravitch, 2004). According to one review of history textbooks, "so much needs to be covered and compressed in the texts" that the resulting prose "strips from the narrative whatever is lively, adventurous, and exciting" (Ravitch, 2004, p. 63). These fact-filled tomes promote a view of history as a "fixed body of knowledge, already discovered by others and not open to investigation or interpretation" rather than a document that provides access to controversial issues or conflicting interpretations (Levstik and Barton, 2001, p. 161; see also Hess, 2001). Since most classroom social studies instruction has relied heavily on textbooks (Levstik, 2008; Wade, 1993), their limitations are particularly troublesome.

Thus, while the discipline of history itself has the potential to help students learn to sort through conflicting evidence and perspectives and to see how individuals' biases and agendas show up in primary and secondary sources, the way history is taught usually minimizes students' access to the conflict and interpretation that are inherent in constructing any historical account. In contrast with the actual work of historians, history textbooks, state standards, and district curricula usually reduce students' opportunities to engage in evidence-seeking, critical perspective-taking, and independent judgment, and thus fail to develop skills needed to thoughtfully choose whether and how to engage in social action.

2. History and change are made by exceptional individuals. A traditional approach to making history more memorable is to teach about heroes, ushering students into the tension and drama of famous individuals' struggles and decision-making (Barton and Levstik, 2004, p. 153). Teaching about U.S. history and government often socializes students to see social and political progress as the product of the great "men" in these stories, but this comes at a price. Historian Howard Zinn argues that "the mountain of history books under which we all stand" is "so tremblingly respectful of states and statesmen and so disrespectful, by inattention, to people's movements" (Zinn, 2003, p. 631). Even when textbooks tell stories of heroes representing social justice or multiculturalism, they may do a kind of harm. For instance, Rosa Parks is often depicted as a woman who, on her own and somewhat arbitrarily, decided one day that she was tired of the injustice of standing at the back of the bus when seats were available up front. Contrary to the details and spirit of this story as it is sometimes told in history classrooms, however, Parks' act was the result of much planning, and it had impact only because it was part of a broader and well-organized movement

by many citizens (Kohl, 1993). To most future citizens, influencing policy will look futile if their only image of participation is individual action. On the other hand, students who learn about the social movements that spurred legislation in different eras in history are provided with a rationale for their own engagement in such efforts at change. To the extent that textbooks and teachers continue to emphasize how presidents and other exceptional reformers produce change, students learn that good citizens need do little more than be personally responsible, keep up with the news, and make informed decisions regarding the next great men to run the government. Social studies textbooks and teaching may deprive students of critical understandings regarding how to effect change through movement building.

3. History and government courses reflect American goodness or exceptionalism. American exceptionalism comprises another recurrent feature of much social studies education that blunts student capacity to resist. American exceptionalism is the belief that the United States, as a polity and society, is qualitatively different from other nations, i.e., that the United States contains some special virtue, mission, or qualities which set it apart from other nations (Lipset, 1997; Hodgson, 2009). This often-unexamined belief seems most evident in conservative critics' championing of history that emphasizes admirable stories of patriots and progress (see Nash, Crabtree, and Dunn, 1997 regarding the history wars of the 1990s). Presenting the United States as a land that enjoys a unique or purer brand of democracy, freedom, and inevitable progress also occurs in less overtly political places. Loewen's study of U.S. history textbooks concluded that "textbook authors present our nation as getting ever better in all areas, from race relations to transportation" (Loewen, 1996, p. 295). Loewen also identifies multiple "lies" that teachers and textbooks tell, distorting episodes of U.S. history to emphasize the virtuous and erase the injustice (Loewen, 1996). Many history classrooms and museums base their narrative of U.S. history around the themes of freedom and progress, which promotes pride and veneration of these unquestioned features of our national story (Barton and Levstik, 2004). Thus, textbooks and curricula not only avoid controversial issues or critical perspectives, they often support a vision of the U.S. society and policy as fundamentally just and good or even exceptional. Such a master narrative, reinforced through multiple means, makes it more difficult to take alternative perspectives (Barton and Levstik, 2004) or to begin to question existing arrangements. Conversely, students are empow-

ered to ask questions when they gain access to multiple perspectives about the goodness, exceptionality, and flaws in U.S. society, government, and history.

4. History comprises rote learning of names, dates, and places. The content of typical social studies teaching may socialize citizens to see history as conclusions already reached, as change wrought only by exceptional people, or as stories that usually reinforce the unique qualities and goodness of the United States. A fourth way that social studies teaching blunts individuals' capacity for social action comprises the common use of didactic rather than participatory methods of instruction. A careful look across extant documents led educational historians and authors to conclude that patterns of social studies instruction have been fairly consistent since the 1900s (Cuban, 1993; Levstik, 2008). The majority of teachers have engaged in teacher-centered instruction akin to Freire's "banking model" of education (Freire, 2000). Teachers and textbooks are the sources of information (Ravitch, 2004; Wade, 1993); teachers engage in recitation, i.e., initiating lower-order thinking questions requiring short student responses; and much of the remaining time in classrooms is used for tests and individual seat work (Cuban, 1993; see also Levstik, 2008). Such teaching reinforces the notion of history as memorizing "one damn thing after another" (Rescher, 1997, p. 203). A small number of teachers have developed a hybrid approach, which combines these teacher-centered activities with more active student involvement in debate, role-playing, small group activities, inquiry activities, and more authentic discussions (Cuban, 1993; Levstik, 2008). Most efforts to shift traditional patterns of instruction, however, have been adapted in ways that turn them into incremental rather than fundamental changes (Tyack and Cuban, 1995).

The widespread use of teacher-centered pedagogies further discourages the kinds of critical literacy, thoughtful disagreement, or capacity to engage in social action that are required for more active citizenship. Such instruction probably also discourages interest in social and political matters. When students were asked to rank subjects in terms of which they find most interesting, social studies ranked last (Wiley and Race, 1977). It is possible that students' negative attitudes toward the subject result in part from textbook and lecture-heavy pedagogy. Students turned off by this experience seem less likely to have the interest, knowledge, or skills to become thoughtfully engaged in social and political issues later in their lives.

Counter examples from the history of the social studies

Much social studies curriculum and instruction have traditionally discouraged taking a critical stance or action with regard to current conditions and controversies; however, there have been countervailing forces seeking to empower critical thinking. Indeed, when the National Education Association asked historians to report on the place of history in schools, the Committee of Seven in 1898 called for a history that went beyond "acquiring facts" to encompass promoting "judgment" and "the scientific habit of mind," i.e., open-minded questioning and evidence-seeking (Saxe, 1992, pp. 59-60). The new social studies of the 1960s called for students to engage in discovery or inductive learning and to use the modes of inquiry employed by historians and social scientists (Hertzberg, 1981). Values clarification exercises from the 1960s and 1970s and the promotion of higher order thinking skills in the last decades of the 20th century are other examples of social studies approaches that build individual capacity to think independently and critically about social and political issues.

WHAT IS A COMMUNITY OF PRACTICE, AND WHY BUILD THEM IN SOCIAL STUDIES CLASSROOMS?

How might we create classrooms equipping students with the ways of thinking, the skills, and the dispositions to thoughtfully and effectively decide when to resist existing policies, injustices, and orthodox beliefs? Having a clear theory about how students acquire new ways of thinking and acting in the world could be very helpful to envisioning how social studies classrooms could produce such outcomes. The notion of a "community of practice" provides just this kind of practical guidance.

The community of practice, or CoP, is a way of explaining how people learn to do things in the world. As envisioned by Jean Lave and Etienne Wenger, CoPs occur wherever people are engaged in a shared enterprise (Lave and Wenger, 1991). Pediatricians who share a practice, National Writing Project teachers who engage in their own writing response groups, or members of Alcoholics Anonymous who engage in specific approaches to improving their lives all constitute COPs. At the center of CoPs are practices, shared ways of getting things done in the world. Experienced members of a CoP will know how and why they do things in a certain way. Newcomers—to the pediatric practice, a response group, or the Alcoholics Anonymous meeting—would ideally have the chance to observe the practices at the core of the CoP and then to ask questions. Rather than immediately trying to perform all the practices unaided, they would ideally have support and supervision in performing and then learning from limited components of the practice: A pediatric intern practices doing a physical exam under the watchful eye of an experienced practitioner, or a new member of AA tries participating in just one ritual with the encouragement and guidance of a sponsor. As newcomers to a CoP grow in skill, understanding, and judgment, they are given increasing opportunities to engage in shared practices with less support and increasing real world challenges (Lave and Wenger, 1991; Wenger, 1998). The concept of a CoP reminds us that much of our most powerful, enduring, and enjoyable learning occurs when we are engaged in activities with other people. (For a more detailed exploration of the affordances and limitations of CoPs, see Levine, 2010.)

The next section of this chapter identifies four approaches to social studies education that could be at the center of a social studies classroom working as a community of practice. For each of these four approaches, the teacher might act as the most experienced member seeking to determine when and how to introduce specific new ways of thinking and acting. He or she can help students, as newcomers to the practice, to see models and then to begin to experiment and learn from their fledgling efforts performing small pieces of the practice. Students learn not only from feedback from the teacher, as a more experienced practitioner, but also from their engagement in the practice, their observation of examples of skilled performance and peers' performance, and from the mutual learning that comes when surrounded by others who are talking about and working on shared goals. While some may think these kinds of practices are more possible or relevant for secondary students, scholars and teachers have shown how primary and intermediate grade students can also work as communities that engage in the kinds of critical inquiry, action, and efforts to impact the social world described below (Cowhey, 2006; Levstik and Barton, 2001; VanSledright, 2002).

APPROACHES TO SOCIAL STUDIES THAT COULD BE ENACTED WITHIN SOCIAL STUDIES CLASSROOM COPS

In the following text, I introduce four approaches to social studies teaching which are promising in terms of creating citizens with the capacity and inclination to work thoughtfully and collaboratively to improve social and political conditions if these citizens believe that is necessary. Each of these approaches is a current manifestation of the tradition of social studies as promoting critical thinking. Simply including these practices in social studies classrooms would build skills useful to thoughtful engagement in social and political issues. When implemented in the context of a community of practice—in a classroom intentionally organized to help newcomers to engage in each practice with support, reflection, and increasing sophistication over time—such participatory activity can also build the confidence, skills, and dispositions to contribute to a "small group of thoughtful committed citizens" that can "change the world," according to Mead (Lutkehaus, 2009, p. 34).

1. Acquiring critical literacy through "doing history"

The approach

A number of scholars hope that elementary and secondary students will get the opportunity to "do history." (Brophy and VanSledright, 1997; Levstik and Barton, 2001; Marcus and Levine, 2007; Wineburg, 2001). This approach to history engages students in historical inquiry and modes of making meaning akin to the work of real historians. Such work can prepare future citizens with critical literacy—the ability to read critically within and across texts—thus equipping future citizens with habits of mind that include recognizing all texts as constructed, partial, and biased in their accounts (Wineburg, 2001; Levstik and Barton, 2001). Such critical reading of primary sources is a core activity of historians, and one that is recurrently proposed for younger students learning history. History continues to be a particularly promising subject area for building critical literacy skills, i.e., the ability to interrogate texts regarding their point of view and potential sources of bias and inaccuracy.

Enacting the approach in a community of practice

How might a history classroom as a community of practice develop students' ability to engage in historical inquiry? Whether students are new to a practice or are deepening their proficiency, they need the chance to observe more skilled performance of the shared practice. Seeing professional historians or their own teachers "think aloud" as they interact with various types of documents creates public access to new ways of thinking. For instance, students might see that historians, when they first encounter primary sources, often start reading at the bottom of the document, learning about the author, the date, the audience, and/or the period when the document was written (Wineburg, 2001); this sourcing heuristic (Wineburg, 2001) helps a skilled reader adopt a more critical stance by letting them think about the trustworthiness and positionality of a text's author before they read the author's words. (See Chapter 3 of Wineburg, 2001 for a nuanced look at "skilled reading of history" and the use of think-alouds.) Students would then need activities and exercises that give them scaffolded opportunities to practice aspects of such critical reading. For instance, worksheets with focused questions can accompany documents that take conflicting views; such worksheets might help pairs or groups of students to critically evaluate the trustworthiness of sources. As students learn from each other's efforts and insights, and gain skills in critical inquiry, they might graduate to Socratic seminars, a model for teaching that looks deeply within texts and helps students raise and explore authentic and pressing questions (for a fine short introduction online, see Adventist Education, 2004–2009). They might also respond to document-based questions, which require critical reading across primary sources to construct answers to complex and important historical questions. In any of these cases, the presence of a community that is working together to model and develop such skills can provide invaluable support and learning opportunities otherwise unavailable in a teacher-centered classroom.

2. Learning to engage in civil discussion of controversial issues

The approach

Social studies textbooks and teaching often avoid controversy (Cuban, 1993; Hess, 2001). Citizens in a democracy, however, must learn to constructively engage with difficult social and political issues. Thus, some social studies scholars are developing specific pedagogies and broader lines of thinking about how social studies teaching can prepare students to engage in individual deliberation, joint conversation, and constructive negotiation relevant to past and present controversies.

One example of such pedagogy comprises "structured academic controversy." Where traditional classroom debates force students to take only one side and motivate students to win at all costs, structured academic controversies put pairs of students on opposing sides of a controversial issue. After participating in scaffolded reading and preparation, students take turns arguing one view, and then they also engage in active listening to opposing arguments; they are even required to briefly try arguing the topic from the other side than the one they initially took. This activity structure concludes by requiring students to drop the forced roles and work with the pair that had the opposing view to craft a joint response to the problem; they may synthesize points of view or propose a third position (for more regarding this pedagogy, see Johnson and Johnson, 1993).

Enacting the approach in a community of practice

The concept of a community of practice reminds us that fostering students' ability to engage in controversial issues is best taught by observing and then actually practicing a new skill in the company of peers and a more skilled practitioner. As with historical inquiry, teachers need not feel expert to have more expertise than their own students. It is possible to view good examples of structured academic controversies and historical inquiry on the web via the Persistent Issues in History Network (http://dp.crlt.indiana.edu/ to request membership). Such videos provide students with access to models of effective discussion. As in any community of practice, more skilled practitioners should help novices to explicitly recognize desired features of the performance and to discern the kinds of preparation or behavior that contribute to successful outcomes. Thus, teachers should explicitly identify conversational moves that facilitate dialogue and disagreement, including active listening, responding to ideas rather than people, using questions to clarify others' ideas, and inviting participation of quiet peers. Students then would benefit from scaffolding, i.e., structured exercises and materials that provide students with content and ways of preparing to engage in discussion. After trying such conversations, classrooms as communities can learn from their developing efforts through joint reflection. Audiotape or videotape of specific conversations can provide more opportunities to observe the shared practice and can help the emerging CoP to understand and build on its current progress. Students who gain multiple opportunities to participate in and reflect on such conversation can learn how to engage with those who disagree with their views, to reason, and to compromise; these are all the skills which would enable more active citizenship. (For further suggestions about practice, see Hess, 2001; Hess and Posselt, 2002; Parker and Hess, 2001.)

3. Promoting students' ability and desire to understand multiple perspectives

The approach

History may be taught in ways that lead students to empathize with people whose era, socio-economic position, and/or culture are very different from their own. When students study history, cultural geography, and other social sciences, they may be given the chance to deeply enter the perspectives of those traditionally left out of traditional history; this can empower individuals to move beyond passive acceptance of prevailing beliefs and practices. Use of first person accounts of history or historical fiction can be particularly effective in promoting individuals' ability to empathize with others whose lives, beliefs, and context are unfamiliar. The ability to take others' perspective may be critical in building the kinds of coalitions and movements required for effective social action. This ability is also important if we are to avoid having citizens who narrowly seek gains only for themselves or their sub-group.

Students could read first person accounts in isolation, as homework exercises or seatwork. Individuals, however, are likely to bring their current concerns, values, and ways of seeing the world into such foreign realms. When first person accounts and historical fiction are at the heart of a community of practice, teachers may help students learn how to enter such works while practicing suspension of their preexisting assumptions and biases.

Simulations and role-play exercises are another example of pedagogies that require students to understand and explore a perspective different from their own, and which can have a lasting impact when implemented among a group of people. For example, while studying the Industrial Revolution in U.S. history, students might offer testimony to Congress from the point of view of immigrant laborers, farmers, industrialists, urban machine politicians, social reformers, and others; students could understand proposals regarding limiting child labor, enacting regulations for food and drugs, or regulating monopolies from multiple points of view. If a community of practice focuses explicitly on coming to empathize with others' situations and comprehending their values, or on making sense of a historical period on its own terms, future citizens may develop skills and dispositions that help them understand others different from themselves in the present. Decisions about engaging in social action would ideally be based upon such comprehension of current issues from multiple views. Those engaging in social action will also be able to build more effective coalitions if they can comprehend the concerns and values of others.

Enacting the approach in a community of practice

In the context of a CoP, to help students learn to actively seek out and understand others' perspectives, teachers could provide the initial examples of skilled performance by thinking aloud. Teachers should explicitly identify how their thinking, values, and understandings from their own era affect their efforts to comprehend an immigrant as presented in a short story or document. Teachers could also demonstrate how they can look within and beyond a short story or document for help identifying values and concerns of an individual, group, or era. Small group exercises in class could then give students practice in developing empathy with those whose views are unlike their own. Witnessing peers engaged in simulation or role play can provide further examples of the practice; classrooms that create such collective opportunities to try taking multiple perspectives also create opportunities for collective reflection on the challenges and desirability of seeing from various viewpoints.

4. Providing students with the opportunity to engage in social action

The approach

Freire has proposed that students must go beyond achieving understandings, or even awareness of their own consciousness and their era; Freire proposes that education must create dialogue and praxis, a cycle of theory, application, evaluation, and reflection that can produce social transformation (Freire, 2000). In some places, social studies is enacted in ways that look like praxis, putting theoretical knowledge into action. Indeed, service learning has emerged as an approach to education which helps youth become "capable, productive, and essential contributors to their communities," engaging simultaneously in service and in learning (Wade, 2008, p. 110).

A number of service learning and social service projects are incorporated into high school curricula or serve as stand-alone experiences equivalent to courses. Other schools offer opportunities to do work in local or international communities as a co-curricular activity. An example of one current approach is community mapping, which scaffolds groups of students' ability to enter the community and to measure and describe features of a community, including problems and potential resources for solving those problems. As students "map" a community, service learning and other scaffolded projects beyond the school can build citizens' skills and affinity for undertaking collective efforts of resistance or change. Effective service learning—to maximize both the impact of the service and of the learning—should include the following elements: thoughtful preparation for the service; integration with curriculum, creating intentional opportunities to use or develop skills; respectful collaboration with peers; opportunities and scaffolds for reflection; assessment of both the service and the resulting learning; students' sense of ownership; and community celebration (Wade, 2008). Ultimately, service learning promises to integrate the development of some traditional kinds of literacy and conceptual understanding into projects that have real world impact and produce civic attitudes unlikely to develop solely in an isolated classroom; such dispositions include care for others and for social issues, tolerance, respect, integrity, and fairness (Wade, 1997, p. 15).

Enacting the approach in a community of practice

Whether students solicit donations and expert help to create a new playground for an elementary school, lobby state legislators to fund summer arts programs, or network with other schools to affect global climate policy, they will need to develop a number of new skills. Teachers might at first need to be more active in modeling and assisting, but should see themselves as seeking to promote competent practitioners of the required skills, and thus offer opportunities for students to think and do with decreasing levels of support. The teacher also might structure feedback—from the teacher, peers, or self-reflection—to promote more skilled action in the world; the classroom could become a place where students talk about how they collect donations, contact busy politicians, or motivate others to participate in a joint effort, and learn together from the strengths and weaknesses of their efforts. Teachers might view themselves as mentors or coaches helping students master practices necessary to collaborate, build coalitions, persuade, and find the necessary information and resources to achieve impact in the world.

Suppressing Resistance: How Social Studies can Contribute to the Problem or the Solution

Across the United States, schools and school systems often have mission statements that include, in their objectives, promoting active citizenship or preparing individuals for citizenship. This chapter takes that notion seriously, and argues that such citizenship should include the capacity to question or challenge existing social and political arrangements based upon critical analysis and thoughtful engagement. Schools should give future citizens the tools with which to think objectively about their world, and to decide for themselves whether and how they should resist injustice and engage in social action.

There is reason to worry that our schools are mostly failing to produce such citizens. High school and college students today, compared with young people in earlier generations, know less about politics, vote less, and self-report feeling less civic obligation (Wade, 2008). This chapter has focused on the school subject directly associated with fostering citizenship, the social studies. It has suggested how common features of typical social studies teaching and learning in K-12 education can contribute to apathy and the predominant, passive forms of citizenship in the United States.

To address political apathy and the limits of typical social studies instruction, this chapter has proposed that social studies classrooms should work as communities of practice that foster specific skills and dispositions enabling resistance. In such communities, teachers model—and students develop—a host of skills that allow social engagement. Students learn to ask and answer their own questions. They conduct research and critically evaluate sources. Students learn to engage both in civil disagreement and efforts to collaborate and compromise. By allowing room for learning that goes beyond unquestioning acceptance of a textbook, such communities can promote the inclination to take critical perspectives and to find answers and viewpoints beyond the ones offered by a single source. When such communities actually publish work by students, seek to influence others, or take social action, students learn lessons relevant to getting things done in the social and political world. Teachers in such communities, rather than being a source of unquestioned factual knowledge, guide students into having experiences and gaining repeated practice to develop critical thinking skills, empathy, and the ability to speak publicly about controversial issues. Students experience school as modeling the kinds of collaboration, compromise, and thoughtful decision-making required to decide whether and how to engage in social action.

If we are to equip students with the understandings, skills, and dispositions required for resistance, who must ultimately be responsible for this work? This chapter argues that teachers, schools, and school leadership must provide the experiences that help students develop knowledge, skills, and dispositions enabling the possibility of resistance. Again, school must not tell students what to think or resist, as this ultimately undercuts the development of students who can decide for themselves whether and how to resist. While schools can create the context within which students might develop the relevant skills, students must have an agency in deciding the content, direction, and nature of the work they do in classroom communities.

Given the many pressing questions raised by the study of history and the social sciences, it is a shame that social studies has been seen as the most boring of school subjects (Wiley and Race, 1977). Organized differently, social studies classrooms could become the crucible within which students learn the power and joy of having a voice, having agency, and being able to change the world in which they find themselves. Working as a small group of thoughtful, committed citizens in social studies classrooms, students can learn how to make a difference.

References

Adventist Education (2004–2009). Socratic Seminars. Retrieved August 24, 2009 from http://www.journeytoexcellence.org/practice/instruction/theories/miscideas/socratic/

American Textbook Council (1994). *History textbooks: A standard and guide*. New York: American Textbook Council.

Anderson, C., Avery, P. G., Pederson, P. V., Smith, E. S., & Sullivan, J. L. (1997). Divergent perspectives on citizenship education: A Q-Method study and survey of social studies teachers. *American Educational Research Journal*, 34 (2), 333–364.

Barton, K. C., & Levstik, L. S. (2004). *Teaching history for the common good*. Mahwah, NJ: Lawrence Erlbaum.

Brophy, J., & VanSledright, B. (1997). *Teaching and learning history in elementary schools*. New York: Teachers College Press.

Cowhey, M. (2006). *Black ants and Buddhists: Thinking critically and teaching differently in the primary grades*. Portland, Maine: Stenhouse.

Cuban, L. (1993). *How teachers taught: Constancy and change in American classrooms, 1890–1990* (2nd ed.). New York: Teachers College Press.

Freire, P. (2000). *Pedagogy of the oppressed*. New York: Continuum.

Hertzberg, H. (1981). *Social studies reform, 1880–1980*. Boulder: Social Science Education Consortium.

Hess, D. (2001). Teaching students to discuss controversial public issues. ERIC Digest. Bloomington, IN: ERIC Clearinghouse for Social Studies/Social Science Education. ED 457106.

Hess, D., & Posselt, J. (2002). How high school students experience and learn from the discussion of controversial public issues. *Journal of Curriculum and Supervision*, 17(4), 283–314.

Hodgson, G. (2009). *The myth of American exceptionalism*. New Haven, CT: Yale University Press.

Johnson, D. W., & Johnson, R. T. (1993). Structuring academic controversy. In S. Sharan (Ed.), *Handbook of cooperative learning methods* (pp. 66–81). Westport, CT: Greenwood.

Kohl, H. (1993). The myth of "Rosa Parks the tired": Teaching about Rosa Parks and the Montgomery Bus Boycott. *Multicultural Education*, 1(2), 6–10.

Lave, J., & Wenger, E. (1991). *Situated learning: Legitimate peripheral participation.* New York: Cambridge University Press.
Levine, T.H. (2010). Tools for the study and design of collaborative teacher learning: The affordances of different conceptions of teacher community and activity theory. *Teacher Education Quarterly, 27* (1) 109–130.
Levstik, L. S. (2008). What happens in social studies classrooms? Research on K-12 social studies practices. In L. S. Levstik & C. A. Tyson (Eds.), *Handbook of research in social studies education* (pp. 50–64). New York: Routledge.
Levstik, L. S., & Barton, K. C. (2001). *Doing history: Investigating with children in elementary and middle school.* Mahwah, NJ: Lawrence Earlbaum.
Lipset, S. M. (1997). *American exceptionalism: A double edged sword.* New York: W.W. Norton & Company.
Loewen, J. W. (1996). *Lies my teacher told me: Everything your American history textbook got wrong.* New York: Touchstone.
Lutkehaus, N. (2009). Margaret Mead: Public Anthropologist. *Anthropology Now,* 1(1), 29–39. Retrieved August 19, 2009 from http://www.anthronow.com/mead1.pdf
Marcus, A. S. & Levine, T. H. (2007). Exploring the past through feature film in Alan S. Marcus (Ed.) *Celluloid blackboard: Teaching history with film* (pp. 1–13). Information Age Publishers: Charlotte, NC.
Marker, G., & Mehlinger, H. (1992). Social studies. In Jackson, P. (Ed.), *Handbook of research on curriculum* (pp. 830–851). New York: Macmillan.
Nash, G. B., Crabtree, C., & Dunn, R. E. (1997). *History on trial: Culture wars and the teaching of the past.* New York: Knopf.
Parker, W. C., & Hess, D. (2001). Teaching with and for discussion. *Teaching and Teacher Education,* 17(3), 273–289.
Ravitch, D. (2004). *A consumer's guide to high school history textbooks.* Washington, DC: Thomas B. Fordham Institute.
Rescher, N. (1997). *Predicting the future: An introduction to the theory of forecasting.* Albany: State University of New York Press.
Saxe, D. W. (1992). *Social studies in schools: A history of the early years.* Albany: SUNY Press.
Sunal, C. S., & Haas, M. E. (2008). *Social studies for the elementary and middle grades: A constructivist approach.* Boston: Pearson/Allyn & Bacon.
Tyack, D., & Cuban, L. (1995). *Tinkering toward utopia: A century of public school reform.* Cambridge, MA: Harvard University Press.
VanSledright, B. A. (2002). *In search of America's past: Learning to read history in elementary school.* New York: Teachers College Press.
Wade, R. C. (1993). Content analysis of social studies textbooks: A review of ten years of research. *Theory and Research in Social Education,* 21(3), 232–256.
Wade, R. C. (1997). Community service-learning: An overview. In Wade, R. C., & Wood, G. H. (Eds.), *Community service-learning: A guide to including service in the public school curriculum* (pp. 19–34). Albany: SUNY Press.
Wade, R. C. (2008). Service learning. In Levstik, L. S. & Tyson, C. A. (Eds.) *Handbook of research in social studies education* (pp. 109–123). New York: Routledge.
Wenger, E. (1998). *Communities of practice: Learning, meaning, and identity.* New York: Cambridge University Press.
Westheimer, J. & Kahne, J. (2004). What kind of citizen? The politics of educating for democracy. *American Educational Research Journal,* 41(2), 237–269.

Wiley, K. B., & Race, J. (1977). *The status of pre-college science, mathematics, and social science education: 1955–1975, Vol. 3: Social science education.* Boulder, CO: Social Science Education Consortium.

Wineburg, S. (2001). *Historical thinking and other unnatural acts: Charting the future of teaching the past.* Philadelphia: Temple University Press.

Zinn, H. (2003). *A people's history of the United States.* New York: HarperCollins.

CHAPTER TEN

The Challenge of Bullying in U.S. Schools

Resistance and Reaction

JO ANN FREIBERG

THE BACKGROUND

On April 20, 1999, in Littleton, Colorado, a tragedy now known universally simply as "Columbine" became the crucible for a targeted awareness on school safety. Schools are by far the physically safest places any person can be in a 24-hour period. Winning the most competitive lottery is actually a better bet than being killed in a school. Schools are not, however, the safest places in our communities when it comes to emotional or intellectual safety. Too many schools foster toxic climates that allow, and in some cases even promote, the unethical treatment of school community members. The phenomenon of the "rampage school shooting" actually began a quarter century prior to Columbine, during which time over 30 such incidents took place, in which dozens of individuals were killed or wounded. Then there was Columbine High School. Schools and communities have not been the same since, but why? Why was the April 20, 1999 tragedy in Littleton, Colorado, the one that so shocked the entire nation? Arguably there are two main reasons. First, it was truly a school shooting of a magnitude never seen, or even imagined, before. But second, it was the first school shooting to happen in an upper middle-class, suburban community. This aspect is central to explaining why Columbine was so significant in raising our awareness. Columbine demonstrated that *no* school in our nation could assume that it was immune to the risks of school shootings. Such tragedies were no longer just a southern or rural problem. They were a national problem, and one that might occur in any school. Hence, Columbine was a "wake-up" call that the problem of school shootings, and issues related to school climate and safety could no longer be ignored.

Initial reaction and recommended remedies focused exclusively on the physical aspects of school safety: the presence of firearms and other weapons in schools. What has subsequently become clear is that no combination of metal detectors, sign-in procedures, ID tags, clear backpacks, and so on would have stopped these determined and driven young men. Subsequent research has sought to uncover the roots of the problem and combat the knee-jerk reactions. We now know that the real problem was and continues *not* to be about keeping dangerous individuals out of schools; it has always been about ministering to those students legitimately in attendance *within the school* who became outcasts from the school culture in large part because of toxic school climates in which they were treated inappropriately. Such climates saw students alienated and pushed to their limits.

The root causes of these rampage school shootings are now widely known. *All* of the "shooters" were marginalized by their peers by being teased, taunted, excluded and called names mercilessly and maliciously, and this had escalated over time. Most, if not all of the "shooters" were accused of being "gay," whether or not they were. Such cruelty was overlooked at the very least and condoned in far too many cases. All of the students tried desperately to get help from adults who supposedly were there for them, and sadly, were not. They all had layers of personal problems, from serious mental health diagnoses[1] to depression and anxiety to family issues that none of us should ever have to endure. A feature of their personal psychology in many cases appears to have been some form of psychosis, schizophrenia, or malignant narcissism. The fourth thing they all shared is that they all learned in schools where the cultural boundaries for acceptance were narrow and their differences were simply too great to allow them to fit in. All of these students were too "different" and strange for the school that they attended. Finally, they were all able to acquire guns with relative ease.

Up to this point, I have not yet used this word, "bullying," choosing instead to use the words "cruelty" or "being marginalized." I have done this purposefully. It has been widely reported that bullying was a major contributing factor for the rampage school shooters. It is also interesting that in one seminal report, the conclusions were that "most of the shooters were bullied." It is now well known that they were *all* subjected to unimaginable peer cruelty, but in some notable cases, it just was not called bullying. The word itself is highly problematic both in theory and in practice. This is one of the most critical barriers in managing the problem with bullying and cries out to be addressed.

Research and targeted concern about the arena of bullying began in Scandinavia in the 1970s. The Norwegian researcher Dan Olweus of Norway first studied this phenomenon in earnest (Olweus, 1978, 1993, 1994). His landmark work led to related research other countries, particularly Britain, Australia, and New Zealand. This level of interest and attention did not come to the United States until the post-Columbine era. Immediately after Columbine, the Secret Service National Threat Assessment Center engaged in research that found that most of the "shooters" were targets of bullying (Vossekuil, Fein, Reddy, Borum, and Modzeleski, 2002, p. 31). More recently, a group of Harvard researchers confirmed the same (Newman, 2004). Additionally, *The Journal of the American Medical Association* (*JAMA*) conducted a survey of youth in grades 6 to 10 in all demographic arenas throughout the country in 2001 again to discover the same: bullying is widespread and a serious problem for school-aged youth (Nansel, 2001).[2]

Throughout all of this well-respected research and in countless other studies, books, and articles, bullying is portrayed as a critical problem in American schools. What seems to be missing from the conversation is any recognition that there is no real consistency in what is called "bullying," either in the literature or in terms of how the word "plays" in schools and communities, not to mention for the families that comprise them. Until such awareness is taken into consideration, there is little chance that schools will actually become safer places, physically, emotionally, and intellectually.

ANTI-BULLYING LEGISLATION

Effective July 1, 1999, Georgia enacted the first anti-bullying law in the United States, only two and a half months *after* Columbine. Not one state in the country had passed such a law before Columbine. As of the tenth anniversary of Columbine, thirty-seven states had some form of anti-bullying legislation, six more were working their way through their respective legislatures and nearly every other state was considering doing so. America *reacts*; we are unfortunately not as good at prevention. Columbine and the arrival of state anti-bullying laws are analogous to "9/11." There had been many terrorist attacks on American interests around the world prior to the planes hitting the Trade Towers in New York City; there had even been earlier attempts on the Trade Towers themselves. But such attacks on American soil had not been successful, so lives continued uninterrupted and without concern or sacrifice, and for the most part the nation was not really prepared for such a devastating attack.

The passing of the states anti-bullying legislation is an attempt to react to and "solve" the "bullying" problem that has taken so many lives physically and emotionally over the past few decades. It is often as we believe that merely *having* the law will in some way diminish the amount of bullying in schools. But this is demonstrably false. The number of allegations of bullying being tried in courts of law since 2000 is only increasing. And, of course, bullying seems to have been around as long as childhood has been chronicled. Prior to Columbine, the phenomenon of "bullying" was generally seen as a common part of growing up, which seemed always to have been a part (though perhaps an unpleasant part) of American schooling. Historically, "bullying" was treated more as a childhood "rite of passage" than as something to give to the courts or about which to legislate.

Why is the issue of "bullying" one that has only recently been brought to the forefront and tackled more systemically? The simple answer is that in very recent times, the stakes have become alarmingly high compared to past eras, and the rampage school shootings have brought this into clear focus. Children have access to myriad ways to hurt and kill themselves and others that were not options decades ago (weapons, drugs, technology, etc.). In the 18th, 19th, and first half of the 20th century, a "bully" might break an arm, bloody a nose, or make another feel the pains of marginalization; family members and community neighbors were much more likely to provide the care, connection, and concern that would buffer the harm. The current 21st century social milieu is far different, and there is much more likelihood that the ravages of a "bully" will go untreated.[3] However, merely attempting to legislate "bullying" away does not in any way on its own impact the existence or severity of bullying. A fuller understanding of this reality is sorely needed.

THE LETTER VERSUS THE SPIRIT OF THE LAW

It is true that laws addressing bullying, which are often tied to relatively severe consequences for the perpetrator, have brought increased awareness for this pervasive childhood "disease." Any individual state law can be easily read and reviewed to assess the legally required elements to which schools are held to account. This can be described as the *letter of the law*. Ultimately, however, schools must look beyond the legal (and often minimal) requirements to what is the overarching intent in passing and implementing all these individual state laws. The bottom line is that each and every one of these laws is attempting to achieve the *spirit of the law* which is a very simple concept: to legislate that each and every child has the right to learn and socialize in a physically, emotionally, and intellectually safe environment. Throughout the country, in every school district and the individual schools residing in those districts, *all students*, not just some students or a subset of the population, but each and every student has the right to spend his or her time in school in a safe place. And, importantly, the nation, the individual states, school districts, schools, and the personnel who work within them have important legal and moral obligations to make this happen. Unfortunately, in far too many educational settings, these obligations are not being met; there is real resistance in practice to close the gap between the *letter* and the *spirit* of the law. This resistance can be attributed to certain barriers which can, if properly understood, be removed, with the practical result that bullying really can be diminished if not completely eliminated.

Barrier #1: Understanding the goal: Climate and culture considered

Without a clear destination or goal, it is virtually impossible to travel down the appropriate path. This is true in virtually all settings, inside and outside of schooling. Leaving home to travel to a museum requires knowing where the museum is and figuring out how to get from the starting point (home) to the destination (museum). With classroom lesson planning, the process is no different: educational goals/objectives work in collaboration with specific subject matter, to determine the appropriate methods to employ in working toward reaching the ultimate learning objective. Countless examples of this sort could be provided. The point is that in order to diminish and ultimately eliminate bullying (our goal), a clear map must be provided, complete with the meaningful steps that must be taken to reach the destination. Far too often in practice, the goal of diminishing bullying is dealt with by using the "whac-a-mole" (named after a popular game) philosophy: when a case of bullying pops up, intervene with some form of punishment for the perpetrator. The "punishment" often takes the form of detention or suspension from the regular school setting, which serves to eliminate the problem while that student is not in the setting, but does nothing to change behavior when they return…and the "mole" pops up again. This process of *intervention* with the "bullies" (moles) continues, rarely yielding any significant positive changes over time. Another comparison might be that when dealing with the historical epidemic of smallpox, treating one case at a time did not work to eradicate the disease. Eradication only came when the *system was inoculated:* the road map to eliminate bullying is flawed if the pathway to reach the goal focuses on intervention. Further, the majority of the legal requirements for diminishing bullying throughout the country take this flawed approach: when bullying incidents appear, intervene.

Research points in a clear, single direction: the ultimate remedy for bullying is to have a school culture that is foreign to such behaviors and, simply put, will not allow them. In order to create such a culture an understanding of what is meant by "culture" is fundamental. Culture and climate are often taken to be the same concept. They are not synonymous and, importantly, should be distinguished so that improvement in this wide arena can be achieved.

School Culture

The culture of a school can be defined in two related, albeit distinct ways: as descriptive goals or as positive goals. In both cases, the "culture" of a school is about the wide standards and norms that embrace what the school stands for. So, in the first sense, a school culture is what is *descriptive* of the school. In other words, when a school community member (student, parent/guardian, faculty/staff member) *describes* what is distinctive of the school, how others might see it or what is characteristic, this would be to understand the school culture *as it is*. For example, it was widely reported in the days after the Columbine High School shooting tragedy, the school supported a "jock" culture, which meant, "sports ruled!" In the words of teachers at Columbine, this was confirmed with the additional description of the school as hosting a "culture of homophobia." This is definitely a *description* and few, if any, would argue that this is what the culture of this or any school *ought* to be. This leads to the second way in which school culture can be articulated.

In the second sense of the term "school culture," *description* is not relevant. Instead, the mission or vision of the school is what matters. School culture is not about what the school *is*, but rather *what the school is striving to become*. In 21st century [public] schools, in virtually every school district and school, there is an articulated school mission: a lofty set of goals toward which the district and school is aspiring. In this second meaning of culture, what the school *ought* to be is central. The mission/vision should set the tone for what the school or district hopes *will be* the description and should be working toward becoming reality for each and every school community member.

Most, if not all, schools experience a gap (and often a substantial one) between the *descriptive* sense of school culture and the second sense of school culture as *goal*. The vehicle that is used to close the gap between these two meanings of culture (working toward arriving at the second or *mission* sense) is school *climate*. Often schools embrace district-approved "mission statements," which may or may not match any kind of *real* goal. Cleverly worded "mission statements" that adorn hallways and offices may represent the outcome of exercises serving to satisfy accreditation requirements but never practically viable or attainable. If school culture is correctly understood as being along a continuum (description at one end and mission/goal at the other), then any real gap between these two meanings can only make sense if the "mission" (goal) sense of culture is not merely a hollow proposition.

School Climate

Simply defined, climate boils down to the nature of the interrelationships among the people in the school community physically, emotionally, and intellectually; *how the people within the school community treat one another* (adult to adult interactions, adult to student interactions, and student to student interactions) through their actions, verbal and non-verbal exchanges, tone of voice, and the use or abuse of inherent power advantages. And, far too often, *"[s]chool climate is an ever changing factor in the lives of people who work and learn in schools. Much like the air we breathe, school climate is ignored until it becomes foul"* (Freiberg, 1998, p. 22). Climate is the "engine" that functions to close the school culture gap. When school community members treat one another appropriately and with respect, it is possible to have the description of the school culture actually be synonymous with the stated school mission (vision).

Barrier #2: Defining "bullying"

Defining "bullying" is an initial hurdle and without attention, potentially an insurmountable barrier. No matter what definition is used, in schooling *practice*, administrators, faculty, staff, students as well as parents and guardians are hard pressed to describe with clarity what bullying looks, feels and sounds like. Generally, individuals "know it when they see it." The challenge here is much like that identified many years ago by the historian Carl Becker, who observed that:

> Now, when I meet a word with which I am entirely unfamiliar, I find it a good plan to look it up in the dictionary and find out what someone thinks it means. But when I have frequently to use words with which everyone is perfectly familiar—words like "cause" and "liberty" and "progress" and "government"—when I have to use words of this sort which everyone knows perfectly well, the wise thing to do is to take a week off and think about them. (1955, p. 328)

But, in reality this is not good enough. Getting a handle on bullying with an honest intent to diminish it begins with knowing what it is. It is impossible to eliminate something that is ephemeral. In order to tackle this *a priori* element, it is necessary to understand how definitions work.

A standard analysis of the anatomy of definitions rests with Israel Scheffler (1960). Definitions fall into three main categories: descriptive/reportive, stipulative, and programmatic or persuasive. In reality, there are only two categories. There are definitions that describe or report on experience, how people actually use terms in context, and then there are definitions that stipulate how words will be used in identified contexts. Stipulative definitions can be viewed as restricting a definition for the purpose of clarity or to lay out the boundaries of understanding and use. Sometimes stipulating a definition takes the form of a new word or acronym for a particular context.

In practice, all descriptive/reportive and stipulative definitions are *prescriptive*; they guide what one does in practice by adhering to that definition. Even a simple definition such as for "stool" as "A low bench or support for the feet or knees in sitting or kneeling, as a footrest" (*The American Heritage Dictionary*, 1982, p. 1200) would suggest that standing on a stool is not to be done; only sitting or kneeling are appropriate. This same analysis can be done for all other definitions, be they descriptive of experience or stipulative. Every definition has some kind of implication of what should be done in practice by accepting and living by the definition. In this sense, definitions are a potentially insidious and dangerous form of a statement because they all guide practice implicitly. They are not often clearly and explicitly directive. To that end, there are no definitions that are programmatic or persuasive on their own; they are all either descriptive/reportive or stipulative and programmatic or persuasive.

There is no standard or consistent definition of bullying; all extant definitions are "stipulative" and appear to honor Olweus, who was the first to provide a formal definition: A person is "being bullied or victimized when he or she is exposed repeatedly and over time, to negative actions on the part of one or more students" (Olweus, 1978). In an analogous way, as Alfred North Whitehead (Whitehead, 1979, p. 39) said about philosophy, "the safest general characterization of the European philosophical tradition is that it consists of a series of footnotes to Plato," defining the term comes down to a series of footnotes to how Olweus first laid down the term.

Definitions of bullying seem, not surprisingly, to share a few characteristics. Most include acts of harassment or intimidation that continue with regularity for a certain period of time, often for as long as six months or more. In a schooling context, bullying seems by definition to be restricted to *student* behavior, implying that adults do not engage in such acts, which is, of course, not simply silly but also counterfactual.

Definitions of bullying vary widely in terms of their ambiguity and vagueness. For example, the landmark 2001 study conducted by *JAMA*, defined bullying simply as "intentionally harmful behavior that occurs repeatedly over time" (Nansel, 2001). Contrast this definition with the one found in the Connecticut bullying legislation for example: "any overt acts by a student or a group of students directed against another student with the intent to ridicule, harass, humiliate or intimidate the other student while on school grounds, at a school-sponsored activity, or on a school bus, which acts are repeated against the same student over time" (*Connecticut General Statutes* 10–222(d), 2006). Interestingly, in 2008 this definition was changed once again. The Connecticut definition of bullying thus reads, "any overt acts by a student or group of students directed against another student with the intent to ridicule, harass, humiliate or intimidate the other student while on school grounds, at a school-sponsored activity or on a school bus, *which acts are committed more than once against any student during the school year.* These progressive changes were made intentionally to try to use the definition to do a better job in practice of eliminating bullying, though simply tightening the definition alone is insufficient as will be discussed.

The *JAMA* definition is overly simplistic and is both vague and ambiguous. The 2002 Connecticut definition, slightly changed in 2006 and again in 2008, is much more restrictive but is still open to a great deal of wide interpretation due to its inherent vagueness. What counts as an *"overt"* act? How is *"repeated...over time"* or *"more than once against any student"* translated into practice? How do you prove *"intent"*? Why should adult behavior be excluded? These are important questions that impact practice in significant ways. Definitions are not just a group of words put together to *describe* practice. Definitions *guide* and in actuality *dictate* practice. In this case, depending upon how vague or restrictive, the definition determines how many individuals are involved in bullying in schools. Empirical studies suggest that anywhere from 5% to 30% of students are determined to be bullies and targets according to the definitional parameters.

Both the *JAMA* and Connecticut definitions were among the earliest to be created and used in the United States. More recently, other states have benefited from the practical lessons learned in these early years. Recent definitions have moved farther and farther away from Olweus.' Consider two more contributions. In 2006, South Carolina passed its "Safe School Climate Act." In South Carolina, the arena is defined as follows:

> "Harassment, intimidation, or bullying" means a gesture, an electronic communication, or a written, verbal, physical, or sexual act that is reasonably perceived to have the effect of: harming a student physically or emotionally or damaging a student's property, or placing a student in reasonable fear of personal harm or property damage; or insulting or demeaning a student or group of students causing substantial disruption in, or substantial interference with, the orderly operation of the school. "School" means in a classroom, on school premises, on a school bus or other school-related vehicle, at an official school bus stop, at a school-sponsored activity or event whether or not it is held on school premises, or at another program or function where the school is responsible for the child. (Code of Laws: Section 2, Chapter 62, Title 59, 2006)

This South Carolina definition introduces the use of the terms "reasonable" and "substantial" in reference to how a student would *perceive* something. Although open to interpretation, at least there is a standard that would more clearly rule in and rule out certain actions experienced by a student or group of students. It is also important to note that in the case of South Carolina, adults are implicitly held to account.

It is interesting that the focus is not on the negatively charged "bullying" arena but rather on the ultimate remedy for ameliorating bullying which is to create a school climate that does not support these behaviors. Additionally, the South Carolina definition seems to recognize that practice in schools is directly impacted by how bullying is defined in their stipulation. States that are passing legislation at present appear to be less concerned with honoring Olweus and more concerned with impacting school practice.

Finally, in 2008, Delaware passed their "School Bullying Prevention Act." Expressly,

> [T]he goals of this Act is [sic] to provide a safer learning environment for students attending…schools. In their definition, bullying "means any intentional written, electronic, verbal or physical act or actions against another person that a reasonable person under the circumstances should know will have the effect of: (1) Placing a person in reasonable fear of substantial harm to his or her emotional or physical well-being or substantial damage to his or her property. (2) Creating a hostile, threatening, humiliating or abusive educational environment due to the pervasiveness or persistence of actions or due to a power differential between the bully and the target; or (3) Interfering with a student having a safe school environment that is necessary to facilitate educational performance, opportunities or benefits; or (4) Perpetuating bullying by inciting, soliciting or coercing an individual or group to demean, dehumanize, embarrass or cause emotional, psychological or physical harm to another person." (14 *Delaware Code* §4112(D), 2007)

Delaware's definition elevates the notion of "reasonable" beyond what the targeted student would perceive to what "any reasonable person under the circumstances would know." This is a significant change, and one that provides more clarity to assessing whether or not something is considered an act of bullying. This definition also includes a "hostile environment," which is a central feature of protected class harassment (sexual and racial) but was not considered by Olweus and does not show up in any prior legal definition of bullying in the United States. And, as with the South Carolina definition, adults are held accountable.

As mentioned earlier, one of the hallmarks of most common definitions of bullying is the difficult vague notion articulated in a variety of ways of "repeated over time." This condition is missing from both the South Carolina and Delaware laws, and the significance of its exclusion cannot be underestimated. Logically, if something is "repeated over time," or even "more than once," then there must have been a *first* time. Why would any reasonable person want to wait to intervene until some arbitrary time *after* an initial inappropriate incident of hurtful behavior? Why is *any* number…even *one* act of hurtful behavior satisfactory? Clearly it is not. The earlier in the cycle that "bullying" can be stopped, the better off everyone is. South Carolina and Delaware appear to reflect this understanding. Managing bullying is not merely about *intervention*, but more importantly about *prevention*. Both of these definitions are objectively superior to early U.S. attempts to define the term in an effort to manage the territory.

Despite the definitional improvements, there still remains a serious flaw in both the South Carolina and Delaware definitions: the word "bully" itself. No amount of restrictive linguistic clarity will change the fact that "bully" and "bullying" are so inherently negatively charged. If the goal really is to create physically, emotionally, and intellectually safe schools where all children can thrive intellectually and socially, then rather than continuing to refine and hone in on better ways to assign the word, "bully" to certain behaviors, why not change the conversation entirely?

Barrier #3: The loaded nature of the word "bullying"

Labels matter. "Bully" or "bullying" is a negatively charged word. No student wants to be called a bully; no parent will claim that his or her child is a bully, and no school happily admits that there is any bullying taking place in that school. This reality stems not from the fact that certain *behaviors* have been experienced but rather because of the connotation of the concept itself.[4] In addition, *No Child Left Behind* (*NCLB*) emotionally paralyzes schools. Aside from worrying about meeting "adequate yearly progress" (AYP), there is language in *NCLB* that is equally bothersome: schools can be labeled "persistently dangerous" (PDS) and there is a common perception that if the school has any "bullying" that they could be so labeled not necessarily legally but by the communities in which they reside.

In practice, there is a wide gulf between the legal and policy definitions that school lawyers have given to the terms "bullying" and PDS and how families would hope these would be defined. Schools are overly cautious and tend to create vague and difficult to satisfy definitions. For example, in Connecticut, to be labeled "persistently dangerous," a school would need to "meet the conditions in *two of the following three categories of offenses, in each of three consecutive years,* (1) Two or more gun-free schools violations (possession of a firearm or explosive device that resulted in expulsion from school); or (2) One 'Other Weapon' incident resulting in expulsion per 200 students with a minimum of three such incidents; or (3) One violent criminal offense resulting in expulsion per 200 students with a minimum of three such incidents" (Sergi, 2003). Families, on the other hand, want definitions to provide clarity and embrace the goal of achieving truly physically, emotionally and intellectually safe schools.

Another way to say this is that in ordinary language, one might well assume that a PDS is one in which bullying is rampant. Each individual state determines its own legal definition of "persistently dangerous." As with the Connecticut example, the definitional bar is typically set so high that it would be almost impossible for a school to be put on such a list. These definitions focus exclusively on *physical* safety. Bullying may or may not be physical and in any case, bullying is not part of states' definitions of PDS. However in practice, there is widespread reluctance on the part of schools to label inappropriate behaviors as being bullying, in part because they worry that such a link between bullying and being a PDS will be made. Further, if a school were to claim that bullying was a common occurrence, public perception would likely be that, legal definitions aside, the school *is* persistently dangerous and thus unsafe.

What is actually happening in the school may or may not reflect what a reasonable person would consider to be bullying or a PDS. The bottom line is that schools, and individuals, are much more comfortable describing inappropriate behaviors *without* assigning a label. Neutral description is palatable; emotionally coloring a behavior with a label that has a negative connotation is not.

On the other hand, schools actively seek to be labeled "Blue Ribbon Schools." The designation is enough to provide the "Good Housekeeping Seal of Approval" into perpetuity, regardless of when the award was given and how many administrative, demographic, or school climate changes have occurred since. Being a "Blue Ribbon School" is another loaded term, albeit one with a positive connotation. Receiving the label of being a PDS or a school that has any bullying is the opposite.

Barrier #4: (The highest hurdle of all) Responsibility and blame

Those who chronically treat others inappropriately generally come by these practices honestly. In other words, as they have moved through their lives from the time they were young and as they have grown, they have observed others—their role models and mentors—interact with others. Everyone learns how to treat others not only by how they were treated but also as keen observers of interactions between and among others. When these individuals come into schools, their behavior patterns come with them. The path of least resistance in dealing with them is to admonish and punish with some form of blind assumption that this will change their habits. It does not take a "rocket scientist" to learn that nothing changes (until something does change). Blame for this inappropriate behavior is placed on the shoulders of perpetrators (He/she did it and must pay!). Faculty and staff in schools are implicitly saying, "this is not *my/our* problem!" In reality, it is our problem, and the solutions rest not on the shoulders of the offending student (or for that matter the targeted student who "just needs to self-advocate").

Return for a minute to the elements that the rampage school shooters all have in common. To date, some states in the country have been spared experiencing a school shooting, although there is no state that has been spared experiencing student suicides caused in part by youth who fit the profile but took their own lives rather than those of others. Girls are more likely to do so, which is why the "shooters" are almost universally boys. And, more and more we are experiencing firearms, among other weapons, being brought into our schools by younger and younger students "for protection." We may not be able to change their accessibility to firearms or the fact that their personal circumstances and family situations are lacking, but we *can* impact the other three areas. And yet, traditionally, *this is where the blame is placed which absolves adults in school of any responsibility*. Even the authors of the books published around and after the tenth anniversary of Columbine who argue that the "shooters'" mental health diagnoses are true "causes" of the rampage shootings reluctantly admit that "[t]hey lacked resilience, supportive relationships, and other assets that might compensate for their deficits" (Langman, 2009, p. 100). The fact that they experienced appalling treatment by their peers, that adults in school were not there for them and that the perimeters of acceptance within the school culture were narrow is not only useful information but also a loud and very important wake-up call which is as clear a mandate as can be given for what must be changed in schools where it is easy to fall through the cracks and be virtually invisible even though the warning signs were all too obvious. We've seen these "red flags" every time another school shooting happens when we look back and analyze "what went wrong."

It is important to realize that these big events did not start there. The seeds had been planted for all of these young people many years before they ended and ruined so many lives. We all need to manage and stop the little things that hurt while we can. Seemingly innocent instances of "meanness" escalate. We can and *must* debunk the myth that "sticks and stones can break my bones, but names will never hurt me." The scars from emotional pain last far longer than childhood cuts and bruises. Physically and emotionally scarred brains present identically. It matters. We must become better listeners and observers of the things children say and do, and what is left unsaid. And finally, it must become acceptable to be different, however that looks, feels, and sounds. None of this is easy, but it is doable, and more importantly, if we do not give it our best, rest assured that school shootings and student suicides will continue to happen and ruin more lives needlessly.

Resisting Bullying No More: Putting the Puzzle Pieces Together

Whether for research or legislative purpose, defining bullying contains an implicit goal: creating safe, respectful and "bully-free" schools. In the decade since Columbine, defining the term has evolved from simplistic and vague descriptions to increasingly complex and confining ones. What is happening in schools with respect to realizing the goal is likely the reason for such definitional changes. Legislating what bullying *is* has not yielded the hoped-for result. What now? Another way to state this problem would be to ask not how the *letter* of the law can be satisfied, but what must be done to honor the *spirit* of the law?

No amount of definitional refining will ever change the *connotation* of the term. "Bullying" will always be so negatively charged that even with increasingly careful and targeted stipulations, it is virtually impossible to get past how the word "plays" in practice. If we can exchange the term for one less offensive ("mean" or "peer cruelty") there is a better chance of bringing relevant groups together in an effort to ameliorate the phenomenon. Consider the following. Ask any parent/guardian if they are purposely raising a bully and no one will answer "yes." Ask any child if he or she is a bully and the result is the same. However, if you survey the same group of adults and inquire if their children are ever "mean" to anyone else (call someone a name, make fun of someone, laugh at another person or tell someone they can't sit with or play with someone), honest affirmative admissions are common. The very same child who says they don't "bully" will admit that the very same behavior was "mean" and "not nice." *Everyone* is mean from time to time. For some reason, owning up to being "mean" is perceived to be more descriptive and neutral and far less threatening than describing the very same person or act as being "bullying." "Bullying" carries heavy negative emotional baggage; "mean" does not. A crucial additional benefit from eliminating the words "bully" and "bullying" in school settings is that when adults are charged with intervening during inappropriate student interactions, it is patently clear (especially compared with "bullying") what "mean" looks like, feels like and sounds like. If adults should take responsibility, and they *must*, it is far easier to stop the "mean," or "cruel." Adults would be far more likely to provide a consistent and viable front against bullying if they abandoned this unsavory label in practice.

Aside from the issue of the loaded nature of the words, "bully" or "bullying," there are a number of other reasons why abandoning these words in deference to others makes sense. First, "bullying" is an inflammatory label, and that label does not provide a clear picture of the behavior(s) in question. It is highly likely to tell a child to, "Stop bullying!" and for that child to respond by saying, "What did I do?" The conversation might continue with, "You called him a name." And, the child would just as likely answer, "That wasn't bullying!" However, if the conversation began with, "Stop being mean," there would much more likely be immediate understanding. Second, using "mean" avoids the problem of waiting to deal with behaviors until they are "repeated over time." One of the leading reasons why "bullying" is not consistently subject to meaningful intervention is that adults do not know what bullying looks, feels and sounds like. Adults do, however, know what *mean* looks, feels and sounds like. Adults *do* care about the safety and well-being of children in school and they want to work toward this end. They want to intervene when children are inappropriately treated, but they do not recognize that if they used *mean* as the measure rather than bullying, the goal would be much easier to achieve.

All of the empirical research validates the view that catching the lower level antecedents to bullying and stopping those mean incidents when they are initially experienced, results in arresting the potential pattern of escalating cruelty (Wessler, with Prebble, 2003). Thus, dealing with "mean" in practice is much more helpful in reaching the implicit goal of creating safe and respectful schools.

Words matter and in the case of the terms "bully" and "bullying," this is particularly true. Educators would do themselves a great service if in *practice* these words were treated as are other offensive and inappropriate language, such as "swear" words. Think of them as just another couple of "four letter words" that have no place in school. It is actually quite simple. There is little, if anything to be lost by doing so and a great deal to gain: satisfying the spirit of legislating against bullying to create physically, emotionally and intellectually safe and respectful schools.

Conclusion: Resistance and Responsibility

Resisting bullying requires an assumption and acceptance of responsibility of a systemic sort at the district and school levels. No one person or constituency is singularly responsible, but everyone collectively must share the burden of resistance. The path of least resistance, so to speak, is *not* an option. Educators must resist the urge to deny that mean-spirited ("bullying") behaviors exist in their schools and instead, tackle the problem head on and begin by changing the conversation away from "bullying" toward mean or cruel and welcome and invite open and frequent communication from families. Educators must also recognize that mean-spirited actions happening *outside* the school in community settings directly impact the learning and socializing *inside* the school, and especially what is known as "cyber-cruelty." As long as educators resist embracing this growing arena that has potentially tragic consequences, the longer "bullying" in brick and mortar settings as well as in cyber-space will continue. Educators must embrace rather than resist gaining an understanding about the multi-dimensionality of how individuals are capable of hurting others. In doing so, they must reach out and communicate, inform, teach, and work collaboratively with parents/guardians. Once *real* parent/guardian involvement in the "bullying" arena is achieved, that is when children will benefit on so many levels.

Parents/guardians of those who hurt others physically or emotionally must resist the attitude that their own child does not have the capacity to be mean ("bully") and instead work collaboratively with the school to improve their child's treatment of others and communicate openly and respectfully. Parents/guardians of those who would be targets of mean-spirited ("bullying") behavior must resist the desire to demand that their injured children are better off once the label of "bullying" has been attached to their child's circumstances and instead work as partners with the school to create concrete and realistic safety plans for their targeted children. Without embracing such collaborative communication and problem-solving strategies, schools and the children who inhabit them risk perpetrating the circumstances that have yielded so many anti-bullying laws and little if any progress toward actually eliminating "bullying" in practice.

The rewards of reframing the "bullying" territory by looking down the lens of creating safe school climates are large and incontrovertible. On both practical and moral grounds, children—all children, not just some children—will have the opportunity and ability to soar academically and socially and experience overall success. Resistance itself, both theoretically and practically, presents something of an oxymoron in the context of efforts to eliminate bullying. What is actually being resisted? Are schools and communities resisting the acknowledgment that bullying actually exists? Or, rather, are we talking about resistance to understanding the context and the toxicity of "bullying"? Or, finally, are we concerned with resistance to efforts designed to enable schools to focus on creating safe climates and thus truly eliminate of all forms of violence, no matter the severity? I hope that we are trying to address all of these possible senses of resistance.

Parents and guardians send their best children to school every day, and each and every adult school community member has an obligation to make each and every one of these children physically, emotionally, and intellectually safe. At the heart of the historical "resistance" of bullying is the pointing of fingers of blame every other place than inward at the school. Parents and guardians are to blame, the media and technology are to blame, communities are to blame, the wider culture is to blame, a weapons-rich country is to blame, an individual student's mental health issues are to blame, and on and on. There is definitely plenty of blame to go around…educators must resist the urge to assume all of the causes of bullying are out of their control and make schools safer for children by targeted focus on the school climate: how people treat one another. Doing so will not only diminish and potentially eliminate bullying, but importantly the life outcomes for children will improve exponentially.

Notes

1. Coinciding with the tenth anniversary of the Columbine rampage school shooting, a number of books have been published focusing primarily on the personal psychologies of school shooters. Three works are noteworthy in this regard: Ceremonial violence (Fast, 2008), *Why Kids Kill:*

Inside the Minds of School Shooters (Langman, 2009), and *Columbine* (Cullen, 2009). The authors collectively come to the conclusion that of those "shooters" studied (the majority of rampage school shooters are not discussed), all have extremely pathological conditions, which fall into three categories: psychopathic, psychotic, and traumatized, and that these personal conditions were the primary causal factor of the rampage shooting.

2. All three authors writing about the psychology of school shooters cite Katherine Newman's 2004 seminal work *Rampage: The Social Roots of School Shootings*, and essentially argue that "[H]ad they been safely maintained through their crises, there is no reason to assume they would have become murderers" (Langman, 2009, p. 154). The thrust of these works, and others, seems to be to place blame on the personal psychologies of the shooters themselves for these tragedies, despite a wealth of information that is more tempered. A question of great practical import ought to be raised. What role does the school, and do school community members play, in either fueling or diminishing the occurrence of rampage school shootings? If "shooters" are psychologically predisposed to commit tragic acts of violence and are on a trajectory that is unstoppable, then schools can really do nothing to mitigate disaster. If, however, as Newman's more balanced analysis suggests, the personal circumstances of a would-be shooter are just one piece of the puzzle, then schools *can* and *should* be taking their share of responsibility. There seems to be an almost primal need to place blame on someone or something after a rampage school shooting and the tenth anniversary of Columbine was a dark reminder. As one telling example, despite definitive evidence to the contrary, 83% of the public places blame for Columbine squarely on the shooters and their parents. (Cullen, 2009, p. 340). Focusing on access to guns, perceived flawed parenting and serious mental illness deflects blame away from the school and its social culture. From a school perspective it is understandable why this might seem desirable. However, the "blame game" must take a backstage to serious practical efforts to understand that "[S]tudents need to feel safe [physically and emotionally] in school. Although bullying itself does not cause school shootings, anything that contributes to students' misery, fear and rage can play a part in driving them to violence" (Cullen, 2009, p. 192). At Columbine, for example, "Kids would either assimilate quickly or spend four years struggling to fit in" (Cullen, 2009, p. 273).

3. The harm caused and now recognized by bullies in the post-Columbine era is often less visible to the naked eye and takes the form of insidious injuries of an emotional variety. Thus, "treatment" is an interesting notion. As of Spring 2009, the American Pediatric Association has called for their members to take a more active role in this school-based "disease" primarily through careful and targeted screening as well as direct communicating with educators within their patients' schools (Sklaire and McInerny, 1990).

4. Throughout Langman's (2009) *Why Kids Kill*, the words and phrases such as, "teasing," "harassment," "picked on," and "bullying" are used repeatedly. Whenever "teasing," "harassment," or "picked on" are used, even if there is clear admission that it was repeated and mean-spirited, this is not considered "bullying," and is part of growing up, and therefore above reproach. When "bullying" is used this is not the case. Examples include: "At school, Cho (Seung Hui) was made fun of as a foreigner who could not speak English. His older sister was also teased, but she was able to take it in stride" (Langman, 2009, p. 93); "There are multiple reports that Jeffrey (Weise) was teased or harassed by some of his peers, as well as multiple reports that he was not picked on. The evidence is so mixed that it is impossible to know for sure what really happened to him at school." This is also an excellent example of what happens in many schools with respect to investigations. The conclusion of the multiple and conflicting "reports" often leads away from a label of "bullying" (Langman, 2009, p. 121); "Although Dylan (Klebold) was teased at times, his envy

or normal kids appears to have been more devastating" (Langman, 2009, p. 149); "What about Jonathan's (last name not known) level of social acceptance? Was he picked on or marginalized? Jonathan's sense of insecurity and low self-esteem was not a result of harassment by bullies but of his own troubled identity" (Langman, 2009, p. 157); "He complained he was severely picked on at school, but his reports were vague and the school contradicted his stories. Kyle (last name not known) said that he had been harassed for seven years…he claimed he was picked on wherever he went…Kyle was odd….His strangeness could easily lead peers to avoid him or to tease him….He was so disturbed by the alleged harassment that for a period he was home-schooled to avoid his peers….The school continued to maintain that there was no *significant* (my emphasis) mistreatment" (Langman, 2009, pp. 161–162); "There were mixed reports about harassment. Michael (Carneal) felt like a victim. He reported being harassed about his clothing and glasses, being threatened, and even being spit on. Perhaps the most devastating event was when a gossip column in the student newspaper implied that Michael was gay. As a result, he was called 'gay' and 'faggot' at school" (Langman, 2009, p. 75). Finally, a very interesting passage suggests that whatever mistreatment Dylan Klebold experienced, it wasn't "bullying." "In the videos the two boys made, Dylan complained about the 'stuck-up' kids who hated him, going all the way back to feeling mistreated since daycare….He complained about being picked on by his older brother and the brother's friends. He also said he was put down by his entire extended family, excluding his parents…nowhere does Dylan single out jocks or bullies" (Langman, 2009, p. 66).

REFERENCES

The American heritage dictionary. (1982). (2nd college edition). Boston: Houghton Mifflin.
Becker, C. (1955). What are historical facts? *Western Political Quarterly, 7:* 327–340.
Connecticut General Statutes. (2006). Hartford, CT: State of Connecticut.
Cullen, D. (2009). *Columbine.* New York: Twelve.
Fast, J. (2008). *Ceremonial violence: A psychological explanation of school shootings.* New York: Overlook Press.
Freiberg, J. (1998). Measuring school climate: Let me count the ways. *Educational Leadership, 56:* 22–26.
Langman, P. (2009). *Why kids kill: Inside the minds of school shooters.* New York: Palgrave Macmillan.
Nansel, T. (2001). Bullying behaviors among U.S. youth. *Journal of the American Medical Association, 285:* 2094–2100.
Newman, K. (2004). *Rampage: The social roots of school shootings.* New York: Basic Books.
Olweus, D. (1978). *Aggression in the schools: Bullies and whipping boys.* Washington, DC: Halsted Press.
Olweus, D. (1993). *Bullying at school.* Cambridge, MA: Blackwell.
Olweus, D. (1994). Annotation: Bullying at school: Basic facts and effects of a school based intervention program. *Journal of Child Psychology and Psychiatry, 35:* 1171–1190.
Safe School Climate Act. (2006). Safe School Climate Act, South Carolina Stat. Ann., 59 § 63-2.
Scheffler, I. (1960). *The language of education.* Springfield, IL: Charles C Thomas.
School Bullying Prevention Act. (2007). School Bullying Prevention Act, 76 Del. Laws 14 § 4123a.
Sergi, T. (2003, August 27). The unsafe school choice option of the No Child Left Behind Act of 2001. (Circular Letter C-12). Hartford, CT: Connecticut State Department of Education.
Sklaire, M., & McInerny, T. (1990). The role of the pediatrician in school health. *Pediatrics in Review, 12:* 69–70.

Vossekuil, B., Fein, R., Reddy, M., Borum, R., & Modzeleski, W. (2002). *The final report and findings of the Safe Schools Initiative: Implications for the prevention of school attacks in the United States.* Washington, DC: United States Secret Service and United States Department of Education.

Wessler, S., with contributing author W. Prebble. (2003). *The respectful school: How educators and students can conquer hate and harassment.* Alexandria, VA: Association for Supervision and Curriculum Development.

Whitehead, A. N. (1979). *Process and reality.* New York: Free Press.

CHAPTER ELEVEN

"We Want To Be Heard"

Using Instructional Technology to Resist Student Silence

KATHLEEN P. KING

GRAMMAR CRUSHER TRANSFORMED

Ms. Remarko was a well-respected English teacher in her middle school. She had been in Phoenix Middle for 10 years, and her students consistently scored highly in the school-wide grammar competitions and tests. However, very few of her students had any enthusiasm for writing. In fact, when it came time to lessons which included writing, journals, essays, and short stories there were continual moans, groans, and absences in Ms. Remarko's classroom. The students' resistance and apathy plainly stymied her.

For the holidays, Ms. Remarko received a portable digital video player. She liked technology well enough for personal use and her newly resumed graduate courses, so she hooked the video player up to her computer and downloaded some of her photos and music. That worked just fine, so she began looking for online material she could include. She had heard from a friend that she listened to conference sessions and radio shows on their players, so she did an Internet search.

Fast forward to just three busy weeks later and you see Ms. Remarko and her class using her old digital camera in class to have students video record their pre-written and approved book reports. They were so excited because they had created a class blog site, and Ms. Remarko had figured out how take their very own video reports and put them on their blog! Their teacher, who had been solely absorbed with grammar, now used technology to let them tell their research reports for their video series, "As The Page Turns: Phoenix Rising Stars," instead of having to write out a research book report. But their work sure had to be good, because their whole class would hear their report! In fact, their family would too, including Grandma in California, because of the blog!

What happened? How could this be? From traditional, dry reports and lectures to discussions and creating blogs and videos, from book reports to book trailers, from book reviews to podcasts about books. Their class was exciting now; there was always something new happening. In fact, they would sit in other classes and during lunch, thinking about the class and race down the hall to get there. Questions and energy consumed the students: what were they doing next? What did people have to say about the books and topics? They needed to get all the information so their reports could be top-notch.

Undoubtedly though, the biggest question was what had caused the transformation of Ms. Remarko "Grammar Crusher"? Would they ever know? That would make a great video episode!

INTRODUCTION

In a world of educational traditions, instructional technology continues to be a fount of innovative instructional strategies, teaching perspectives, and teacher-student dialogue. By using technology to cultivate voice among learners of all ages, educators introduce experiences, perspectives, skills for independent lifelong learning, and participation (Jonassen et al., 2008; hooks, 1994; King, 2002; King and Gura, 2007).

Much like Ms. Remarko's class in our opening scenario, traditional classrooms in the United States have been teacher centered (Joseph and Burnaford, 2001). Yet, new media, such as podcasting, blogging, wikis, video podcasts, and social networks, provide a vastly different opportunity to enable learners to take center stage (King and Gura, 2007, 2009). Similar to the meaning and purpose of new media, integrating technology in instruction in problem-based learning or dialogue may facilitate learners' transformation from "knowledge consumers" to "knowledge creators." For example, using blogs and wikis in meaningful ways provides multitudes of opportunities to cultivate critical thinkers, researchers, and literary giants as they engage as *immediate* participants in global dialogue (Jonassen et al., 2008; King and Gura, 2007, 2009).

This chapter provides a "resistance perspective" of innovative technologies, specifically new media technology, applied to teaching perspectives and practice. Not only does the chapter describe and demystify new media technology, but it also illustrates practical classroom examples, application, outcomes, and changes. Written with a strong philosophical and practical perspective of radical pedagogy, social change, instructional methods, and personal transformation it synthesizes topics that are infrequently articulated in teacher education literature (Freire, 1976; Giroux, 1988; hooks, 1994; Jonassen et al., 2008). Growing from the teacher and classroom experience and building on learning experiences which engage students as vital voices in a connected world, the chapter will provide a fresh perspective, inspiration, and application for philosophers, theorists, educators, researchers, and practitioners (Berge and Collins, 1998; King and Gura, 2007). Digital natives are primed to express their voices and opinions; therefore, educators need to innovatively and pedagogically capture this potential to build vital participation and voice across content areas through freely accessible technologies.

THEORETICAL PERSPECTIVES

Constructivism

Constructivism is the perspective at the very basis of many approaches to teaching and learning in ways that are relevant, authentic, and situated in context (Argyris and Schon, 1974; Lave and Wenger, 1991). This theory and philosophy builds upon the traditions of Dewey's pragmatism (1938) and Kolb's experientialism (1984). Rather than transmitting knowledge and being solely invested in didactic teaching, constructivism has a learner-centered orientation of discovery, experience, and problem solving (Von Glaserfeld, 1991). The basic premise is that learners who experience, discover, and construct knowledge will have a better understanding, longer retention, and greater abilities to interpret, apply, and generalize (Jonassen, 1981; Jonassen et al., 2008).

Numerous familiar, and effective instructional approaches have grown from this perspective over recent years alone including problem based learning (Jonassen, 1997; NCTEM, 2008), project based learning (Wilhelm, Sherrod, and Walters, 2008) ,and inquiry based learning (Llewellyn, 2001), to name a few. As a body of practices, they reveal the power of learner-centered instruction in developing knowledge, skills, and agency (Jonassen et al., 2008; NCTEM, 2008).

21st century learning skills

In the 21st century, technology and problem solving permeate our lives. From requesting books at the local library, to researching information, taking online courses, and purchasing gifts online technology is ubiquitously embedded (eSchool News, 2008; Lessig, 2001; Rich, 2008). Therefore, in order to be successful in their educational pursuits, daily lives, and the workplace, people of all ages need to be information literate, critical thinkers, and problem solvers.

It is not enough to need information, 21st century people must find it. Indeed, we cannot solely retrieve information; we must assess and analyze it. Furthermore, understanding the explicit and implicit meanings and purposes is insufficient without valid and substantiated interpretation and application. These needs briefly describe the abilities now termed "21st century learning skills" (Partnership for 21st Century Skills, 2004). These relevant and empowering skills include critical thinking, problem solving, creativity, flexibility, coping strategies, collaboration, self-direction, multiple literacies (language, information technology, information, visual, cultural, and more), and research strategies (Backborby, Wagner, Camero, Davies, Levine, Newman, Marder and Sumi, 2005; Partnership for 21st Century Skills, 2004).

Information literacy skills

In considering the roots of resistance through new media technology, we also need to identify clearly "information literacy skills." In fact, information literacy is a more specific level of expertise than the above described 21st century skills. Today, people must deftly determine what information or resources they need to find, evaluate, analyze, and interpret. In addition, they must apply the content and understand the issues, which surround the use of information (ALA, 2000). Furthermore, they need to understand and be adept with research and logic, visual literacy, technology literacy, copyright laws, and more (King and Sanquist, 2009). Such a broad spectrum of skills is well beyond the scope of 21st century skills or technical know-how. Instead, they incorporate more interdisciplinary connections such as understanding of issues, ethics, and responsibilities related to technology and information use in a digital age and global society (Backborby et al., 2005; Giroux, 1988; Gordon, 2003).

Learner-centered

Three joint cornerstone concepts of radical pedagogy are the safety, respect, and co-learning which are essential for genuinely learner-centered classrooms. To create an inviting and learner-friendly environment, teachers have to unlearn much of what they know. While by default, we may "teach like we were taught," reflective practitioners engage in observing students, seeking to understand learning styles, understanding learning obstacles, and both academic and personal strengths of students (hooks, 1994; Schön, 1987; Shor, 1992). Such a focus decidedly orients toward learner centeredness, and one realizes quickly that this environment can afford many best practice instructional approaches. Learner-centered classrooms powerfully support, even unleash differentiated instruction, collaborative learning, problem based learning, the development of sociocultural understandings, and meaning making (Project 2061, 1993; Vygotsky, 1978).

The fundamental definition of a learner-centered classroom is that the learner, not the teacher is the focus of choices made (Jonassen et al., 2008). For example, one may observe that instead of an emphasis on teacher preferences for teaching, learners' needs are heavily weighted; instead of teacher only monologues, student discussion is promoted; and rather than the focal point always being the teacher, small group activities are frequently selected. Learner-centered classrooms are student-focused, active, busy, and dynamic. They afford opportunities for educators to be responsive to learning needs and cultivate inquiry (Project 2061, 1993). One can see this is a prime environment to enable students to explore their ideas, consider their choices, and make decisions. Returning to the point of our chapter and book, all of these characteristics are vital ingredients for empowerment, voice, and resistance.

Engagement

At the same time that the literature acclaims the characteristics and varied benefits of learner-centered classrooms, it also clearly documents that *engaging* learners is a powerful means to improve outcomes. Specifically, assignments which engage students foster greater involvement and participation (Backborby et al., 2005; Dewey, 1938; Gordon, 2003). As they appropriate more of their whole person, so to speak, students begin to use their full intellectual and emotional capacities to learn (Backborby et al., 2005).

So very often formal learning lacks this holistic engagement and learners appear to dissociate from the experience. Blank stares, heads on desks, doodling, and daydreaming: these are all signs of students not fully invested in the lessons at hand. Compare these images to the one of students huddled around a computer, researching, choosing, and arranging quotes, text, content, graphics, and images they want to include in their academic weekly blog. It can be the same content, but different delivery, and decidedly different impact.

Philosophical Bearings

Constructivism

Not only is constructivism a strategy of teaching and learning practice, it is also has deep roots in the philosophical development of the educational field. In order to appreciate fully the basis for developing projects and experiences where students construct knowledge, one may return to the work of Dewey (1938), and Kolb (1984). Here we see an emphasis on doing as well as learning, personal experience as the basis for knowledge, and concrete experiences scaffolded into abstract understandings. From the known to the unknown, through the windows of their eyes, ears, and hands, learners can discover anew, and personally, critical principles of Math, Earth Sciences, Life Sciences, Language Arts, Music, Art, etc.

Experiencing learning as *exploration* provides learner agency, ownership, and persistent understanding (Gordon, 2003). Engaging students in constructivist learning cultivates not only deeper understanding but also additional interdisciplinary observations, alternate perspectives, critical thinking, and community (Gordon, 2003; iEARN.org, 2008). Furthermore, Vygotsky (1978) describes significant learning and meaning making as taking place in a social context and coupling that with constructivist learning, provides powerful dialogue opportunities that can afford new insights about values, beliefs, and perspectives.

Such dynamic experiences are the foundation for radical change: being able to examine information and situations, posing questions, searching for answers, analyzing information and resources, and evaluating unexamined beliefs and values. Learners engaged in constructivistic learning experiences have the foundation for critically examining themselves and their world, therefore being able to recognize issues, instances, and systems of oppression (Freire, 1976; Giroux, 1988; hooks, 1994; Shor, 1992). New media may fuel not only discovering and analyzing such understanding but also making meaning through dialogue (audio, video, presentations, etc), discovering new personas, and disseminating alternative findings and views.

Radical pedagogy

We have seen that constructivism provides a foundation for learner-centered, project based engagement. There are many opportunities for a perspective of radical pedagogy in which the goal of education is seen to be social change (hooks, 1994) to be powerfully experienced in new media technology instructional use. In addition, radical pedagogy provides a solid platform for critical thinking, critical inquiry and contextualized, or situated learning (Argyris and Schon, 1974; Freire, 1976; hooks, 1994). Indeed, this philosophical perspective can be a most informative framework for providing learners the ability to gather information, articulate needs, make decisions, and transfer learning, all of which are essential for 21st century learning (King and Sanquist, 2009; Partnership for 21st Century Learning, 2008).

Furthermore, there are many examples in the literature of how such critical perspectives combine to create learning experiences. In fact, these learning experiences often exemplify qualities of engagement during delivery and outcomes of social action, empowerment, and voice (Freire, 1976; Giroux, 1988; hooks, 1994; King, 2008a, 2008b; King and Sanquist, 2009; Partnership for 21st Century Learning, 2008). A perspective of radical pedagogy is about critical perspectives, power, oppression, social responsibility, and action. Due to its grassroots origins and continued use, new media technologies have been used effectively to introduce and promote not only these understandings but also the work (King and Gura, 2007, 2009; King and Sanquist, 2008; Walch and Lafferty, 2006).

Personal transformation

Not least of all is an essential element that I experienced in my teacher professional development experience and research early on. That is, when teachers realize empowerment they want to share the experience (King, 2002, 2005).

How often do we hear the call for develop learner-centered classrooms, integrate more technology, and cultivate critical thinking skills in our schools (Jonassen et al., 2008)? And yet, we are still teaching in traditional formats. Research has shown that the most effective way to help teachers learn about and adopt these radical changes in practice is just like the need for students to appropriate and construct knowledge-experiential learning and constructivism.

In fact, the model of the Journey of Transformation (King, 2002) does not even explicitly discuss critical thinking and learner-centeredness. Instead, it focuses on teachers' needs, their teaching context, and their professional development goals. When faculty developers invest time in teaching learning, their professional growth and their cultivation, they invest in the depth, roots, and perspectives of those who envision and shape student learning experiences (King, 2008a). Rather than patching the outward appearance, this approach addresses teacher concerns, needs, and perspectives. In addition, it blends autonomous freedom with facilitation skills, additional resources, demonstration, modeling, project based learning, lesson development, and abundant dialog and reflection (King, 2008a; King, 2002, 2008a; Schön, 1987).

Rather like the slogan "truth in advertising," we engage educators in the context, and *experience*, rather than just speaking about it. The results have never disappointed. In fact, as this chapter explains a recent teacher education short course that did just this; it reveals how such changes in perspective result in change in practice, choice, empowerment, voice, and radical change (King, 2008a, 2008b; Schön, 1987; Shor, 1992).

Just as we desire students to develop confidence, voice, and 21st century skills as they grow through our schools, so do these educators. They want to be heard, they want to be *creative*. Furthermore, they are ready to *create content* of their own (King, 2008b; King and Gura, 2009; Richardson, 2006; Williams, 2008). Our goal is to open the door of opportunity wider through new media learning experiences.

WE WANT TO BE HEARD!

Technology to facilitate empowerment and voice

Blogs, wikis, podcasts, and video podcasts: as new media have progressively grown in popularity since 2001, the general public has become increasingly enamored with the power and ease of globally distributing their opinions and perspectives (Prensky, 2001). No longer just content consumers, they expect to be content *creators*!

While some people have been late coming to the realization, others quickly embraced the opportunity to make their voices heard by every means possible. The next sections of this chapter illustrate how these inexpensive and convenient new media are being used in educational and public settings to test, discover, and celebrate voice. No longer are minority opinions regulated to the margins of society. Today anyone can take center stage and invite a global audience to watch or participate.

Blogs—global audience

One of the easiest ways for educators and students to develop a web presence is to create a blog. A blog may serve as a dynamic, easily updated webpage or a collaborative forum. Basically, a blog can be instantly developed with a choice of template. Then users, bloggers, add their information by filling in the fields, or blocks, on the screen.

With so many free blog sites available, the choices are many. Blogspot.com, owned by Google, wordpress.com, gaggle.net, 21classes.com, classpress.com, and livejournal.com are just a few of the many sites, which are available for use. Some of these sites offer different features including password protection, no advertisements, and privacy. Therefore, educators should verify the features of the blog platform they are considering using and make choices based on their instructional needs and organizational requirements [Electronic Frontier Foundation (EFF), 2006].

As a few general introductory examples, educators can use blogs to create a home page for the class, or a specialized site for a topic or lesson. In addition to the plug-n-play ease of blogs is the capability to instantly archive and categorize entries. These web 2.0 features make the blog searchable for any word, entry, category, and timeframe with no additional effort or coding by the blogger (King and Gura, 2007, 2009; Richardson, 2006).

Blogging platforms enable educators to focus on learners' needs, content, and creativity rather than the technology. In working with classroom instructors, they create their first blog framework in 30 to 60 seconds. Then they begin to plan the focus, content, and scope they want to develop.

For example, we see educators and students get very excited about creating blogs, which express their cultural heritage, communities, favorite books, countries' views related to government studies, politics, current issues, or technology. They typically master the ability to post content to the blog within about three minutes—even without formal instruction.

Podcasts—resistance rules

Illustrative of the radical/revolution emphasis of podcasting is the slogan which has accompanied the movement since its dawning in 2004, "Democratization of the Media" (Walch and Lafferty, 2006). This phrase trumpets one does not need wealth, influence, or prestige to be broadcasted and syndicated through the podcast directories. In fact, one of the hallmark directories is Libsyn.com, whose name stands for *Liberated Syndication*. Again, the freedom and power of voice have been the impetus for this media.

One example of this experience within education is a teacher education classroom (King, 2008a), where students explored, embraced, and articulated their perspectives and voice on key issues in education. Rather than a Foundations of American Education course rehashing history and philosophy, this format enabled the students to research, analyze and form arguments to support their opinions on current manifestations of historical trends and philosophical perspectives (King and Gura, 2009). In collaboration with the instructor, they chose such critical topics as political, policy, and educational issues through individual, peer, and collaborative learning.

The class was developed around the concerted effort to collaboratively create online resources on these topics. Therefore, the students knew as they researched their topics and wrote their papers or presentations, they would have a global audience. In this way, they collaborated on creating a class blog which was publicly accessible and would continue to be a valuable resource for other teachers and students. Not only did the class post their critical essays to the class blog, but they also engaged in extensive private discussion board dialogue on selected topics related to class experiences and course content. They also used the private discussion board as a space to conduct class discussion building upon their research papers, which they posted there.

The professor incorporated the different new media features in an organic and participatory format. That is, at the first session she introduced the possible projects and explained them. However, she worked with the students to build a community, which had clear respect and validation of varied opinions and perspectives. This transparent and accepting classroom climate proved to be a strong base for the risk-taking the students undertook in using the new media and in their engagement in the critical questioning nature of the course.

Not only were the students surprised by the several technology components of the course but also by the abundant dialogue, flexibility, and learner-centeredness. However, the results were surprisingly substantial.

While students attended 14 classes of 2 hours each, they also

- ~ Posted 249 posts in the discussion board
- ~ Wrote a draft and final philosophy of education paper
- ~ Posted three critical essays to the class blog or three blogs plus a podcast
- ~ Created and posted to the blog a multimedia presentation on a significant educational philosopher
- ~ Created and took two exams

In final reflections about their experiences, students described the impact of the course on their professional development and many referred to the empowerment and technology components of the class. Student observations included

- ~ Amazement at self-efficacy and personal accomplishments
- ~ New visions of learner-centered classrooms
- ~ Commitment to using new media with their students
- ~ Realization of empowerment and voice
- ~ Appreciation of many benefits of learning communities in classrooms

This example was a traditional classroom transformed into a participatory learning community. It was in large part due to the vision of the teacher but also through the power and ease of new media. Students who had never experienced this model of learner-centered instruction were able to grasp it and thrive in it. In addition, those who had not used the technologies became adept and ultimately proponents of technology use in education based on their experience. Experiential learning provides the possibility to "break the mold" firsthand.

The LGBTQ community is an even more vibrant example of the liberating power of the revolutionary podcasting media in a study conducted by King and Sanquist (King, 2008b). This study traces the evolution of an underrepresented and often times oppressed community and their use of podcasting to gain voice and control globally. Indeed, the LGBTQ community seemed to dominant this media in its early years.

Many LGBTQ individuals were among the first wave of podcasters, and some of those most popular shows are still in production in their original or different format and focus. Nevertheless, what is so significant is that over the 4 years of podcasting, the LGBTQ community has continued to be a significant representation in the public podcast directories.

An important distinction is drawn here—because LGBTQ issues are related to sexual identity, the popular podcast directory of iTunes.com will not list many of these shows. This denial of access and inclusion is an important issue because at least 75% of the public seems to draw their podcast choices and understanding from iTunes now (eMarketeer, 2007).

If one were to use iTunes.com as the only representation of the podcast world, little in the way of this alternative perspective is evident. However, in reality, there are over 100 other podcast directories available, and people are increasingly relying on web searches to find podcasts on specific topics. In these directories, one finds scores of LGBTQ podcasts.

As far as the content, focus, and progression of the LGBTQ podcasts, the insights are most telling. King and Sanquist (2008) found these podcasts were originally one person shows with focus on making their sexual identity journal, personal concerns, lifestyles, and interests more visible to the public. Many were unknown people, not celebrities or experts, who wanted their own podcast to talk about their personal life and opinions. In more ways than one, there is the impression that the LGBTQ community, one by one, was rushing up to center stage and grabbing the mike, because they *could*.

Certainly mainstream media is not a platform for the non-expert. Additionally, content and word choice are closely governed by the FCC for radio and television. Hence, the combination of free, public access, and no censorship brought many outspoken people to the forefront of the podcasting movement. How prolific was the production of these new series? So great was the demand that LGBTQ podcasters created and sustained specialized directories (such as Qpodder, http://qpodder.com/) in addition to listing their series in the general podcast directories (e.g., Libsyn.com, PodcastPickle.com, PodcastAlley.com, Odeo.com, etc).

However, over the next four years, while the LGBTQ community and others were enjoying the freedom and fame of having an instant global audience, some shifts in focus and formatting occurred. From King and Sanquist's research (2008) it appears that the LGTBQ podcasts began to be hosted by support groups who were trying to reach out to marginalized and needy constituencies. Indeed podcasting and all new media are powerful vehicles for reaching niche interests (Walch and Lafferty, 2006). However, in this case podcasting was used to address the needs of a niche *community* which was underrepresented in the media.

This development of podcasting as a distribution vehicle is most informative because these organizations and individuals discovered and pursued a course of action to deliver critical messages through a global, uncensored, public, and free media for the first time. A sense of responsibility to use the media for facilitating change and help the community emerged. From the podcasts which provide questions and answers for LGBTQ youth about identity development, to community groups with updates of activities (the Lesbian, Gay, Bisexual & Transgender Community Center, 2008), to LGBTQ support groups providing messages about overcoming drug addiction, suicide thoughts, alienation and prejudice, to those disseminating speeches from LGBTQ rallies and meetings (South Carolina Gay Lesbian Pride Movement, 2007), LGBTQ people captured podcasting and sought ways to broadcast and disseminate information to reach those who are alienated and disenfranchised.

On the user side of the scenario, podcasting listening offers the benefits of being free, private (you can listen in your own home), anonymous (you do not need to sign in or register anywhere to listen to episodes), vast choices [e.g., nearly 2 million podcast feeds available through one site (Feedburner, 2008)], convenient access (24 hours a day), and flexibility (listen at computer, a MP3player, or some cell phones). And the characteristics of geographical location, economic, race, and socioeconomic status would no longer be barriers for listeners in these cases. Many of the obstacles are overcome. Resistance to mainstream images and messages rules, as it were.

Wikis—Collaborative dynamo

Wikis are another vibrant example of new media technologies that have many powerful educational opportunities and are usually free, and easy to use. One of the best explanations of a wiki is that it is a web page that is easy to edit *together* (King and Gura, 2009; Richardson, 2006). Consider the following scenario for instance.

> Mr. Ruiz finds it very effective for language arts skill development when his students can collaborate in the entire writing process and have a platform integrated with a global audience. While he used to have them work in their groups on writing assignments together, he found it difficult for the actual writing, editing, and reviewing process to happen efficiently in this manner. Remember, only so many hands can work on a keyboard at once or write on a single page.
>
> What a difference the wiki has made with his students' participation, collaboration, and learning outcomes. The wiki he created for his class is set up much like a blog. He made it private in the sense that only he and the students can see and enter information in certain areas. The empowering capability of the wiki is seen in that all students can enter ideas and whole paragraphs of text and edit the content on their "page." And when they do so, an edit-

ing trail is left behind. Therefore, any of them can click a button and see either the current state of the product, or click again and a "review screen" which has a list of all the edits and who entered them, when.

Students enjoy using wikis in learning experiences because it is real time, technology driven, and ubiquitously available 24×7. Its web 2.0 instant-communication format is part of their world perspective. The concepts that they can express themselves whenever and wherever they like, freely and fully with their classmates, are critical to the ownership and motivation of the learning activities.

Furthermore, the capability to review and assess their progress at any moment is a tremendous benefit to any teacher. Teachers do not have to ask students to hand in the next version of their draft or wait for them to deliver their forgotten assignments—if they have done the work, it is all there, always. Moreover, the review screen makes the work of assessing group participation much more objective and convenient. The review feature also provides documentation to help assess student learning needs because the work of *individuals* can still be reviewed although the product is collective.

Examples of some of the free wikis that are available for educators include pbwiki.com, wikispaces.com, and www.wetpaint.com. These sites include user-friendly tutorials for educators and public areas where one can experiment freely. Teachers and learners can discover the potential for collaboration and expression together by using the wiki format. This unique, free, and convenient technology platform fuels opportunities to incorporate research, critical dialogue, and dynamic collaboration.

Discussion boards/threaded discussions—electric learning

A more integrated approach to using new media and web-based technology in education is the discussion board, often referred to as threaded discussions. Indeed, such platforms are frequently used to facilitate discussions across a wide range of participants, views, and topics. People "sign in" to a common website, choose which issues they want to discuss, and engage in global dialogue. In this manner, discussion boards may be used for both formal and informal learning. Examples of formal learning being used among higher education and K-12 settings include platforms such as Blackboard (http://www.blackboard.com), Desire2Learn (http://www.desire2learn.com), and Moodle (http://www.moodle.org). These vehicles can support distance *only* learning and enable web-enhanced classroom experiences.

Regarding informal learning, one may look at such varied subject areas as medical support and health information discussion boards, and community support groups, to name only a few. Thus, public discussion boards can provide interactive dialogue with experts and a focused community for information and support (examples of such discussion boards include http://www.healthboards.com, http://www.apparelyzed.com/, and http://www.medhelp.org/). Because the health industry is widely recognized as ruled by big business, health education is an area where resisting dominant practices, opinions, and policies is much needed. Providing health education through this grassroots, participant-driven format can quickly and collectively cultivate and suggest alternative support, treatments, and options, and challenge the demigod, authoritarian foothold of the medical establishment. Informal education leverages the potential to foster perspectives and practices of medical advocacy, both individually and collectively.

Many people are familiar with the use of discussion boards in distance learning as educators post questions, and students respond. However, when we break away from the Socratic model, teaching and learning have great possibilities here. More innovative strategies, which are popular in this online collaborative space, include

- ~ Collaborative case study solving by learners, with each person offering a different piece of the solution
- ~ Small group role playing
- ~ Learner-created scenarios
- ~ Rotation of group roles (e.g., facilitator, leader, rater, etc.)
- ~ Group governance (King and Griggs, 2007; Rovai, 2007)

Additional distinctions of discussion boards are that they are usually private to a specific community and moderated by group norms. Because educational contexts suggest and advise privacy and ground rules for appropriate discussion, discussion board protocol is an easy fit. Furthermore, by building and sustaining a safe and respectful environment for group members, even greater facilitation of communication, critical discussion, and transparency can occur in these virtual forums.

Indeed, a very simple example of the power of peer learning may be seen in using a discussion board for students to privately post their assignments. By using this procedure occasionally in the learning experience, learners gain much greater benefits from sharing their work with the whole class, rather than just with their teacher. Indeed, the first few times educators experience this with students, they are often surprised by student enthusiasm, empowerment, and learning (King, 2008).

In this discussion board case, one might ask students to build on others' responses, scaffold ideas, and critically consider perspectives of others. Such open critical dialogue being the focus rather than critique can create a powerful experience of voice, validation, and empowerment. Based on the recent research, students gain many benefits from being able to see and respond to one another's work, including content knowledge, academic skills, writing skills, interpersonal skills, community building, professional identity development, and personal development (King, 2008; Rovai, 2007). Specifically, students remarked that they read helpful, alternate explanations of difficult topics; learned different approaches to assignments; saw the quality of work of their peers for the first time; benefited from the research done by their classmates, rather than only their own paper; better appreciated the insight, experiences, and expertise of their colleagues; delved deeper into class discussions because of the questions and observations offered; and appreciated the opportunity to engage in deeper peer dialogue on course content.

Creating such learning opportunities through new media epitomizes the goals of cultivating lifelong learners who have critical perspectives. Indeed, they are living the reality of a vibrant learning community as they experience a less teacher-centered, more independent, self-directed opportunity to exercise their critical thinking and insight (Rovai, 2007). The validation which emerges from such experiences does not emanate from a grade book, instead it flows from self-validation as they improve their ability to think, respect, and dialogue with one another. The experience is nothing short of electric. This is educational practice through web 2.0 technologies, which can cultivate current and future generations of great minds of radical pedagogues, scientists, philosophers, and political leaders.

Video blogs/video podcasts—new legs for creative expression

Video blogs are the final example in this chapter of new media that can be used to vibrantly bring the inner thoughts, dreams, and voice of students alive. Much like podcasts, they are hosted on Internet servers and globally distributed via a push technology RSS feed; however, video blogs are digital video rather than audio.

To realize the power of web 2.0 video, consider the emergence of YouTube.com since 2005. It rushed into existence and swiftly dominated the lives of most people under 30. As of late 2010, we expect to find any current news event announced on Twitter.com and available for instantaneous viewing in YouTube.com because the global community of "every person" is contributing their choice selections of content nonstop. From the famous to the infamous, Twitter and YouTube are iconic cultural experiences that typify our expectations for instant access and unfettered expression.

Really though, how widespread is this phenomenon? Consider just one example: "Evolution of the Dance." This is a six-minute video by comedian Judson Laipply (2006) in which he performs the last 50 years of dance, predominately from a U.S.A perspective. While this is funny enough to watch, the phenomenon is not even only that it was watched 97,236,529 times from April 2006 to August 2008, but that it spawned a tidal wave of copycats (Giuffo, 2007). From comedians, to children, puppets, to brides and grooms, everyone feels the need to not only make their own "Evolution of the Dance" video but also upload it to the global hall of video fame (YouTube).

How did this happen? No doubt, because someone recorded Judson Laipply's six-minute routine with a cell phone and uploaded the video clip to YouTube.com. This illustration documents that instant creativity and self-expression have new *legs* and expectations in the culture of YouTube.

Even with this cultural landslide in mind, the point is that uploading digital video is something students expect to do in their everyday life. However, we as educators too often keep it segregated from their education. Why is this? It might often be because our schools do not have the equipment. But it might also be because our teachers are not as comfortable with the medium, purpose, and technologies as the students are. However, if we as educators examine the possibilities, embrace the opportunity, and take the leap, we stand to gain so many educational benefits. What is more, we will engage students in exciting creative, in-depth, and critical learning experiences.

While many classes are creating movie trailers to develop self-expression as a first level of video development, others are reaching into dynamic expression of critical views and topics. Consider the "Eye to Eye" or "Kindred Spirit" projects, which gather students together from around the world to answer critical issues about friendship, community, and responsibility (Frates, 2008; iEARN Media Gallery, 2008). Students log into the site to see what the community topic will be, they then research and develop their response. Once that has been prepared, they decide how to video record their responses and the format. (Will it be a monologue, a performance or a role play for instance?) When finished, they upload their collective expression of their perspective to the global site alongside that of all the other classes from around the world. One among many, authentic researcher in the world; these students realize this is a rich lesson in much more than technology or current events. These are lessons of voice, empowerment, collaboration, and global citizenry. They are learning experiences that may forge their sense of identity and being, and ones they will not forget soon.

If all these individual videos were strung together in a series, it would be a video blog or video podcast. It could then be registered with iTunes.com and one could subscribe to it. Then, whenever iTunes opens, the program automatically downloads any new episode/video from the series. Using this technology, the dynamic global conversation could continue right on learners' desktops. This certainly is different from bringing in newspaper clippings for "Show and Tell." Students are creating the message, no longer just looking at it: students are "content creators, not content consumers."

How to Get Started as Content Creators

Once educators and students see how easily they can create, update, and customize their blog site, participate in audio or video podcast broadcasting, or engage in online discussions they begin to invest more time in research, content choices, and content creation. Effective approaches to support this empowerment, voice, and engagement are collaborative groups and project or problem based learning (Jonassen et al., 2008; King and Gura, 2005, Richardson, 2006). Each of these instructional strategies affords the capability for extended opportunities for learners of all ages, to make choices about research and practice as well as develop critical thinking, learn dialogue and negotiation, and engage in every aspect of language arts. A review of the International Society of Technology in Education's National Education Technology Standards (ISTE NETS) for student learning reveals how well such efforts can integrate content and performance standards across disciplines in meaningful ways (ISTE, 2007a, 2007b).

Another vital perspective for considering these issues is that of *multiple literacies*. While the American Library Association (ALA) reminds us of the powerful dimensions of information literacy (ALA, 2006; Rich, 2008), many professional associations demonstrate specific literacies and standards that are embraced through technology integration. For instance, the National Council of Teachers of English has made it clear that multiple literacies may be fully embraced in the Language Arts for instance, while a review of Math standards at the National Council of Teachers of Mathematics (NCTM) and Science standards at National Science Teachers Association (NSTA) repeatedly emphasize the need for technology literacy embedded in content skills and understanding (National Academy of Sciences; 1996; NCTE, 2008; NCTM, 2000; Texley and Wild, 2004).

When educators see that technology use is not isolated from content learning, they are invited to incorporate their expertise and understanding with this new opportunity in vital ways. This "content-grounded" perspective, as it were, also validates the role of the content specialist and the general education teacher in instructional technology processes. Teachers should not entirely abdicate the role of discovering and implementing technology innovations for instructional purposes to technicians. Indeed, the reverse is true; the best technology coordinators seek to have content area specialists develop the most relevant applications and activities for their learners (ISTE, 2007a, 2007b; Jonassen et al., 2008; King, 2002; King and Gura, 2007).

This approach is several steps beyond the traditional model: teachers actively pursue and appropriate opportunities to incorporate new media, dynamic expression, constructivism, and exploration into their content area. Teachers may develop new learning experiences for their learners by starting with simple blogs, discussion boards, or wikis, and let the students be their co-learners. In these ways teachers can leverage this as a powerful opportunity to develop more inclusive learning communities, in which the learners, together with the teacher, question, discover, plan, and grow. These are memorable experiences of developing new knowledge in Math, English or Social Studies, etc. and of

1. Understanding new perspectives
2. Discovering voice
3. Realizing their teachers are also continuing to learn and change
4. Validating their questions, struggles, and opinions
5. Developing an appreciation and vision of lifelong learning

Radical Conclusions

Educational podcasting and web 2.0 new media offer a rapidly growing archive of content which is freely available for hosting or appropriating learning resources. In addition, because these technologies reach vast numbers of people and provide a platform for diverse perspectives, they are valuable for creativity, expression, and instruction. However, which communities will resist the mainstream media, status quo, reified models of learning, increasingly reified technologies and cloned formats of virtual learning?

A review of recent endeavors to launch response to intervention (RtI), virtual K-12 schools, and credit recovery of broad based platforms via technology demonstrates the pressing urgency to educate populations who are not well served by the current educational systems (Dessof, 2009). However, we cannot launch these efforts by continuing the same pedagogical and administrative approaches. As suggested in this chapter, educators and learners alike need to question prior practices and assumptions. We can no longer "teach as we were taught."

Spaces which are not only effective but also welcoming and safe places in which to learn and grow, are urgently needed for special populations of students across race, gender, abilities (gifted) and disabilities, (physical and learning), sexual orientation, class, and more (Miners, 2009; Rose and Blomeyer, 2008). Learners who are not well represented in the dominant society and schools and/or who in any way see themselves perceived as "the Other" need new paradigms of representation and participation in teaching and learning (Taylor, 2002). For instance, to begin with we need new paradigms of entry to education, the removal of barriers, and communities of learning which allow learners freedom to grow and learn. We need new ways to allow all students to speak aloud, write, and portray the questions of their hearts and minds as well as to discover, explore and create new knowledge. The technology is available at all price points including free, moderate, and high-end luxury versions. This technology-assisted and virtual platforms include the means to support standards and facilitate inclusive learning experiences and communities.

However, where are the dedicated, forward-thinking, resistant educators prepared to fight for change? Can we find those who will resist the reified system of "one-size fits all" standards of technology modules? Are they willing to demand the formats, individualization and transformations required to meet the needs of an inclusive society? We need leaders who will resist homogenous technology solutions. And in doing so, open the doors to opportunities for persuasive, global resistance across educational philosophies and domains.

Technology is moving beyond the digital divide of the 1990s and 2000s (NTIA, 2007), but our educational applications are slow to transform it to address the needs of the 21st century. Visionary activist pedagogues need to be problem solvers, critical thinkers, and creators of the future! These acts of resistance mean standing against the swelling waves of broad-based roll-outs, which exclude differently abled students, minority experiences, and iconic educational philosophies.

Quandary of resistance

Educators, learners, and the public have the means to create new waves of revolutionary thought and action parallel to the days of Paulo Freire (1976), because there is a huge void in serving diverse needs and the free technology engines to disseminate the message. Yet at the same time that technology is our means of resistance, to effect educational revolution, it is also the focus of resistance. Why does the very means of our dialogue and freedom (technology) erupt strong and persistent resistance among some sectors of society and schools (Christensen, Johnson, and Horn, 2008; King & Griggs, 2007)? The means to disrupting the status quo is by definition a disrupting experience. Technology is a disruptive force which can further our educational transformation. Let us not kill the messenger; technology can be leverage for equity and community or continue to be the target of frustration, rejection, and resistance by those who choose not to change or relinquish power.

Twenty-first century living and learning is about *constant* change. Nowhere is the need for responsive change to these 21st century new conditions more evident than in education. Our older methods of teaching will not work without substantial transformation to reach deeper and wider across diversity lines and dimensions of content and learning (Christensen, Johnson, and Horn, 2008; King and Griggs,

2007). Digital media and web 2.0 technologies afford this deep, critical thinking, community building and platform for dialogue and education. However, we must resist the vocal remnant who are hanging onto the last threads of archaic classroom power structures, and embrace the means of equal voice, empowerment, and validation.

Vision

Introducing people to the freedom to challenge the status quo does not happen in an instant (Freire, 1976; King, 2005). However, varied technology tools can provide ubiquitous access, voice, and empowerment on worldwide private or public forums. Digital media which embraces all abilities and perspectives stands to offer greater democratization of *education*, if we as educators will challenge the status quo of education and appropriate its transformation to inclusiveness.

REFERENCES

ALA (American Library Association). (2000, Sept. 1). *Information literacy competency standards for higher education*. Retrieved July 23, 2009 from http://www.ala.org/ala/acrl/acrlstandards/information literacycompetency.cfm

Argyris, C., & Schon, D. (1974). *Theory in practice.* San Francisco: Jossey-Bass.

Backborby, J., Wagner, M., Camero, R., Davies, E., Levine, P., Newman, L., Marder, C., & Sumi, C. (2005). *Engagement, academics, social adjustments, and independence.* Palo Alto, CA: Stanford Research Institute.

Berge, Z., & Collins, M. (1998). *Wired together: The online classroom in K-12.* Cresskill, NJ: Hampton Press.

Christensen, C., Johnson, C. W., & Horn, M. B. (2008). *Disrupting class.* New York: McGraw-Hill.

Dessof, A. (2009, Oct). Reaching graduation with credit recovery. *District Administration,* 43–48.

Dewey, J. (1938). *Experience and education.* New York: Collier Books.

Electronic Frontier Foundation. (2006). *EFF: Legal guide for bloggers.* Retrieved on August 10, 2009 from http://w2.eff.org/bloggers/lg/

eMarketer. (2007, May, 21). Podcast user demographics. Retrieved October 20, 2009 from http://www.emarketer.com/Article.aspx?id=1004938

eSchool News. (2008). Schools try to reach students via podcast. *eSchool News* 11(28), 4.

Feedburner. (2008). *About Feedburner.* Retrieved October 2, 2008, from http://www.feedburner.com/fb/a/about#stats

Frates, L. (2008). *Eye to eye.* Retrieved August 25, 2009 from http://media.iearn.org/node/188

Freire, P. (1976). *Pedagogy of the oppressed.* New York: Seabury.

Giroux, H. (1988). *Teachers as intellectuals: Toward a critical pedagogy of learning.* Westport, CT: Bergin & Garvey.

Giuffo, J. (2007, April 30). *Ten videos that made YouTube famous: Forbes.com Special Report.* Retrieved August 26, 2009, from http://www.forbes.com/2007/04/30/youtube-videos-hits-ent-cx_jg_07networks_0430tube.html

Gordon, D. (Ed). (2003). *Better teaching and learning in the digital classroom* Cambridge: Harvard Education Publishing Group.
hooks, b. (1994). *Teaching to transgress: Education as the practice of freedom.* New York: Routledge.
iEARN Media Gallery. (2008). Collaborative centre of EARN.org media projects. Retrieved July 1, 2009 from http://media.iearn.org
iEARN.org (2008). International Education and Research Network. Retrieved July 1, 2009 from http://www.iearn.org
International Society for Technology in Education (2007a). *National Educational Technology Standards for Students* (2nd ed). Eugene, OR: ISTE.
International Society for Technology in Education (2007b). *National Educational Technology Standards for Teachers* (2nd ed). Eugene, OR: ISTE.
Jonassen, D. H. (1981). Designing constructivist learning environments. In C. M. Reigeluth (Ed.), *Instructional theories and models* (2nd ed.), (pp. 215–241). Mahwah, NJ: Lawrence Erlbaum Publishers.
Jonassen, D. H. (1997). Instructional design models for well-structured and ill-structured problem-solving learning outcomes. *Educational Technology Research and Development* 45(1): 65–94.
Jonassen, D., Howland, J., Marra, R., & Crismond, D. (2008). *Meaningful learning with technology* (3rd ed). Upper Saddle River, NJ: Pearson Merrill Prentice Hall.
Joseph, P. B., & Burnaford, G. E. (2001). *Images of schoolteachers in America.* (2nd ed.). Mahwah, NJ: Lawrence Erlbaum.
King, K. P. (2002). *Keeping pace with technology: Educational technology that transforms. Vol. One: The challenge and promise for K-12 educators.* Cresskill, NJ: Hampton Press.
King, K. P. (2005). *Bringing transformative learning to life.* Malabar, FL: Krieger.
King, K. P. (2008a, May). Introducing new media into teacher preparation. *ISTE SIGHC* 3(4), 4–7.
King, K. P. (2008b). Slamming the closet door and taking control: Analysis of personal transformation and social change as LGBTQ podcasting. In T. Bettinger & J. Gedro (Eds.), *Proceedings 2008 Adult Education Research Conference, LGBTQ&A Pre-Conference.* St. Louis: University of Missouri.
King, K. P. & Griggs, J. K. (Eds.). (2007). *Harnessing innovative technologies in higher education: Access, equity, policy and instruction.* Madison, WI: Atwood Publishing.
King, K. P. & Gura, M. (2007). *Podcasting for teachers: Using a new technology to revolutionize teaching and learning. Series: Emerging technologies for evolving learning.* Charlotte, NC: Information Age Publishing, Inc.
King, K. P. & Gura, M. (2009). *Podcasting for teachers: Using a new technology to revolutionize teaching and learning* (2009 edition). *Series: Emerging technologies for evolving learning.* Charlotte, NC: Information Age Publishing, Inc.
King, K. P., & Sanquist, S. (2009). 21st century learning and human performance. In V. Wang, & K. P. King, (Eds.), *Fundamentals of human performance and training issues. Series: Adult education special topics* (pp. 61–88). Charlotte, NC: Information Age Publishing.
Kolb, D. A. (1984). *Experiential learning.* Englewood Cliffs, NJ: Prentice-Hall.
Laipply, J. (2006). Evolution of dance. YouTube.com Retrieved August 28, 2009 from http://www.youtube.com/watch?v=dMH0bHeiRNg
Lave, J., & Wenger, E. (1991). *Situated learning.* Cambridge: University of Cambridge Press.
Lesbian, Gay, Bisexual & Transgender Community Center, The (2008). Out at The Center podcast. Retrieved August 25, 2008, from http://www.gaycenter.org/out
Lessig, L. (2001). *The future of ideas.* New York: Random House.
Llewellyn, D. (2001). *Inquire within: Implementing inquiry-based Science standards.* Thousand Oaks, CA:

Corwin Press.

National Academy of Sciences. (1996). *National Science education standards.* Washington, DC: National Academy Press. Retrieved August 25, 2009, from http://www.nap.edu/catalog.php?record_id=4962

National Council Teachers of English (NCTE). (2008, Feb. 15). *The NCTE definition of 21st-century literacies.* Retrieved August 28, 2009 from http://www.ncte.org/print.asp?id=129117&node=65

National Council Teachers of Mathematics (NCTM). (2000). *Principles and standards for school mathematics.* Retrieved July 28, 2009 from http://standards.nctm.org/

National Telecommunications and Information Administration (NTIA). (2007). Networked Nation: Broadband in America. Washington, DC: NTIA. Retrieved November 11, 2009 from http://www.ntia.doc.gov/reports/2008/NetworkedNationBroadbandinAmerica2007.pdf

Miners, Z. (2009, August 7). Virtual school hopes to offer welcoming community for gays. *US News and World Report.* Retrieved November 15, 2009 from http://www.usnews.com/blogs/on-education/2009/08/07/virtual-school-hopes-to-offer-welcoming-community-for-gays.html

Partnership for 21st Century Skills. (2004). Learning for the 21st century. Retrieved July 23, 2008, from http://www.21stcenturyskills.org/images/stories/otherdocs/P21_Report.pdf

Prensky, M. (2001). Digital natives, digital immigrants. *On the Horizon* 9(5), 1–6.

Project 2061. (1993). *Benchmarks for science literacy.* New York: Oxford University Press.

Rich, M. (2008, July 27). Literacy debate: R U reading online? *New York Times.* Retrieved August 12, 2008 from http://www.nytimes.com/2008/07/27/books/27reading.html

Richardson, W. (2006). *Blogs, wikis and podcasts.* Thousand Oaks: Corwin.

Rose, R. M., & Blomeyer, R. L. (2008). *Research Committees Issues Brief: Equity and access in online classes and virtual schools.* Vienna, VA: North American Council for Online Learning (NACOL). Retrieved November 15, 2009 from http://www.inacol.org/research/docs/NACOL_EquityAccess.pdf

Rovai, A. P. (2007). Facilitating online discussions effectively. *Internet and Higher Education*, 10(1), 77–88.

Schön, D. A. (1987). *Educating the reflective practitioner.* San Francisco: Jossey-Bass.

Shor, I. (1992). *Empowering education.* Chicago: University of Chicago.

South Carolina Gay Lesbian Pride Movement (SCGLPM). (2007). Rainbow Radio: The real gay agenda. Retrieved August 28, 2009 from http://www.scglpm.org/rainbowradio/2007/index.html

Taylor, C. (2002). Understanding the other: A Gadamerian view on conceptual schemes, In J. Malpas, U. Arnswald, & J. Kertscher (Eds.), *Gadamer's century: Essays in honor of Hans-Georg Gadamer* (pp. 279–297). Cambridge: MIT Press.

Texley, J. & Wild, A. (2004). NSTA Pathways to the Science standards: Guidelines for moving *the vision into practice.* Arlington, VA: NSTA.

Von Glaserfeld, E. (1991). *Radical constructivism in mathematics education.* Dordrecht, Holland: Kluwer Publishing.

Vygotsky, L. S. (1978). *Mind in society.* Cambridge, MA: Harvard University Press.

Walch, R., & Lafferty, M. (2006). *Tricks of the podcasting masters.* Indianapolis: Que.

Wilhelm, J., Sherrod, S., & Walters, K. (2008, March 1). Project-based learning environments: Challenging pre-service teachers to act in the moment. *Journal of Educational Research* 101, 220–233.

Williams, B. (2008). *Educators guide to podcasting.* Eugene, OR: International Society for Technology in Education (ISTE).

CHAPTER TWELVE

Resisting an Unbecoming Science

JOHN CRAVEN & TRACY HOGAN

> There is the standing danger that the material of formal instruction will be merely the subject matter of the schools, isolated from the subject matter of life experience. The permanent social interests are likely to be lost from view.
> JOHN DEWEY, DEMOCRACY AND EDUCATION, 1916

There are persuasive arguments arising from the discourse of educators and scholars alerting us to, and opposing, a dominating ideological doctrine permeating schools and society today (Porfilio & Malott, 2008). Extending back over the past several decades, that doctrine, Neoliberalism and Global Capitalism, the analysts contend, exerts powerful political and economic forces on the educational landscape that transform schools into anything but centers of learning (Spring, 2008). Described variously as "knowledge factories" (Aronowitz, 2000), "marketplaces" (Slaughter & Rhodes, 2009; Bok, 2003), and/or "warehouses" (Wacquan, 1997), these altered places (schools) have become dehumanizing centers in which knowledge represents the power and students are "[robbed] of their individuality and, instead, trained to become cogs in the corporate capitalist machine" (Aronowitz, 2000, p. 3). Indeed, the authors, as science teacher educators, all too often walk into science classrooms today only to find students sitting in their chairs being fed prescripted pabulum developed and fueled by the textbook and testing industries with the endorsement of policymakers. Some groups seeking to resist such hegemony of corporate and political influence may find the research and rhetoric of critical theory and critical pedagogy enlightening or perhaps empowering. Others may place hope in a public science education that creates a critically-oriented citizenry. Indeed, the broader science education community has long sought to enhance inquiry and question-generation in the classroom. However, resistance educators say such a focus is too limited if we are seeking to promote activism in society. Giroux (2004), for example, calls for a pedagogy that goes beyond the promotion of a culture of questioning by educating people to assume "public responsibility through active participation in the very process of governing and engaging important social problems" (p. 124). Unfortunately, the current concentration on content acquisition in science education usurps a much needed focus on the development of habits of mind that promote and support critical stances through skeptical, empirical, and independent thinking. Moreover, the current movement driving the myopic focus on content acquisition is not likely to disappear anytime soon.

In as much as science and technology are serving as powerful weapons in the competitive race for global economic, military, and political dominance by the United States as well as other nations, for many decades science education at the K-12 level has been identified as a ground to seize early advantage—through targeted programs of "reform" (Duschl, Schweingruber, & Shouse, 2007). Despite what has been learned about human development and learning during the same period, science education has seen little change in form and function over those years. With disregard to years of failed reforms and lessons supposedly learned, policymakers expect students to learn more—more content, more advanced sciences, and more powerful technology. And with a collective call that is louder and more influential than ever, these policymakers demand that they do it faster, at an earlier age and with more accountability in the hope of gaining and maintaining scientific and technologic superiority over other nations.

And yet, at the same time, we see increasingly brighter public light shed on the megalithic barriers to freedom of thought, inquiry, and voice imposed upon science teachers and students by testing, accrediting, and political agencies across the nation. We also see a mounting number of instances in the American society in which the perceived "authority" associated with a positivistic science is being exploited in an effort to control the beliefs and actions of others; manipulate values held by individuals and society; censure knowledge and information; control the questions that can and should be asked; and dictate modes of inquiry. At the same time, the moral obligation on the part of schools to provide youth with opportunities to make meaningful contributions to society is often neglected. Considering these conditions, the need to promote a citizenry with the habits of mind needed for the growth and development of democracy is greater than ever (Carr & Thésée, 2008;

Hogan & Craven, 2008). Thus, the authors contend that a critical stance and resistance pedagogy approach is particularly necessary in science education wherein mandated curriculums represent increasingly oppressive forces in the classroom. Perhaps, in fact, we should be teaching toward an entirely different kind of science—a more liberating science described by Martin (2000, 2006) as centering on citizen action and empowering the disenfranchised.

We are inspired and informed by the advocates of critical pedagogy and resistance education such as Henry Giroux, bell hooks, Lisa Delpit, Michael Apple, Peter McLaren, Jean Anyon, and Joel Spring, as much as we are educated by the sociologists of science, critical media journalists, and activist bloggers who help chronicle the often hidden, many times nefarious, aspects of the scientific enterprise. Yet the authors also spend considerable time in high school science classrooms in the metropolitan New York region. And our experience observing teachers in marginalized, disadvantaged settings keeps us grounded in the realization that for many of the science teachers with whom we work, the discourse on resistance education and critical pedagogy remains abstract or inaccessible if not perceptually irrelevant, particularly in the context of a discipline widely portrayed to the public as objective, pure, socially neutral and unbiased. Therefore, from our perspective there is an enormous gap between the vision of a science education that prepares students for, and has them take action on, scientific controversies confronting society (Hodson, 2009) and the current practices in urban classrooms scrutinized for "poor performance" and schools threatened with closure, dismantling and/or restructuring. Yet we acknowledge that the "action curriculum" or "resistance pedagogy" described, for example, by Bencze and Alsop (2009) represents a more compelling and relevant direction for science education and youth development than traditional practices have allowed. This dilemma raises the question of where to begin the dialogue of resistance education with teachers who work in environments shown to promote if not reward resistance to change and yet who teach the very populations that are most likely to be written off as failures from the start of their young lives.

We hope this chapter responds to that challenge by offering entry into a tangible discussion on resistance in science education that focuses on the identification of, and advocates resistance to, a few modest yet compelling factors influencing classroom practice. We do so by sharing some vignettes drawn from authentic experiences and dialogue with teachers in the field. The vignettes reveal ways in which the prevailing system of education has shaped the thoughts and actions of science teachers and we interpret the stories from a resistance education stance. Similar to Schmidt (2000) who asserts that the structure of training programs for science are designed to deliberately shape the students into conformists, we acknowledge a research-supported assumption that the current educational system has indoctrinated many new science teachers to ways of thinking about the discipline, their roles as teachers, and the capacities and abilities of their students that are detrimental to the habits of mind needed to (1) "reflect, form opinions, evaluate, oppose [and] reconceptualize information in a meaningful way," (Schmeck, 1988, p. 335) and/or (2) respond to controversial, ill-defined problems in sophisticated ways (King and Kitchener, 2004).

Specifically, as science teachers, we should know, understand, and confront our personal belief systems that have been tacitly yet inexorably shaped by our own educational experiences. For these powerful belief systems all too often shackle our ability to teach a pedagogy of freedom by constraining our capacity to reshape the goals of the discipline and limiting our potential to envision a different kind of science education. Hence, we offer this chapter as one vehicle for sparking discussions on all too often unexamined forces shaping teaching behaviors in the classroom.

The reader should note that we are not implying that the teachers with whom we work do not have altruistic motivations of helping adolescents rise above the limits of possibility placed upon them by the current economic, political, and cultural forces that have determined them to be "disposable" (Giroux, 2003). Nor do we intend to trivialize the very real pressures placed on them as teachers by the current zeitgeist of accountability. However, we do understand that people often hold conflicting theories and ideas. Kegan and Lisa Laskow (2001), for example, describe a psychological dynamic called a "competing commitment." Consistent with the research on naïve conceptions (misconceptions) and their negative influence on science learning (Driver & Easley, 1978), competing commitments are described as tacitly held cognitive conflicts (or conflicting beliefs) that can account for the lack of progress toward change (Wagner et al., 2006). Hence, while we see teachers profess to have goals targeting the self-actualization and engagement of their students as well as "teaching for science literacy," we find all too many conscripted to didactic, content-focused, test-oriented pedagogy—models of pedagogy that have dominated their own educational experiences. In reference to Carl Rogers, they end up teaching the way they were taught (Rogers & Freiberg, 1969).

The messages many teachers have received through such educational models have produced misguided belief systems that very often negatively impact practice such as setting low expectations or limiting the role of the learner to listening, receiving, remembering, and doing (Fang, 1996, pp. 50–51). In our own work with teachers, the commitments include (1) an all too often unjustifiable belief and unexamined confidence that they have a deep, robust knowledge of their subject and that their knowledge of content is sufficient to teach students about the discipline; and (2) a belief that students generally do not have the ability, if not interest, to engage in complex, socially and ethically bound issues associated with the production and application of scientific knowledge. We first briefly explain these beliefs and then explore their manifestations in dialogue and practice.

Firstly, all too commonly new as well as seasoned teachers have come to think that they have mastered the content of their discipline. And they point to their wealth of facts, their ability to recall information and perform well on standardized tests as fundamental measures and evidence of having done so. It follows, in their view, that their own scores and their students' performance on standardized tests are the true and valid benchmarks of success and learning in the discipline. Through their educational experiences, many teachers have also "learned" their content in decontextualized environments—that is, as isolated sets of facts and principles. Schwab (1962) called this practice teaching science as rhetoric of conclusions. The presentation of "pure" facts and principles in isolated form and absent of connections to social, political, economic, and justice frameworks appears to have disallowed many science teachers an understanding of fundamental relationships between science and society and, thereby, absolved them of the responsibility to engage their own students in such topics and issues.

Secondly, it is not uncommon for science teachers to hold the belief that their students generally do not have the ability (and many times interest) in dealing with controversial issues. Simply put, "the students just can't handle it." This belief may be rooted in their own experiences in science and science education. For example, an unacceptably large percentage of science teachers have not had educational experiences within the sciences that have dealt with ethical and social justice issues associated with the production and/or application of scientific knowledge. We know this by having reviewed transcripts of hundreds of applicants to science education programs over the past 12 years. Therefore, it is not surprising to find them unfamiliar with organizations, public advocacy and activist groups dedicated to social justice issues tangential to socio-scientific controversies (groups opposing, for example, genetically modified food industries, global agricultural companies marketing seed crops with "terminator genes" to farmers in developing countries, genetic patent and price gauging practices of pharmaceutical giants, or plastic bottle manufacturers using bisphenol A). Nor have they had sufficient training, as education majors in a school of education, in developing and implementing the more advanced forms of action-based curriculum described by Hodson (2003). Consequently, these science teachers usually have as much trouble grappling with, and disentangling, the very complex science-based issues imposed upon society by multi-national corporations (through enterprises such as chemical and biological engineering operations or hazardous waste operations or energy exploitation enterprises) as would an average citizen. Furthermore, we expect that ethical controversies likely invoke visceral and emotional responses in humans searching for understandings of, and solutions to, troubling socio-scientific problems—particularly those imposed upon society by powerful global industries. And knowing how to manage social and personnel conflict in the adolescent classroom requires specialized knowledge. Yet comparatively little time is devoted to equipping teachers with deep understandings of adolescent development in their education programs in comparison to teaching the technical aspects and demands of the profession (Nagle, 2009). Therefore, we suspect that their own inexperience and an absence of understanding of the psychology and sociology of adolescents may be the reason why so many of the teachers with whom we work believe that students can't handle complex, science-based social justice issues. Or, perhaps, there are those science teachers who are simply reluctant to have students see them fail in the role as knower and, very often, as provider, of answers to all questions (albeit rather mundane and trivial) routinely posed in the classroom. It would, after all, be easier to avoid ill-defined, multi-dimensional, real-world messy issues altogether.

We suggest, therefore, that an entry point to resistance education in the discipline of science may be found through introspective study of personal belief systems influencing practice. Specifically, we encourage science teachers to reflect on their practice and consider whether a personal resistance to a belief in any of the following is warranted:

1. Students cannot, should not and/or will not engage in deeply complex, ethically bound scientific and technological issues.
2. One's content knowledge is deep enough and sufficient to teach discipline to the students.

In the following section, we share ways in which we have seen these beliefs manifested in the dialogue and experiences we've had with teachers in the field.

Belief 1: Students Can't Handle It

In our science methods courses we often show the documentary, *Gene Hunters* (Holland & Taylor, 1995). The film centers on a research project, the Human Genome Biodiversity Project, designed in the late 1980s to collect DNA from the blood of indigenous peoples in a lot of nearly isolated villages around the world. We use this documentary in our secondary science teaching methods course for a multitude of reasons (as we must do for all our activities given the very limited number of pedagogical content knowledge classes that are taken by pre-service teachers). The purposes include: to spark discussions on links between science, technology, and society; to explore the nature of science and technology; and, most importantly, to motivate our students to consider using science-based issues that have roots in moral and ethical dilemmas currently confronting local and global communities as context for learning. As a prelude to the film, we ask the students a question: Would you support a project that proposed a genetic bank to store and preserve the DNA (or genetic code/sequence) of endangered species around the world? Our assumption that their conception of endangered species does not include unique people and their cultures has held true to date. Most commonly, the students share a widespread support for such a program. We then follow the gene hunters' journey through the film.

The Television for the Environment (TVE) documentary tracks scientists into remote villages in the rainforests of northern Colombia and elsewhere as they seek to convince members of the tribes living there that the team of researchers is on a humanitarian mission. The researchers tell the Ahuaco and Asario Indians of Colombia, for example, that they are there to diagnose whether or not members of the tribe have diabetes; they also offer to conduct some routine dental health and other basic medical examinations. What the scientists don't tell the locals or any of the other 700 members of tribes contacted in remote corners of the world is that they (the researchers) are primarily there to collect DNA from blood samples. The scientists hope to identify and isolate genetic sequences that may hold the keys to new drugs and treatments for diseases such as AIDS, motor neuron disease, or cancer. Nor do they reveal that their funding comes from a very large global pharmaceutical giant that will patent the newfound genes. At a point in the film, one man describes how pharmaceutical companies have successfully won court cases in the United States to maintain their patent on human genes despite the protestations and objections of those people whence the genes are derived.

Dr. George Annas, Professor of Medical Ethics at the Massachusetts Institute of Technology, argues that process "is, in fact, taking total advantage of the tribal people by taking from them what Westerners value most." He continues by saying, "This is exploitation…and it represents the worst form of colonialism." Meanwhile, Ray Apodaca, of the National Congress of American Indians, adds this example of exploitation to a long, historical list of cases in which native people have been used as laboratory rats for the sake of Western "learning" and the quest for "knowledge." Many refer to this process of harvesting genetic material in a global fishing expedition as "bio-prospecting." In fact, by 2005, roughly 20 percent of human genes were patented (Jensen & Murray, 2005). These patents subsequently require payment forms of royalty fees to the patent holder by those seeking to do any research involving those genes (Koepsell, 2009). Indeed, one research scientist linked to the project in the documentary is now on a vastly more industrious bio-prospecting project—one that is attempting to catalog and patent hundreds of thousands of genes of micro-organisms in the ocean. The Human Genome Diversity Project was eventually shut down following a vast human outcry of indigenous voices from around the world.

Not surprisingly, many of our students (prospective as well as practicing science teachers) find the film interesting and provocative. Though versed in the "science content" of the film (i.e., DNA sequencing, HLA Typing, cloning, etc.), we have yet to find one of our teachers having prior knowledge of this particular project. And, though most are familiar with the Human Genome Project (after all, that project has and continues to have broad media attention, the gene hunter project—the one designed to deceptively "steal" and "commercialize for profit" the genes of indigenous people—never surfaced in their studies or content courses). We eventually ask our students whether or not they would ever use this film in their current or future high school science classroom and, if so, what role would it serve in their curriculum. Their responses are all too often disappointing if not disturbing. The typical responses include: My students couldn't handle this controversy. There's no way that my students have the emotional stability to deal with the ethical and moral issues raised in this film. My students would get too riled up watching this film. They [the students] wouldn't get it or would lack interest in the debate. Worst of all? My job is to teach science content—not social studies or philosophy. Yet, these same teachers expect those same students to master the content and vocabulary of sophisticated concepts such as polymerase chain reactions, recombinant DNA, Euaryotic gene regulation, phosphate, and dexoyribose groups within the respective purines and pyrimidine structures of DNA, etc. They will, in fact, teach them how to extract the DNA from fruits and insects and even the students' own epithelial cells found within the mouth, but few will accept the belief that their students have the intellectual capacity or social maturity to tackle issues and questions posed by the director who questions the enormous profits harvested by pharmaceutical companies and wonders who will benefit and who will lose from the technology. Yet fewer believe it is their role as a science teacher to get into such topics especially as they face the school, parental, and political pressures relating to pass rates on state tests.

Ironically, this belief that students are not sophisticated enough to comprehend the complexity of these deep moral and ethical conflicts is not so very different from the beliefs expressed by the researchers in the documentary regarding the capacity of the indigenous people to understand the technicalities of the science behind their project. In short the researchers say there's no point in explaining what they're doing for the locals couldn't understand or know what is meant by "cloning," "HLA Typing," or "DNA." As a consequence of this belief, the researchers do not even attempt to explain the real purpose behind their work. Instead, they mislead their subjects and try to convince them that they are on this humanitarian mission for the greater good of mankind.

In our view as teacher educators, this belief that "students can't handle it" is as pervasive as it is misguided. Duckworth (1996) describes a very similar problem in her chapter, "Either we're too early & they can't learn it, or we're too late & they already know it: The dilemma of 'applying Piaget.'" In essence, Duckwork argues that Piaget's work had shed tremendous insight into the cognitive development of children and rightly so. However, she continues her argument by saying that educators make a mistake when they assume that children are locked within academic brackets that are constrained by rather meaningless diagnoses of intellectual development (Duckworth, 1996). Such assumptions limit the instructional frameworks and potential learning situations to rather narrow exercises. Similarly, teachers all too often misapply Bloom's Taxonomy in the belief that "higher orders" of thinking must be preceded by "lower orders" of thinking. Such beliefs provide a rationale for educational practices that focus on "knowledge" and "comprehension" far more so than on those aspects of cognition that are conducive to critical thinking or critical stances (evaluation, synthesis, analysis, and application).

In retrospect to our initial question regarding the support for a genetic bank for endangered species, we have yet to hear our students raise clarifying and critical questions such as: Who would control the storage and access to such a bank? Who would benefit most from the endeavor? What are the incentives for those associated with the enterprise? If there are gains to be had in such an enterprise, then who are the winners (those on the upside of the gains) and who are the losers (those on the downside of the gains)? What are the potential unintended consequences of establishing such genetic repositories? Might, for example, the bank encourage invasive excursions into the more pristine parts of the world in a for-profit search for rare or endangered species much in the same way as poachers currently invade national and international preserves in search of ivory and other valuable biological artifacts (ranging from bird eggs to gall bladders)? Or, as Koepsell (2009) warns, might we forfeit our rights and identities as we know them to corporate greed? And we have certainly never heard the questions: What happened to those villagers after the scientist left? Were they left with nothing more than the knowledge that they may or may not have diabetes? What influence did this interaction with the westerners have on their culture, society, or way of life? For it is in our view that such questions represent ways of thinking, habits of mind, and critical orientations that are all too often absent among the science teachers we teach. However, we have found that we can use the documentary to foster discussions of the types of ethical and social justice questions that should indeed be considered as necessary when learning about genetics.

Unfortunately, dependent solely upon the questions recommended within sidebar notes to the teacher in nearly every textbook, instruction will remain limited to a generic set of questions regarding the engineering of human genetics. Drawing examples from a widely distributed biology textbook, those questions include: Should scientists try to make people taller or shorter? What might be the consequences if scientists clone a human being?, and Should biologists try to change human appearance (hair color, gender, etc) through genetic engineering? We note to the reader that we have yet to see connections between global corporations and their financial interests questioned—neither explicitly nor implicitly—in these sidebar notes. And the questions certainly do not address the concerns and questions that the general public might have about scientific studies in terms of access to data, knowledge, and full disclosure of intent/purpose and outcomes of research. And the questions needed to help students gain the knowledge intimately linked to political literacy and activist stances described by Hodson (2009) will surely not be found in the textbook. The knowledge of social, legal, and political systems within communities and the authorities and processes associated with science-based issues identified by Hodson (2009) must be obtained somehow else for students in classrooms we visit.

Resistance to the belief

We often have discussions in schools with teachers about moving away from textbook-driven instruction and getting students engaged in socially and personally relevant, meaningful issues and creating learning environments that promote a frame of mind among young adolescents wherein critical questions come naturally. In doing so, we ask teachers to resist the belief that their students are not capable of participating in the kinds of ethical issues we've raised above. And we talk about the success that schools in Chicago and elsewhere have seen using "authentic pedagogy" (Newmann & Associates, 1996). Newmann and his colleagues, we explain, use the term "authentic" to describe the type of teaching and learning associated with a high degree of intellectual quality found in successful schools. In such schools, the construction of knowledge, disciplined inquiry and value beyond school serve as focal points for evaluating instruction, while student outcomes ("authentic achievement") are measured by their creativity, meaningfulness, and intellectual integrity. Hence, authentic achievements require students to produce something new and express their ideas through "elaborated communication" in creations that have value beyond school.

We explore the possibility, for example, of getting students involved in a project like one recently highlighted in the *New York Times*. In that example, students from a high school in the city conducted a study of seafood restaurants from which they analyzed fish DNA using simple genetic fingerprinting techniques to determine whether consumers were actually eating the type of product being advertised on the menu. In the study, the students had found, indeed, that one quarter of the fish samples successfully identified through the techniques were mislabeled (Schwartz, 2008). In other words, people were being told they were buying (and eating) one type of fish, but in reality were paying for and eating something entirely different.

Alternatively, we might ask them to consider, for example, the work produced by students in High Tech High in California. Responding to local school conditions characterized by very low student engagement and low academic achievement, High Tech High School started as a charter school by a partnership of San Diego business leaders and educators. Today, the school is recognized as an exemplar school that engages, challenges, and gets students to succeed through high quality intellectual endeavors. Students in the science program, for example, recently produced an award-winning series of books on the ecology of the San Diego Bay system with forewords by esteemed scientists including Jane Goodall and E.O. Wilson (Students of The Gary and Jerri-Ann Jacobs High Tech High, 2007).

Or, we might share how students in lower Manhattan present the findings of their marine research projects conducted under the auspices of environmentalists at the River Project to the New York City Council and other public forums as they advocate for more protections for the Hudson River estuarine system.

Then again, we could share the example of a project in Yonkers, New York, wherein the students in elementary science classrooms across several schools in the district have begun an environmental study of the river systems in the area—a project funded by fines levied against a large business entity for dumping animal and human waste into the Bronx River. While advocates may or may not agree whether any of the above examples represent "resistance" education, the value in these examples is to open a discussion on a broader conception of the capacities and potential of young people. For often we find it necessary to challenge the rather narrow conceptions we encounter in the field by introducing them to models of education that are often quite unfamiliar to them.

Commonly, such discussions come to a point where a teacher will acknowledge the possibility that her students (at least some) might be able to do (or would like to do) some of the activist work provided in the samples above. We see this as a critical juncture in the effort to resist the belief that students "can't handle it." But it's also then that the teacher nearly always poses to us one of two problems. The first is that they would like to get their students more involved, but too many need much more work preparing for the Regents (the New York State Department of Education's high school assessment test). Typically, the supporting statement that time spent on anything but Regents preparation (i.e. test prep) will result in dismal performance on that year's test follows that point.

The reader should note that the schools in which we have these discussions are schools that historically have "poor performance" on the Regents (anywhere from

50% to 40% failure rates). They also have high dropout rates, poor attendance and low percentages of graduates attending 4-year colleges. To those teachers we reply with the question: And how well are the current instructional practices (Regents-preparation instruction) working? Are you getting more students to pass? The answer is generally found in the school report cards where pass rates generally remain stable despite the perennial efforts on test prep. In other words, it should be clear that doing more of the same is apparently not resulting in a different outcome. It is these teachers, we would argue, who are in need of a departure from traditional pedagogical practices.

The other position typically (though more rarely) expressed is that everything is going well and the current success on the Regents cannot be jeopardized. To those teachers we pose the question, Does the strong performance enable some wriggle room in the curriculum to explore instructional strategies that prepare students to think more critically, creatively and more meaningfully than required by the Regents?

And thus, having tentatively entertained a resistance to the belief that students lack the capacity or interest to engage in action-oriented, ethically bound issues, we see the teachers come to a point where they raise the fear that they risk irreparable harm (in terms of Regent scores) if they depart from the familiar—textbook driven—practices of instruction. And, through questions and dialogue, we urge them to resist that fear. For, especially in the case of those with exceedingly high "failure" rates, simply doing more of the same (using the same instructional strategies and constraining the role of both students and the teacher in a pre-scripted learning environment) and expecting different (better) results is clearly unreasonable (we avoid the term "insanity" that Albert Einstein had preferred to use in describing such behavior, although "inhumane" might be our second choice).

The subject of the discussion, hereafter, usually centers on concerns regarding how the teacher will be able to teach everything expected to be known in the course. This need for content acquisition is, after all, the proverbial three hundred pound gorilla in the classroom. That is, the teachers say there is a lot of science they know that students have to learn. Having been fully steeped in models of education that require extraordinary skills in memorization and recall, far too many science educators think that their own students need to learn what the teacher has learned. Furthermore, there is a perceived responsibility to teach students how to navigate through the system of learning science by developing listening, recording, and organizing information skills (these are generally taught through lectures). Through their own educational experiences they have, in fact, developed a belief that their content knowledge is deep enough and sufficient to teach the discipline to students. But we have found, in many cases, that such a belief should be challenged.

To illustrate our point, we share two vignettes from our interactions with high school chemistry teachers—one working in a school in the Bronx, NY, and two others taking part in a professional development workshop in a non-formal learning environment on nearby Long Island.

BELIEF 2: TEACHERS KNOW THEIR CONTENT WELL

Vignette 1: A compressed gas

One of the authors was working with one new chemistry teacher (we'll use the pseudonym, "Marie") in the Bronx, NY. She was very bright, articulate and working hard to create a classroom that promoted inquiry and engagement among her students. The only curriculum materials she was provided before being thrust in front of her class was a textbook. As with many new to the profession, this teacher's (and that of far too many experienced teachers as well) repertoire of teaching strategies was largely limited to lecture, worksheet-based small groups, and traditional (very) limited laboratories. On one particular occasion, she had asked for help in setting up investigatory "centers" in her classroom. She was planning on using the centers after an upcoming lecture instead of the usual whole-class laboratory exercise. She was hoping that the centers would help her struggling students learn the content that would be covered on the Regents. "Centers" are largely self-guided learning experiences generally designed to accommodate up to six students in various places around the room. While students work in these centers, the teacher's role is to move from group to group strategically asking questions about their developing understandings and skills. Marie wanted to focus on the Ideal Gas Law. The Ideal Gas Law is represented by the equation $PV = nRT$ where P = pressure, V = volume, T = temperature, n = the amount of the substance (i.e., the number of molecules) and R = a constant (a constant used in the typical science class is rarely explained let alone deduced). The big idea behind the Ideal Gas Law is that the pressure, temperature, and volume of an "ideal" gas are related; consequently, a change in one attribute has an impact on one or more of the others. She indicated that she would also be covering Boyle's Law (pressure and volume; $P_1V_1 = P_2V_2$), Charles's Law (Volume and Temperature; $V_1/T_1 = V_2/T_2$), and Gay-Lussac's Law ($P_1/T_1 = P_2/T_2$).

At one point in our conversation, Marie was asked whether she thought her students might become interested in exploring volume, pressure, and temperature of gases using the little canisters of compressed air. The canisters are sold over-the-counter as dust blowers for electronic equipment such as computers, keyboards, and printers. The canisters are relatively inexpensive ranging in size from 4 oz. to upwards of 20 oz. cans. It was suggested that students could design and conduct experiments to determine such things as the pressure of the gas stored inside the canister, the volume of the stored air (at standard atmospheric pressure), or whether a difference in cost per liter of gas is dependent upon canister size. Although Marie had trouble conceptualizing what those centers (and, indeed, the experiments themselves) would look like, she nonetheless expressed interest.

For one center, a large 5-gallon plastic container (like the one used for the office water cooler) would be filled with water and inverted into a pan of water. One end of a tube or hose would be inserted up into the container while the other end would be connected to the nozzle of the air canister. When the nozzle was pressed, the escaping air would bubble up through the inverted bottle of water, thereby getting "trapped" at the top. Marie expressed a measure of surprise with this plan for she had been wondering how we would ever "capture" the air inside the canister. For safety purposes, Marie was warned that the students should be cautious working with the compressed air containers as the expelled gas can feel very cold to the skin. This is when a very startled Marie said that I was mistaken. In fact, she said, the air will be very hot. After all, she continued, according to Gay-Lussac's Law, the temperature of a gas increases as you compress it. She was asked if she had ever used these canisters and, if so, if she had seen "ice" form when the nozzle was held too closely to the surface being cleaned. She had, but admitted being confused and therefore had decided to ignore the problem this phenomenon posed.

Vignette 2: A smelly gas

For a number of personal and professional reasons, we enjoy finding ways to take students (science teachers) outdoors for environmental-based explorations in math/science/technology. On one such occasion, the authors were trailing behind two high school chemistry teachers in an affluent school district on Long Island, New York. We were taking them and 15 other teachers on a trail alongside an inlet of the Long Island Sound to visit a salt marsh. We always like to listen to teacher-talk on such walks for one can learn much about current issues in schools. The two chemistry teachers were complaining about the poor performance of their students and the concerns they had about the upcoming state Regents exam. One teacher criticized his students' inability to solve stoichiometry problems (These are the problems that involve the determination of quantitative relationships between reactants and products in balanced chemical reactions. Determining the value(s) of the question marks to balance the equation: $?H_2O \; ? \; ?H_2 + O_2$ is one example of such a problem.). The other teacher expressed a similar concern and added that his students couldn't even draw Lewis Dot diagrams for covalently bonded atoms. Their gripes went back and forth for a while until one of them stopped to ask me what was that "horrible" smell. Asked whether the smell was familiar, they replied yes, but they still had trouble figuring it out. They were still confused even after being told that they were smelling hydrogen sulfide (H_2S), a common compound investigated in high school chemistry labs. At that point, we gathered the others (biology, chemistry, and earth science teachers) for a highly interactive, impromptu discussion of the chemical, physical, and biological decomposition processes occurring in the anaerobic environment of intertidal mud flats that surround the island on which these teachers live. The two chemistry teachers introduced at the beginning of this narrative finally came to understand why things smelled the way they did during low tide at the beaches they had been visiting since childhood.

Discussion of vignettes

These two narratives capture a common problem among all to many teachers. That is, they hold a deep belief that they really know their subject. Actually, however, their content knowledge is often limited (in the deep conceptual sense) and situated within a narrow context. On the surface, these bright, intelligent professionals appear quite well versed in their discipline, especially when observed in didactic modes of communication. Across the narratives, the teachers were quite (if not extremely) confident in their content knowledge. And all were struggling to get their students to learn what they "knew." But from an external perspective, the inability to apply knowledge, ideas and principles of the discipline to novel situations (i.e., problems that are not usually found within, nor provided by, textbooks or problems of heretofore unexamined phenomena outside the classroom) suggests a lack of expertise in dimensions of the discipline that extend beyond a body of facts and principles. This deficiency typically prevents the ability to transfer textbook knowledge to real-world settings. Among these teachers, the "content" that students are expected to master is constrained to the very same facts and factoids the teachers had to master as students themselves.

This focus on acquisition of content has been shown to promote epistemological orientations that are neither conducive to the development of deep conceptual understandings of the discipline nor meaningful learning (Schommer, 1990; Schommer & Walker, 1995). In a recent publication by the National Research Council (1999), *How People Learn*, much attention was paid to the importance of surface versus deep learning and the need to move science education toward learning for deep understanding. The NRC's position on the matter is supported by the findings of numerous studies examining the relationship between epistemological beliefs, conceptions of learning, approaches to learning, and learning outcomes (Bransford, Brown, & Cocking, 2000). According to Entwistle (1988), follow-up studies to research on conceptions of learning by Marton and Säljö (1976), led to a research that sorted the way people viewed learning into broad categories: (a) increase in knowledge (acquisition of knowledge), (b) memorizing, (c) utilization of knowledge, (d) abstraction of meaning, (e) interpretative understanding, and (f) self-Actualization.

Entwistle (1988) later examined links among approaches to learning (how learners proceed in completing a learning task), motivation, learning strategies, and outcomes. He describes three approaches to learning including surface, deep, and strategic. According to Entwistle (1988), surface learning can be linked to motivations centering on concern with completion of a course or fear of failure. The processes of learning (i.e., approaches to learning) used by learners with such motivations include using routine procedures to memorize facts and idea. In this approach, more passive learners generally end up with little or no understanding and are likely to be able to recall a few facts or details. More active learners, on the other hand, may have substantial knowledge of facts but superficial levels of understanding (Entwistle, 1988, pp. 46–47).

In contrast, deep approaches to learning are motivated by a desire to reach personal understanding. Under optimal conditions, learners seek relationships between ideas and supporting evidence. The learning outcomes, in part, include deep levels of understanding and the ability to construct evidence-based arguments. Collectively, the literature on conceptions of learning and approaches to learning strongly suggests that an instructional and curricular system focused on decontextualized acquisition of content knowledge leads to "little or no understanding"; learners who are "able to only mention a few unrelated facts or unimportant details" (Entwistle, 1988; Marton, 1988). Yet science education has a long, robust history of criticism for curriculum approaches that promote surface approaches to learning. As a consequence, we very often find graduates with substantial bodies of facts with little meaningful understanding. As Schmeck (1988), then Professor of Psychology, Southern Illinois University, wrote

> Teachers who hold shallow, quantitative conceptions of the learning process, defining it as some sort of accumulation of bits and pieces of information, are likely to make demands on students which teach them to define learning, to define their responsibilities as students, in a similar quantitative fashion....we have the students who leave the university physics or economics classes with passing or even high grades and yet have no understanding of the most basic concepts that lie at the root of the various facts and rules that they so successfully memorized. Similarly, we have adults who do not see it as their function to reflect, form opinions, evaluate, disagree, oppose, challenge, conceptualize and reconceptualize, or integrate information in meaningful ways. (p. 335).

Similarly, the teachers like those in the vignettes may have mastered their content to the degree that they can thrive quite well in text-book and test-driven environments, but they really have not created a meaning of their discipline for themselves. And, while some may be able to provide "real world" examples of ideas and principles within the discipline to students, they all too often cannot apply what they know to relevant novel situations outside the classroom. Expressed in cognitive terms, the teachers have not scaffolded their knowledge (facts and details) within their domain around big ideas and principles in such a way that they are able to use them to recognize analogous problems or generate creative solutions.

Conclusion

Any hope for meaningful adoption of resistance pedagogy in a discipline traditionally steeped in content acquisition through memorization and other superficial approaches to learning, we argue, rests within the educators' capacity to resist the widely held "vague quantitative conception" of learning promoted through non-reflective experiences and externally controlled expectations. Schneps and Sadler (1987) produced a film which still reverberates within the science education community. And that film holds lessons for all seeking to confront and resist negatively rooted belief systems. The film, *The Private Universe*, exposed the hidden, yet deeply held, belief systems people across all ages very often hold about how the phenomenological world operates. In the documentary, Schneps and Sadler (1987) explored the connections between these belief systems and their deleterious effects on learning science. Similarly, we see it as a fundamental responsibility on the part of science teacher educators to engage their wards in the process of introspection of their own personal "private universe" regarding conceptions of learning and teaching. For those conceptions—implicitly shaped by years of experience in schools—all too often constrain and limit their thoughts, ideas and practices as teachers. Both pre-services and in-service teachers would do well to sustain that process of introspection by continually questioning deeply held beliefs about what constitutes teaching and what serves as key evidence and/or indicators of meaningful learning. As science teachers in the classroom, there should also be resistance to the temptation to believe that the 1000-plus page textbook—whether handed to them by administrators or sold to them by some globalized publisher—is a curriculum and not a reference encyclopedia. Despite the pressures of the policy-makers and textbook industries to cover the content they expect, we science teachers must not allow our role to be limited to that of an organic text-to-speech machine. We argue that following such recommendations would constitute a profound form of resistance in education and likely open the door for more sophisticated forms of resistance pedagogy in science classrooms.

Our advocacy for an action-oriented, resistance education stance in the science classroom does not obviate the very real pressures K-12 teachers endure regarding student scores and test performance. Indeed, we fully acknowledge the potential risks and consequences teachers may face, particularly those working in schools with traditionally low achievement results on high-stakes tests. For many, poor test scores result in job insecurity or even job loss. However, we also recognize the risk of a Pyrrhic victory with the alternative. That is, we hope teachers would come to question whether the outcomes following a capitulation to a focus on content acquisition, didactic pedagogy, and test score outcomes (largely based on trivial knowledge) is worth the abandonment of efforts to make life and learning meaningful to the children with whom they work. It must be left to the teachers as individuals to discern and decide which entails the greater risk to themselves as professionals and to the society at large.

We also acknowledge that it is particularly easy to succumb to the political and economic pressures emanating from educational policies—particularly those designed to validate commonly held beliefs that high test scores: (a) are indicators of effective teaching, (b) ensure national security and global domination in the market place or, more ironically, (c) can create a more equitable and fair society of educational opportunities. But as Lowell and Salzman (2007), Bracey (2009), Berliner and Biddle (1996), and many others alongside them point out, the calls for higher and tougher standards and more rigorous tests are often tied to the political and economic advantage of an elite class.

Collectively, the advocates we cite above offer compelling evidence that there is no shortage of scientists and engineers in the United States. In fact, there is considerable unemployment of those in the field. Furthermore, international test score comparisons have little validity from a psychometric perspective. The policies founded on myths and misrepresentation that promote a science education aimed at creating a small, very elite pool of scientists at the expense of the failure of thousands of others must be resisted by practitioners in the field.

There must also be a commitment on the part of teachers to engage students in complex, controversial societal issues confronting our increasingly science and technology-based world. Teachers might, for example, consider ways to use controversial topics as the context for introducing content to students. This holds true for science teacher educators as well as for those teaching science below the university level. That is, for science teachers and their students, the ethical and social justice issues associated with the production and application of scientific knowledge should be at the forefront of the curriculum. Indeed, we would argue that one cannot disassociate the ethical and moral fibers from the fabric of the scientific enterprise and its knowledge frameworks if the aim of science education is to promote a citizenry (1) equipped to engage in debates surrounding science-based issues confronting society, (2) empowered with voice to participate in decision-making processes regarding the directions of scientific policies, and (3) predisposed to become active in social justice issues. Therefore, we agree with Hodson (2009) who writes

> The absurdity of some current science curriculum initiatives is that they utilize elements of the history, philosophy and sociology of science to show how scientific inquiry and scientific practice are influenced by the prevailing socio-cultural and economic context but do not use this understanding to politicize students. (p. 4)

Finally, we recommend that teachers continually search for like-minded science educators and community activists that can support collective explorations of ways to embrace the socially critical and political action goals found in action-oriented education (Stevenson, 2007) and to share experiences and lessons learned by such attempts. It is through the stories and discussion in this chapter that we attempted to do just that. Our work in schools as science coaches in very challenging urban schools has taught us that support communities are absolutely crucial to creating a counter culture of resistance to the current zeitgeist of education we view as standardizing, demoralizing, and rather meaningless. In those support communities we find teachers, administrators, and members of the broader community engaging in long-term, sustained discussions about science education reform. We see teachers and administrators solving problems in practice together, sharing classroom strategies and coming together during winter and summer institutes in a united effort to challenge the status quo.

We find hope in an expanding community of science educators seeking to use science education as a vehicle to tap into the vitality, creativity, and capacity of young minds to teach how the phenomenological world operates (science) in the context of understanding and solving the messy, technologically based problems brought about both inadvertently and intentionally by human design. We point to: (a) the web-based *Journal for Activist Science & Technology Education* (JASTE), (b) STEPWISE (Science and Technology Education Promoting Wellbeing for Individual, Societies & Environments), (c) Development Education Association (DEA), (d) The Living Knowledge Network's Science Shops, and (e) The Council of the Environment of New York City as a few of many, many models and resources which are out there and from which inspirations and ideas can be drawn. We have found groups and resources such as these, alongside a myriad of models in environmental education useful in expanding our vision of practical ways of integrating resistance models of education in knowledge rich, science learning environments.

To close, we do not consider the narratives and experiences with the teachers we've worked with and described earlier in this chapter to be anomalies to the profession. Indeed, for those grounded in the professional development of teachers, our stories may likely look very familiar. Hence, while we acknowledge the expansion in recent decades in the science of science learning, perhaps researchers and practitioners in the discipline can also expand the skills and knowledge base required to address the inhumanity that occurs as a result of that science education. As Scott Morris (2009) writes

> We make history and society, history and society make us, therefore we should be very careful about the kinds of history and society we make. Or, perhaps in language more Freirean: our being shapes our becoming, and our becoming shapes our being, therefore we should be very careful about what we become. (p. 4)

To that the authors would add that, as science educators and parents ourselves, we are concerned with what science—as it is typically taught in schools—has become for it is not very becoming indeed. Based on our time in classrooms over the past decade, science education in all too many classrooms appears to be perpetuating a generation of students very limited in their growth and development as active, motivated, creative and meaningful contributors of much-needed solutions to the science-based issues plaguing society today.

REFERENCES

Aronowitz, S. (2000). *The knowledge factory: Dismantling the corporate university and creating true higher learning*. Boston: Beacon Press.
Bencze, L. & Alsop, S. (2009). Anti-capitalist/pro-communitarian science & technology education. *Journal of Activist Science and Technology Education*, 1(1), 65–84.
Berliner, D. & Biddle, B. (1996). *The manufactured crisis: Myths, frauds and the attack on America's public schools*. New York: Longman.
Bok, D. (2003). *Universities in the marketplace: The commercialization of higher education*. Princeton, NJ: Princeton University Press.
Bracey, G. (2009, September). Nine myths about public schools. The Huffington Post: The Internet Newspaper. Retrieved December 2009 from http://www.huffingtonpost.com/gerald-bracey/nine-myths-about-public-s_b_298664.html
Bransford, J. D., Brown, A. L., & Cocking R. R. (2000). *How people learn: Brain, mind, experience, and school*. Washington, DC: National Research Council.
Carr, R. & Thésée, G. (2008). The quest for (Il)literacy: Responding to, and attempting to counter, the neoliberal agenda. In B. Porfilio & C. Malott (Eds.), *The destructive path of neoliberalism: An international examination of education* (pp. 173–194). Rotterdam, The Netherlands: Sense Publishers.
Dewey, J. (1916). *Democracy and education*. New York: The Free Press.
Driver, R., & Easley, J. (1978). Pupils and paradigms: A review of literature related to concept development in adolescent science students. *Studies in Science Education*, 5, 61–84.
Duckworth, E. (1996). *The having of wonderful ideas: And other essays on teaching and learning*. New York: Teachers College Press.

Duschl, R. A., Schweingruber, H. A, & Shouse, A. W. (2007). *Taking science to school: Learning and teaching science in grades K-8*. Washington, D.C.: National Academies Press.

Entwistle, N. (1988). *Styles of learning and teaching*. New York: Routledge.

Fang, Z. (1996). A review of research on teacher beliefs and practices. *Educational Research*, 38(1), 47–65.

Giroux, H.A. (2004). Pedagogy, Film, and the Responsibility of Intellectuals: A Response. *Cinema Journal*, 43(2), 119-126.

Hodson, D. (2003) Time for action: Science education for an alternative future. *International Journal of Science Education*, 25(6), 645–670.

Hodson, D. (2009). Putting your money where your mouth is: Towards an action-oriented science curriculum. *Journal of Activist Science and Technology Education*, 1(1), 1–15.

Hogan, T. & Craven, J. (2008). Disempowering the authority of science: Preparing students for a public voice. In L. Wallowitz (Ed.), *Critical literacy as resistance: Teaching for social justice across the secondary curriculum*. (pp. 65–84). New York: Peter Lang.

Holland, L. (Producer) & Taylor, I. (Director). (1995). *Gene hunters* [Documentary Film]. UK: Television for the Environment.

Jensen, K. & Murray, F. (2005). Intellectual property landscape of the human genome. *Science*, 310 (5746), 239–240.

Kegan, R. and Lahey, L. Laskow, L. (2001). The real reason people won't change. *Harvard Business Review*, 79(10), 85–92.

King, P. M. & Kitchener, K. S. (2004). Reflective judgment: Theory and research on the development of epistemic assumptions through adulthood. *Educational Psychologist*, 39(1), 5–18.

Koepsell, D. (2009). *Who owns you?: The corporate gold rush to patent your genes*. Hoboken, NJ: Wiley-Blackwell.

Lowell, L. & Salzman, H. (2007). Into the eye of the storm: Assessing the evidence on science and engineerying education, quality, and workforce demand. Retrieved October 2009 from http://www.urban.org/UploadedPDF/411562_salzman_Science.pdf

Martin, B. (2000). Directions for liberation science. *Philosophy and Social Action*, 26 (1, 2), 9–21.

Martin, B. (2006). Strategies for alternative science. In S. Frickel & K. Moore (Eds.), *The new political sociology of science: Institutions, networks, and power*. Madison, WI: University of Wisconsin Press.

Marton, F. (1988). Describing and improving learning. In R. Schmeck (Ed.), *Learning strategies and learning styles* (pp. 53–82). New York: Plenum Press.

Marton, F. & Säljö, R. (1976). On qualitative differences in learning: Outcome as a function of the learner's conception of the task. *British Journal of Educational Psychology*, 46, 115–127.

Morris, S. (2009, August 4). Literacy as resistance; Resistance as literacy: An essay review. *Education Review*, 12(9). Retrieved November from http://edrev.asu.edu/essays/v129index.html

Nagle, J. (2009, January 1). Becoming a reflective practitioner in the age of accountability. *Educational Forum*, 73(1), 76–86.

National Research Council. (1999). *How People Learn*. Washington DC: National Academy Press.

Newmann, F. & Associates. (1996). *Authentic achievement: Restructuring schools for intellectual quality*. Hoboken, NJ: Jossey-Bass.

Porfilio, B. & Malott, C. (Eds.). (2008). *The destructive path of neoliberalism: An international examination of education*. Rotterdam, The Netherlands: Sense Publishers.

Rogers, C. & Freiberg, H. J. (1969). *Freedom to learn*. Columbus, OH: Charles Merrill.

Schmeck, R. (Ed.). (1988). *Learning strategies and learning styles*. New York: Plenum Press.

Schmidt, J. (2000). *Disciplined minds: A critical look at salaried professionals and the soul-battering system that shapes their lives*. Lanham, MD: Rowman & Littlefield.

Schneps, M. & Sadler, P. (Producers). (1987). *A private universe* [Film]. U.S.A: Harvard-Smithsonian Center for Astrophysics, Science Education Department, Science Media Group.

Schommer, M. (1990). Effects of beliefs about the nature of knowledge on comprehension. *Journal of Educational Psychology*, 82, 498–504.

Schommer, M., & Walker, K. (1995). Are epistemological beliefs similar across domains? *Journal of Educational Psychology*, 87(3), 424–432.

Schwab, (1962). The concept of the structure of a discipline. *Educational Record*, 43, 197–205.

Schwartz, J. (2008, August 21). Fish tale has DNA hook: Students find bad labels. *New York Times*. Retrieved from http://www.nytimes.com/2008/08/22/science/22fish.html?_r=1.

Slaughter, S. & Rhodes, G. (2009). *Academic capitalism and the new economy: Markets, state, and higher education*. Baltimore, MD: Johns Hopkins University Press.

Spring, J. (2008). Research on globalization and education. *Review of Educational Research*, 78, 330–363.

Stevenson, R. B. (2007). Schooling and environmental education: Contradictions in purpose and practice. *Environmental Education Research*, 13(2), 139–153.

Students of The Gary and Jerri-Ann Jacobs High Tech High (2007). *San Diego Bay: A story of exploitation and restoration*. El Cajon, CA: Sunbelt Publications.

Wacquan, L. (1997). Three pernicious premises in the study of the American ghetto. *International Journal of Urban and Regional Research*, 21(2), 341–353.

Wagner, T., Kegan, R., Laskow Lahey, L., Lemons, R., Garnier, J., Helsing, D., Howell, A., Rasmussen, H.T., & Vander Ark, T. (2006). *Change leadership: A practical guide to transforming our schools*. San Francisco: Jossey-Bass.

CHAPTER THIRTEEN

Being at Crossroads

Resisting the Typical Conference Format to Rekindle Passions and Priorities in Science Education

JULIE M. KITTLESON & ROBERT J. CEGLIE

Fifty years following the post-Sputnik era, science educators find themselves in an eerily similar position to that described a half a century ago: there remains dissatisfaction about the state of science education. Beyond the golden years of science where funding for innovative curricula led to initiatives that fostered science as a necessity in our national curriculum, science has been struggling to maintain its position in schooling. The high-stakes testing and accountability movement has ushered in a new age of emphasis on reading, writing, and mathematics. Only recently has science become part of this accountability movement. In many states, science testing has just begun to become aligned with No Child Left Behind (NCLB) mandates. Therefore, science educators again find themselves playing catch up and grappling with questions about how to support classroom science instruction. The challenges, however, come in the form of elementary school classrooms in which science is de-emphasized in favor of increased time for literacy and mathematics and high school science classes that continue to focus on memorization of facts at the expense of critical thinking skills and inquiry skills that could promote a scientifically literate society. In the face of such challenges, it is important that science educators create opportunities to resist the status quo and examine their work and reflect on their goals both in terms of their commitments to local teachers and classrooms and their responsibilities to broader visions of science education.

Opportunities to reflect on overarching goals of science education can be rare, especially when one recognizes forces rooted in academia and acknowledges that science educators' efforts to respond to educational needs can be stifled by requirements that can dampen the interface between academic settings and school settings. Science educators who are employed by colleges and universities are accountable for institutional demands, such as publishing and maintaining a research agenda. Yet the emphasis on these institutional priorities may inhibit action in places where real change can occur, namely K-12 schools. One can provide service in a local school, but this is not necessarily a route to tenure. Thus, choices are made and in many cases intensive writing and focusing on publishable research become the priority. This, however, should not be an excuse for the dilapidated state of science learning in this country, nor should it absolve science educators of their responsibilities to public education.

In order for educators to find ways to hold ourselves accountable for the state of science education we need to see possibilities for combining our academic interests and our responsibilities to schools. In this chapter we discuss *Science Education at the Crossroads* (henceforth referred to as Crossroads), which is a conference that utilizes an alternative format and provides a venue in which science educators can reconsider the choices made between academic and community responsibilities. Crossroads has prompted discussions about what conference participants feel are pressing issues in science education both inside and outside the college walls. The conference supports such conversations by resisting and reconfiguring conference norms and establishing a context in which participants can explore their concerns about science education and learn about others' concerns.

Aside from being a context in which science educators can collectively explore their concerns, Crossroads also serves as a place where individuals can shed conference expectations and remember why we do what we do. It is important to reconsider what brought us to the profession in the first place and to reflect on our priorities because it is easy for priorities to shift during our indoctrination into academic norms. These norms, at times, work against our aspirations. Both authors of this chapter are science educators; we work in teacher education programs at different universities and are responsible for working with pre-service and in-service teachers. In our positions, we are expected to wear many hats and often become spread too thin and become frustrated with our place in the larger scope of promoting science literacy. We believe it is important to take opportunities to remind ourselves why we pursued, and believed in, science education in the first place. Conferences certainly play a role in initiating one into an academic community. Typical academic conferences provide a venue for showcasing one's work and learning about the work of others. They provide opportunities for networking and familiarizing oneself with the conversations taking place in the field. While these activities are valid, even necessary, for becoming part of the community, the formality of academic conferences is not always enough to rekindle one's passion. Although we appreciate what we gain from traditional conferences, we find it is important to have venues where we can have candid conversations that are not bound by norms associated with traditional conference settings. Crossroads provides this opportunity.

Crossroads was initiated in 2005 by two science educators (Adam Johnston & John Settlage) who saw and envisioned an alternative to traditional science education conferences. Their re-visioning was, in part, instigated by dissatisfaction with the limitedness of honest discussions and the absence of an appropriate venue to garner support of others in similar situations. In response, these science educators decided to establish their own conference and organize it around principles they believed would ease their dissatisfaction. The authors of this chapter have had the pleasure of watching the conference organizers' venture unfold over the past several years. From our vantage point, we have developed insights into how Crossroads itself is an act of resistance, as well as how Crossroads serves as a context that helps us resist the norms we find ourselves negotiating in our own academic lives. Further, Crossroads has provided us with a point of reference for reflecting on our personal and professional aspirations and how we go about meeting our goals while working within academia.

The first year, Crossroads participants were recruited by the conference organizers. The organizers' goal was to bring together approximately 40 science educators who would be open to sharing, listening, and offering critical feedback to other participants. Participants were asked to write a brief paper in which they articulated a success (i.e., an issue they felt was well understood by the science education community) and a vexation (i.e., an issue they felt deserved additional attention). The organizers were able to entice science educators from across the United States to take part in their experiment, and on a cold, rainy Sunday afternoon in Storrs, Connecticut, Crossroads participants convened on the campus of the University of Connecticut. These educators spent the next few days sharing concerns and ideas with one another. As the conference concluded, there was a sense that something different had happened, and the organizers committed to an iteration of the conference.

During subsequent years, conference attendees were solicited by the organizers as well as by conference participants. Thus, the role of selecting attendees was shared by the organizers and the participants themselves. Although a core of attendees has remained constant over the five years, many new participants have been recruited. The recruitment has been targeted toward people who have a strong desire to be open to the type of format and climate expected at Crossroads. After 5 years, approximately 100 different participants have attended. In addition, while the focus has been primarily on issues in science education, classroom teachers, principals, policy makers, informal educators, graduate students and others have attended, thus adding a cross pollination of stakeholders to the conference.

In order to attend Crossroads, each attendee is required to be an active participant. As such, each individual writes a two-page proposal which encourages participants to voice their successes and a related vexation related to their current career challenges. During the third year of the conference, the format changed slightly; participants were required to consider and write about a vexation and venture rather than a success and a vexation. In this way, the conference organizers challenged participants to articulate not only their concerns but also their ideas about how they planned to address this concern. Written proposals are funneled through the two conference organizers who provide significant feedback to each potential participant. This "review" process is designed to force people to move beyond their comfort zones and engage in a form of conversation that will provide critical and meaningful feedback to conference attendees. People do not come to Crossroads to remain in their stagnant situations; they come because they have been asked to attend. Participants have been nominated and invited as colleagues who are looking to make a difference in science education, beyond the traditional venues.

The distinguishing feature of the conference is format of the presentations or "sessions." Each session is called an incubator session and lasts for 75 minutes. During this time, the following format is followed:

- ~ Statement: Ten minutes for the presenter to describe the vexation/venture (without interruption)
- ~ Clarify: Five minutes for the participants to ask clarifying questions of the presenter (with responses from the presenter)
- ~ Incubate: Fifteen minutes for the participants to discuss the venture/vexation of the presenter (without any input from the presenter), and finally
- ~ Rejoin: Five minutes for the presenter to become un-gagged and respond, ask questions, and/or summarize what they've heard. (Settlage & Johnston, 2008)

After one individual presents, the second presentation begins. Thus, two presentations are given during the 75-minute period. The other conference attendees are not allowed to "jump sessions" as common at traditional conferences. In addition, all attendees are also participants and will offer their vexation/venture during the conference. This common shared experience fosters a sense of openness and creates a critical but safe environment for each individual to share his or her concerns. Although, we would like to believe that the participants come and are somehow able to rid themselves of the shackles of the ivy tower, we understand that this conference can only help to promote conversations, actions, and relationships that will offer support for meaningful change in science education. Regardless, the environment and type of support at this conference does offer something different. Something that we argue is lacking at traditional conferences.

Keynote speakers (particularly David Moss, John Settlage, & Adam Johnston) have molded Crossroads and introduced themes that serve as rallying points and anchors for conversations. In the following paragraphs, we describe three of the major themes that have been presented to Crossroads attendees.

One theme associated with Crossroads is *scholar activism*. Here we discuss how scholar activism was established during Crossroads, and then apply the idea to our own perspectives. In particular, we discuss scholar activism as a contrast to our standard partitioning of research, teaching, and service within the academy. This perspective urges us to reconsider the very purpose of our work as individuals and the structure within which we work as an academy. Next, we discuss how *pragmatism* was offered as a foundation to support the ambition of scholar activism at the individual level. Third, we discuss *orchestration* as a means by which we can collectively work together to effect change in our field. We offer these as new possibilities with which to structure cooperation—and offer a mode of resisting the norms in the academy—within our own discipline of science education, and possibly beyond.

At root, "the ideal of the scholar activism pivots around the drive to do something" (Settlage, 2006, p. 2). The conference proceedings make clear that Crossroads participants care about the work they do; the desire to do something meaningful is apparent in their words. Granted, the conference is intended to evoke the emotion tied to one's work. Nonetheless, it is powerful to learn about people's reasons for entering the field. When recalling his career path, David M. Moss, who was the keynote speaker at the first iteration of Crossroads, commented,

> Perhaps like many future academics, when considering career options I found myself drawn to professions that seemed to serve society in some small way. My childhood encounters with activism forged in me a sense of justice and leadership which has driven my professional ambitions. (Johnston, Settlage, Moss, & Carlone, 2008, p. 4)

Many contributions from Crossroads participants echo this sentiment. (All conference papers can be accessed in the Proceedings section of the Science Education at the Crossroads website www.sciedxroads.org) In one example, Felecia Moore (2006) pondered her "purpose" in the following:

> [T]his year at Crossroads, I want to present and discuss a diversity and social justice framework for teacher education. The framework is a work in progress. As I think more about my purpose for teaching and what I want to accomplish as an educator, the framework expands.

As I think about student learning in science as well as the role of teacher education, the framework expands. However, the expansions contribute more to the details, goals, and purposes of a framework that provides possibility and hope for new directions and new possibilities in science education that strongly considers issues of diversity.

During Malcolm Butler's (2007) first Crossroads experience he expressed hope that this conference might offer the type of "conversation" that could lead to improvements in science education for those who have traditionally been silenced. He writes

> I am cautiously optimistic that we as science educators will see our work as more than getting published in the best journals (which is important!), and truly see ourselves as the ones who can speak what we know to be true: *every* one of our children has what it takes to do well in science. But this cannot become a reality if we ignore any of them except at those times when we look at subgroups of data. I know there are other science educators and researchers that are doing and/or have a desire to do great work in this area. I and others welcome them to the conversation.

From these comments, it is evident that Crossroads participants see real purpose in their work, and they see real consequences of inaction. Both authors featured here deal with issues that deserve prolonged and evolving attention. Moore admits that her framework is in progress, and Butler encourages others to acknowledge science educators' responsibilities to all students and he invites others to join the cause. One of the benefits of Crossroads is that admitting that one's work is in progress and unfinished is acceptable and even encouraged, whereas at other conferences it is expected that one's work has progressed to the stage of developing conclusions. The issues raised by Moore and Butler, however, are ones that deserve attention and insight from many stakeholders. Thus, the acknowledged evolution of thought surrounding an issue coupled with the invitation for others to join the conversation creates a context in which matters can be further explored, hopefully with an eye toward action.

The Crossroad organizers have made a concerted effort to spread the word of this conference as a way to both recruit potential participants and also challenge the status quo in science education. During one such conference, David M. Moss articulated his desire to be involved in activism, and Moss acknowledged ways in which academia can work against these tendencies. However, Moss offered an alternative way of being an academic:

> I have perceived a growing movement in recent years to re-consider what it means to bring about impact. What has become clear to me is that the traditional notion of writing up research articles for publication is simply not sufficient in terms of advancing the idea of scholar activism. Thus, the notion of service through scholarship affords one the potential to both generate scholarly products which are indisputably the coin of the realm in acade-

mia while concurrently promoting change within and beyond the ivory tower by making our work accessible in non-traditional venues and better yet, directly engaging as change agents. This is particularly true for those of us who work on the field of education. There seems an endless list of issues, both big and small, which demand our immediate consideration. This may not be true for all scholarly pursuits, where a more traditional life of the mind does not leave pressing issues unattended. For professors of education, the life of the mind must be a catalyst for a life engaged. (Johnston et al., 2008, p. 8)

During the first iteration of Crossroads, Moss challenged conference participants to form their own SWAT team—that is, Scholars with Activist Tendencies. There was a palpable energy in the room following the talk. The following year, John Settlage again invoked scholar activism:

> The prospect of calling oneself a "scholar-activist" has the same energizing effect as the television character Xena may have experienced when labeled a "warrior-princess"—what a delicious juxtaposition of disparate roles. For both personas, the wise and regal is blended with justice and righteousness. Whether wielding a sword or a pen, the mightiness resulting from the unification of knowledge and action can be inspiring. (Settlage, 2006, p. 2)

A particularly noteworthy phrase in Settlage's passage pertains to the "energizing effect" of scholar activism. The entrée to academe and subsequent professional activities can make it difficult to look past the demands of one's work and appreciate the scope and complexity of our responsibilities. Being reminded that you can—and should—pay attention to such issues is refreshing. As powerful as the image of scholar activism may be, it is bolstered by its relationship to other themes associated with Crossroads.

A second theme associated with Crossroads is *pragmatism*. Drawing on Dewey, Settlage (2006) describes a pragmatic philosophy as one that joins ideas with action. Settlage fashions his vision in the following way:

> In order to better appreciate scholar-activism and the relationships among impulse, action, and re-direction, it would be useful to secure a conceptual tool that would give structure to thinking about these dynamics. In short, we should feel obligated to identify an intelligent framework for guiding our analyses. No other framework seems more appropriate, given the circumstances and voices already explored to this point, than pragmatism. (Settlage, 2006, p. 3)

With these words, the theme of scholar activism introduced during the first iteration of Crossroads was continued the following year with the push toward pragmatism. As described by Settlage (2006):

> Pragmatism is being offered as guiding principle to shape our professional actions just as a robust theory is meant to guide educational research. More than a platform to stand upon, these intellectual tools aid in the interpretive process. While research reports too often fail to articulate a theory there are equivalent dangers with undertaking activity without a clear

> sense of purpose. Education professionals ought to not only ground their work in an explicit framework but should draw upon it to interpret new information as projects move forward. Just as Dewey indicated, the desire, actions and consequences must work together. Desire suggests what we should do. But once that is hitched to intelligent purpose, then it becomes evident what it is that we must do. (p. 4)

Whereas scholar activism serves as a call to action, pragmatism provides structure to that action by appealing to a sense of purpose. Again, being reminded that science educators have a stake in something larger than themselves is rejuvenating. Additionally, it is important to remind ourselves that we do not have to act alone. It is perhaps no accident that the third iteration of Crossroads emphasized orchestration, which we will describe in a subsequent section.

With respect to pragmatism, during following years, a number of papers aligned with Settlage's call to pragmatism. One vivid example was offered by Jackie McDonnough, who tackled her concerns about teacher effectiveness. In her conference paper, she asks the Crossroads participants to help her answer a practical question: "Can I legitimately use teacher self-efficacy to measure the impact of using a combination of inquiry-based, culturally relevant science instructional strategies, classroom management strategies, and interpersonal relationship building skills?" (McDonnough, 2007, p. 64). McDonnough then outlined one way that she envisioned being able to address this issue.

A second example is taken from Maria Rivera Maulucci's paper, which dealt with her love of teaching. Questions she posed to Crossroads attendees were the following: "How can I attend to my current students' motivation to learn about social justice teaching? How can I foster opportunities for their questions to drive their inquiry into teaching and learning?" (Rivera Maulucci, 2008, p. 59) Along with a pragmatic perspective, Settlage also urged people to examine problems with a strong sense of purpose. In Rivera Maulucci's quote, her purpose is clearly articulated, and her presentation that followed offered the attendees proof of her strong commitment to issues of social justice.

Many other scholars seem to have taken the pragmatic theme to heart. Evidence of this has occurred through the types of papers that have been offered, as well as the atmosphere that emanates through Crossroads. Although we offer two examples of how participants have incorporated this theme, many other individuals have embraced this idea.

A third theme is *orchestration*, which serves as an invitation to collaborate. The issues facing education are far too great for any one person to address, particularly given the multiple dimensions of schooling. We may accomplish more if we create a collective voice. Crossroads is a setting that fosters collectivity. Johnston (2007) describes orchestration in the following way:

> David and John [the previous keynote speakers] have riled up the Crossroads contingent to be active, to do something, to create ventures that effect change and are personally meaningful. At the same time, we come together as a group. To me, the most natural "next step" is to consider how we can create and coordinate collective efforts. Surely there is something to be gained by connecting our individual experiences and initiatives to one another, if not unifying them in some way. (p. 3)

Hearing that others are concerned with the similar issues and are working toward similar goals fosters a sense of solidarity among participants. Building this sense of community helps combat feelings of isolation that can emerge when attending to the details of research. In sum, Crossroads provides a context for science educators to view their work differently and to have honest conversations about our aspirations and responsibilities. While this venue does not ensure collective action leading to radical change, it at least draws attention to our collective struggles and possibilities for action.

The theme of orchestration or collaboration has been evident through many new relationships that have been formed through Crossroads participation. The unique structure and format of the conference have led to relationships that may have never been created otherwise. One participant from the last year's conference expressed a similar idea when she noted, "I gained knowledge that will benefit me professionally through conversations with conference participants. For example, I was able to speak with [another conference participant] about the Noyce Scholarship program during lunch one day."

In a second example one participant believed he had gained a valuable resource through collaboration with other participants. He noted, "My incubator session was very helpful in both providing suggestions specific to the work and identifying people who may be willing to help."

Finally, one participant commented:

> [Crossroads] facilitated the possibilities of collaboration by allowing me to share what I know about some things. It made me feel like I knew some things too. I am planning on collaborating with another Crossroads participant who I met at the conference. Combining our areas of expertise [which were shared aloud at Crossroads] should prove beneficial to both of us and the discipline.

These examples are just a handful of instances when participants specifically discussed collaboration. Since one of the primary goals of Crossroads is to bring together scholars who are interested in promoting change, new collaborations are an important.

As mentioned, entering and persisting in academia do not always leave room for reflecting on science educators' roles and responsibilities. The typical tenure process requires faculty to attend and present at multiple national or international conferences per year. Conferences a science education faculty member would attend include National Association of Research in Science Teaching (NARST) and American Educational Research Association (AERA), Association for Science Teacher Education (ASTE), and National Science Teachers Association (NSTA). In addition to attendance, a formal presentation is required which necessitates the writing of proposals and preparation of presentations. These efforts require an extraordinary amount of time in preparation and time away from other faculty duties. The irony lies in the type of benefit achieved through presentation and attendance. These conferences are generally not set up to promote meaningful conversation but rather offer an avenue to disseminate research findings. Those who want to seek out meaningful conversations at these large conferences must find ways to get away from the conference and find colleagues who are busy coming and going to presentations.

One solution to mitigate the lack of meaningful conversation at these national conferences is to only attend smaller conferences which will offer more opportunities to converse with other attendees. The catch involves the fact that local or regional conference participation is not seen as important to the tenure process. Thus, the "tenure rules" end up discriminating against meaningful opportunities for faculty to collaborate and learn about others' work.

The second negative factor concerning the influence of tenure relates to the type of academic writing that is required. Multiple publications per year in top-tier scholarly journals are expected. *Science Education* and *Journal of Research in Science Teaching* are generally considered the most prestigious science education journals and typically have very low acceptance rates. To be published in top-tier journals, a research article needs to be working off a substantial research agenda which allows for multiple publications. These types of studies may require external funding through grants or collaborations which provide substantial research findings to allow publication. This has the real potential to limit the scope of studies which may be conducted. For example, a small local study designed to promote social responsibility issues in science education may be unlikely to offer a broad enough collection of data to be accepted in a top-tier journal. These examples may be overgeneralizations, yet they are what science education faculty are aiming for. These aims may be at the expense of more creative, more personal and meaningfull, and smaller scale studies which are more relevant to the researcher but do not have the appeal to a national audience. Thus, the case can be made that rigorous research can define the type of research decisions faculty make, moving against efforts that an individual may deem more important to his/her local issues.

As junior faculty, we believe that in order to ensure our success in academia in research-oriented universities we must follow in the footsteps of our predecessors.

Risk taking is generally unrewarded, especially in a field were the need to increase student achievement is so critical. One option for faculty is to move to a teaching institution, where the research demands are less rigorous. However, even at these institutions, research is becoming a more important part of one's role. This is in addition to high course loads, and service to the college and community. One may be able to become more engaged in the local school communities which may lead to direct positive outcomes in student learning, but this information may be hard to quantify and even more difficult to disseminate without the types of resources that exist at larger research universities.

Our mission as educators is to use our knowledge and skills to provide improved learning opportunities for all children. Our special interests, notwithstanding our goals, are to be leaders. As scholars in our respective fields, our mission should be to combine our knowledge and leadership abilities to promote change in our local, regional, national, and international world. Using the themes describing Crossroads, we articulate how the conference has challenged us to view our roles differently.

In the following sections, we describe our own experiences at Crossroads and reflect on how the conference has shaped how we perceive our roles and responsibilities.

Julie's perspective

Several years ago I was enticed to write a conference paper that was like none I had written before. The crux of the paper involved articulating a "success" (i.e., an issue in science education I felt had been addressed in a useful manner) and a "vexation" (i.e., an issue pertaining to science education with which I was concerned or an issue I felt science educators were still puzzling over). For the success portion, I wrote that I felt science education researchers had built a knowledge base describing effective teaching and learning. For the vexation portion, I wrote that I was concerned that what we know about effective teaching and learning may be washed out by policy decisions, an issue that seems pressing if science educators have some degree of responsibility for public education. At root, my concern was about the apparent divide between research and policy. I wrote

> One of the things I wonder about is how the emphasis on accountability—and we will face this in science in the next few years—will shape science teaching and learning practices. In a worst-case scenario, it could be that measures of science learning will be based on overly simplistic representations of students' understandings of science. This is troubling given what we know about the complexities associated with science teaching and learning. We can hope that the emphasis on accountability will not force us to step away from what we believe to be our best practices. But if we fear that accountability measures threaten what we deem to be productive teaching and learning practices, what are we prepared to do about it? (Kittleson, 2005, p. 39)

When I wrote my first Crossroads paper I was nearing the end of my doctoral program. I believed, and still do believe, that my graduate programs helped me appreciate the scope of science education research as well as helped me understand broader conversations informing science education. I found that articulating a "success" and a "vexation" forced ideas about science education, responsibility for public education, and the role of policy to coalesce. The format of the Crossroads paper—one that strayed from the conventions of an academic paper—prompted me to synthesize ideas in a way I had not done earlier. Further, the ideas with which I was wrestling were ones that were not directly connected to the research I was pursuing. Since Crossroads was a conference where people could showcase struggles rather than findings I knew I could ask people to engage in the conversation even though I did not have many answers to offer. Reflecting on that first Crossroads paper reminds me that I still have the many of the same concerns. Further, I find myself returning to these ideas as I think about my current work.

My enduring image of Crossroads is of John Settlage standing in front of the audience and telling them that the conference could be a place where each person could pull out his or her superhero cape, shake it out, and put it on again. He reasoned that the people at the conference had entered science education because they had a desire to make a difference (thus the superhero cape). Despite these desires, we too easily get caught up in the demands of any given day, whether it be teaching, advising, program restructuring, and so forth. These demands have a tendency to cloud our visions of why we do what we do. Sometimes we need to be reminded of what we believe in and why we pursued the line of work we chose to pursue. Sometimes we need to see that other people in our profession share our concerns, and sometimes we need to hear about the challenges that other people face. Many conferences do not foster these kinds of conversations because they are intended for something else; they are places where people are expected to share research findings. Such conferences have an important place in academic work but so do conferences in which people have opportunities to discuss unfinished ideas and spaces to voice concerns about the work that we do (or could do). As educators, we ask our students to be reflective practitioners. It is reasonable to expect the same from ourselves, but sometimes doing so requires us to resist the tendencies that occupy our academic lives. I have found Crossroads to be a conference that forces me to be reflective in a way that other conferences do not, and I appreciate being reminded that I need to be reflective.

Rob's perspective

I began my Crossroads experiences as a first year doctoral student. In fact, my first proposal was written when I was in my final months of high school teaching.

Thus, my first conference experience was participating in the 2006 iteration of Crossroads which occurred just a few months after starting my doctoral program. I did not know what to expect because I had never participated in a conference, nor had I imagined that this is what a conference was like. Much to my regret, the majority of my other conference experiences have been disappointing. My overall perception of the traditional conference is that it serves the purpose of padding one's vita but does not offer the type of support needed (particularly as a novice researcher) to engage in true scholar activism. Traditional conferences lead to a continuation of the status quo, whereas I began to see the Crossroads experience as a call to resist the norms in academia.

My three years of active participation in Crossroads has mirrored my transformation into a scholar. During my first year, I was beginning to transition into the world of the academy. I found the move to be dramatic but found a support group at Crossroads that helped to guide me. Since many fellow participants had similar background experiences, I found comfort in the personal stories that people shared. I felt that I found a community that I could confide in. My second year was a turning point in my academic career, as my vexation/venture was a presentation of my early ideas about my dissertation study.

I had spent what seemed like a lifetime living the life of a successful student, but I began to consider what factors had given me such a success. With much probing, I questioned my position as a successful white male in science. Could my gender, race, and socioeconomic status be the major contributors to why I had been successful in science? More importantly, as I began to recognize disturbing trends of those who were not "successful" in science, I looked for reasons for this phenomenon. In my venture I asked, "[W]hat can be done for these students who have already been derailed from science?" (Ceglie, 2007, p. 27) With the help of other Crossroads colleagues, I was steered toward an investigation of the construction of science identities among those who established success in science.

After extensive questioning, critiquing, and challenging by the collective group of Crossroads participants, I left those few days with a different perspective of what leads to success, who defines success, and how my role as a researcher can make a difference to those aiming for success. In addition, and perhaps more importantly, I left with a completely different outlook on my place as a researcher. Since my proposed study was to investigate the experiences of minority women in science, I needed help situating my place as an outsider. My Crossroads colleagues were able to lend a critical ear and push me to conduct this research in a much under-researched area.

I contend that my personal experiences at Crossroads have shaped my development as a scholar. I arrived at my first conference as a naive newcomer into the academic world and was supported by a collective group of gracious scholars. As a new doctoral student, I was welcomed by this small community of educators. I never felt that my ideas were unappreciated or naive or my experiences unimportant. Instead, Crossroads participants encouraged me to follow my areas of inquiry regardless of what traditional practices exist. This is very different from how I have felt at other conferences, where individuals counseled me on ways to look for opportunities to add lines to my vita. Crossroads offers a safe place to allow one to be vulnerable and take risks and to push against the traditional norms of academia. Although my experiences have not have been as dramatic as some others who have attended, I am confident that I would have been unable to progress as a scholar at such a rapid pace. Collectively, the Crossroads experience has instilled a hope that I can make a difference in science education.

In this chapter we described *Science Education at the Crossroads* as a conference that offers an alternative to typical academic conferences, and we offered this conference as an example of resistance. We see Crossroads as example of resistance because, in contrast to other academic conferences, it is a context in which participants can discuss ideas and/or projects that are not yet concluded and can expect open and honest feedback from others who are concerned with similar issues. Further, the spirit of Crossroads is one in which scholar activism, pragmatism, and orchestration have been fostered as a way to invite participants to share their successes and struggles with others in the hopes of finding ways to forge new alliances to address what are perceived as pressing issues in science education. While Crossroads will never replace traditional conferences, it is valuable for providing a context in which science educators can have conversations that may not fall within the purview of other conferences. As such, Crossroads represents a site at which science educators can resist norms that often constrain their efforts. Sites such as these are vital for reflecting on the state of our work and the ways in which we are and are not responsive to the needs of communities with which science educators intersect, such as school communities.

On a personal note, both of us were "raised" (academically speaking) with Crossroads as part of our professional repertoire. We have been able to see the contrast between conferences such as Crossroads and other science education conferences. While we recognize that Crossroads will never supplant the conferences we need to attend for our professional well being, we acknowledge that Crossroads has been an important part of our academic identity formation. It has provided us with a network of science educators we may not have otherwise found, and the intersection of these different people pushes us to consider issues in new ways. Thus, for us Crossroads has served as a training ground for considering how our work in science education can fit with our desires to make a difference.

A question remains, however, about the long-term impact of conferences such as Crossroads, particularly when so many university-based science educators rely on traditional conferences in order to build their reputations and vitae. Promotion and tenure guidelines are likely not going to go away, so there is risk associated with deviating from recognized conferences. We do not suggest that science educators should abandon the responsibilities expected by their universities. Nor do we believe that Crossroads alone can support an individual's ability to resist the norms that confine their work. The support and networking offered through Crossroads, however, may promote benefits for participants. Many past participants have discussed how the Crossroads experience rejuvenates their commitment to causes that go beyond their typical university work. It is in this sense that Crossroads allows participants to resist norms that are taken for granted in traditional conferences and see different possibilities in their work. While Crossroads has succeeded in attracting a number of participants, it is unclear whether it would serve the same function if taken to scale. Rather, a niche that Crossroads serves is establishing an intimate setting that fosters listening, conversation, and commitment to issues with which science educators deal. Larger conferences, by nature, include a greater array of interests and agendas, and this situation can make conversations unwieldy. Thus, it is important to recognize Crossroads for what it has to offer—a unique setting in which science educators can come together and share ideas and expertise without being bound by norms of our typical conferences.

REFERENCES

Butler, M. (2007). The invisible science educator. In J. Settlage & A. Johnston (Eds.), *Proceedings of the Science Education at the Crossroads Conference (pp. 18–19)*. Amherst, MA: National Science Foundation [Available online at www.sciedxroads.org/proceedings2007.html].

Ceglie, R., (2007). Why science? Trying to find and define a science identity. In J. Settlage & A. Johnston (Eds.), *Proceedings of the Science Education at the Crossroads Conference* (pp. 26–27). Amherst, MA: National Science Foundation [Available online at www.sciedxroads.org/proceedings2007.html].

Johnston, A., (2007). Orchestrations of science education adventurism. Keynote address given at the Science Education at the Crossroads Conference, Amherst, MA, Sept. 24.

Johnston, A., Settlage, J., Moss, D., & Carlone, H. (2008). *Perspectives of Scholar Activism, Pragmatism, and Orchestration in Science Education*. Symposium presented at the annual meeting of the National Association for Research in Science Teaching, Baltimore, MD. March 30–April 2, 2008.

Kittleson, J. (2005). Responsibility in the Face of Accountability. Paper presented at Science Education at the Crossroads, Storrs, CT, Oct. 9–11.

McDonnough, J. (2007). Measurement of tacher effectiveness: Can it be done? In J. Settlage & A. Johnston (Eds.), *Proceedings of the Science Education at the Crossroads Conference* (pp. 64–65). Amherst, MA: National Science Foundation [Available online at www.sciedxroads.org/proceedings2007.html].

Moore, F. (2006). Mapping the diversity and social justice landscape. In A. Johnston & J. Settlage (Eds.), *Proceedings of the Science Education at the Crossroads Conference* (pp. 52–53). Ogden, UT: National Science Foundation [Available online at www.sciedxroads.org/proceedings2006.html].

Rivera Maulucci, M. (2008). Where's the love in teaching and learning? In A. Johnston & J. Settlage

(Eds.), *Proceedings of the Science Education at the Crossroads Conference* (pp. 58–59). Alta, UT: National Science Foundation [Available online at www.sciedxroads.org/proceedings2008.html].

Settlage, J. (2006). *Prospects of Pragmatism: The Generation of Science Education Adventurists*. Keynote address given at the Science Education at the Crossroads Conference, September 28–30, Ogden, UT.

Settlage, J., & Johnston, A. (2008). *Communities of Learning, Practice, and Scholarship: Applying Social Learning Systems Theory to an Association of Educational Stakeholders*. Paper presented at the annual meeting of the American Educational Research Association, New York, NY. March 24–27.

CHAPTER FOURTEEN

Should We Teach Resistance?

DAVID M. MOSS

"RESISTANCE IS FUTILE"

Fans of the science fiction genre will immediately recognize this statement as stemming from the *Star Trek Next Generation* television series. The overall narrative is a familiar one—essentially good versus evil. In this instance, an aggressive alien super species of technologically enhanced humanoids seeks total galactic domination by assimilating other worldly inhabitants into their own collective consciousness. Basically, think really nasty space people wanting to take over the known galaxy. Enter the human species—just in the nick of time—as a civilization who has the moral authority, tenacity, and clever means to resist such bad behavior from beyond. Although the demoralizing mantra of the aggressors is made abruptly clear (*resistance is futile* is heard again and again throughout this series of episodes), when notions deemed "right" and "worthy" are in jeopardy, it is made apparently clear that we have the unambiguous obligation to make our stand against such forces.

BUT DO WE?

Normative issues are portrayed as fairly straightforward in the *Star Trek* series, you have little question regarding the moral authority of the Enterprise crew to resist—

at all costs—the unruly behavior of these galactic invaders. To drive home the point, even the appearance of these creatures, with their ponderous gait and sinister looking armor, leave little doubt this species needs to be dealt with in a serious way. Perhaps that's what makes good science fiction—people seem to need to know where everyone stands—at least by the end of the story. Although our Earth-bound reality may seem a bit hum-drum at some level when compared to the escapism fantasy of science fiction, it turns out our real world is much more complicated and interesting when it comes to right and wrong—and what we should do about it. Maybe, in part, that's why this genre is so popular. You know where you stand and your decisions regarding how to respond to such events seem apparent. And it's nice to be the hero every now and again.

In our own reality—especially within the context of formal education—the good guys and bad guys rarely come with such overt markers as nasty laser blasters (phasers for the real fans). In fact, in consideration of the overall field of education, one might argue most professionals are working on behalf of students and society at some level, it's just that we have differing experiences, perspectives, and agendas that dictate the focus of our efforts.

Most educators I know have been drawn to the field by some sense of social consciousness. This is even true for those pre-service teachers just applying to our teacher education program at my university who note in their admission interviews that "giving back" and assuming responsibility for social change is a primary reason for considering teaching as their life's work. In part, Giroux (2004), describes this as "...active participation in the very process of...engaging important social problems" (p. 124).

That is, educators often view their work as purposefully addressing issues of social justice. Thus, we—as educators—should be strategically evaluating and assessing our professional circumstances to see where our efforts may be best directed to either resist or advance certain agendas. These ideas of opposing and supporting are very much intertwined. As noted in the introduction of this book, resistance in education creates, or reflects, the multiple counter-discourses that arise to challenge the one or more dominant discourses in any given educational setting. To resist something is to advance something else.

So we are left pondering the complexity of the countless issues underpinning public education and the systems designed to support or oppose it. Where do we turn to begin to unravel the questions of when and how we should resist oppressive and unjust practices? As routinely portrayed in fictional narratives, will an effective course of action present itself such that we can merely follow our apparent destiny?

Unlikely.

Our actions must be planned and purposeful.

Interestingly, a shared reality exists between many fictional stories and public education in that weighty dilemmas and decisions, often with very serious consequences, are commonplace. That is, typical plot narratives are brimming with obstacles to overcome, while in a typical day in the *real world* of education such challenges are also routine. Educators in the midst of instructional time lack the luxury of extended periods for contemplation when facing such challenges. Thus, we must rely upon that which we have at our immediate disposal. We must invoke our *value and belief systems* along with our experiences in the moment to moment consideration of our actions. All too often, when facing the need for resistance and/or advocacy, we look outward to gauge our responses. In fact, much of education is designed to focus outwardly on others. Schools and schooling serve many masters. School boards, administrators (local, state, and national), parent groups, and imposed standards from a host of organizations all have remarkable sway on the autonomy of teachers. In contrast, the notion of turning inward demands we know a little something about ourselves and trust that as a valid source of guidance. In my own professional practice, such a focus on *self* is paramount. In my role as a director of a study abroad program which places pre-services teaching interns overseas in urban schools throughout London, England, I emphasize the notion that although one travels abroad to experience other cultures and norms, the real value of such a program is learn about one's own culture and oneself. Gomez (1996) nicely articulates the interplay of others and self in teacher education:

> Among the most promising practices for challenging and changing pre-service teachers' perspectives was their placements in situations where they became the "Other" and were simultaneously engaged in seminars or other ongoing conversations guiding their self-inquiry and reflections. (p. 124)

However, it is Hall (1998) who states most succinctly the ultimate need to look within:

> *Culture hides much more than it reveals and, strangely enough, what it hides, it hides most effectively from its own participants.* Years of study have convinced me that the ultimate purpose of the study of culture is not so much the understanding of foreign cultures as much as the light that study sheds on our own. (p. 59, italics in original)

The notion of self in these examples is not synonymous with selfish behavior, it is more aligned with the idea of being informed regarding your own knowledge and belief systems as a guiding principle for your decisions and actions. Ultimately, it is not merely external demands that should drive our decision making but our perceptions and values as they relate to a given context which should guide one's actions. If and when we resist in a given context should, to a large extent, be a value judgment we make grounded in our own sense of equity and what we deem to be an appropriate response.

For me, being a child of the sixties has undoubtedly influenced my perceptions of the world. The notions of resistance in many ways are synonymous with this time period in American history. My first brush with activism—and all that it may invoke—came as a small boy, specifically at my father's college graduation, there were soldiers stationed on the roof of the building adjacent to the ceremony. It was not until years later that such memories prompted a question or two for my parents, and I learned that this ceremony took place shortly after the killings at Kent State in the spring of 1970. My next encounter was more experiential and came when I was in high school. Along with my best friend I wanted to take a stand against what seemed a lack of policy or diplomacy with regard to what was known as the Hostage Crisis in Iran. We planned a school-wide walk out to begin in the passing time between classes. Talking it up with our peers in the days prior, we envisioned bursting out the front doors of the school and rallying at the flag pole, chanting slogans borrowed from the evening news. However, words travel fast in high schools, and we found ourselves called to the principal's office shortly before the planned walk out. I'm still encouraged by the response of the administration as we calmly sat in the school office and received supportive logistical advice to ensure no one would be injured and were even offered names of a few teachers who might like to say a word or two. Although the protest lost its edge of being a rebellion per se, for a brief moment as a teenager I felt as if I had a voice and could perhaps make a difference.

My childhood encounters with activism forged in me a sense of justice and leadership that has driven my professional ambitions. Articulating a sincere interest in a career in which I could engage in work that was meaningful to me, a mentor of mine explicitly steered me to life in the academy. That feeling of making a difference has stayed with me all these years and in no small way helped me find my path to the professoriate. Embedded deeply within the program which I teach in the Neag School of Education at the University of Connecticut are the ideals of leadership and change agency. At the core of our teacher education program are the following ideals (see Moss et al., 2005 for a complete program description):

1. A liberal education promotes tolerance, welcomes diversity, celebrates human ingenuity, encourages critical thinking, provides knowledge, and fosters creativity. It helps students place themselves in a context, to see what has come before and, most importantly, what might emerge in the future. Teachers who lack a strong liberal arts background and a firm grasp on what they teach all too often find themselves trapped by the standard curriculum—unable to use their own knowledge to expand upon and enrich the experiences of students. They teach what they are told to teach, unable or unwilling to advocate for changes that better serve their students.

2. Subject-specific pedagogy is essential for a program of teacher education. Students must be aware of specific beliefs and practices unique to their chosen disciplines. An understanding of the nature of science is necessary in the context of science education, just as an awareness of the competing theories and techniques underlying writing instruction is imperative for the informed and effective teaching of English. These two notions of a broad liberal arts education combined with subject-specific approaches to teaching and learning serve as the foundation for the capstone year of our program. While the first two years of our program focus on learning and teaching respectively, the final year is dedicated to leadership. It is in this year that ideas underpinning resistance are brought to the forefront—and ostensibly taught.

To that end, course work focuses on the nature of the teaching profession and explicitly encourages reform-minded thinking. The students read and reference the works of key theorists in education—Dewey, Noddings, Freire, and a host of others. They and their classmates explore answers to such questions as "What does it mean to be a professional educator?" "How can teachers reclaim the power they have lost, as evidenced by popular perceptions of teachers and reduced autonomy?" and "What is the role of research in the educational community?" As noted in Moss et al., (2005):

> They explore how the action research process might help teachers reflect upon and improve their practice, as well as empower them as decision-makers capable of bringing their own agendas, grounded in their good research, to the table. (p. 82)

We want our students to serve as teacher leaders—as educators willing and able to elicit real change in their schools and communities. We want them to be empowered, to recognize, and feel comfortable knowing that they have both the tools and obligation to advocate for reform. Thus, in response to the title of this chapter (Should We Teach Resistance?), my resounding response is "YES!," but many issues remain regarding how to do this in an effective and respectful manner.

Various chapters in this book have specifically dealt with the notions of resistance and activism. For many, these notions exist as sort of cousins. For me, they are more like twins as I see the need "to act" as an essential component of resistance. But as noted earlier, against whom we resist and for what reasons often remain ethically and logistically challenging. As I have briefly described, our teacher education programs at the university are directly and explicitly designed to foster leadership for the reform of public education. We make use of school-based research as an avenue into such territory. The seminars, theoretical course work, and clinic experiences are all designed to foster reflective thinking by our teacher candidates.

That is, they are crafted to promote thinking about oneself and one's role in the vast milieu of the educational enterprise. As noted, the notion of self and one's beliefs should be the jumping off point for considering one's actions. On the surface, our program is successful, at least as measured by our graduation and retention rates and anecdotal stories where we hear and see from the field. At the time of the writing of this chapter, we as a faculty are considering significant revisions to our teacher education program. More courses, different courses, new schools, etc...there are numerous decisions to be made. I have argued that prior to any logistical or structural planning, we need to ensure that our conceptual house is in order. My primary issue in this regard centers around the notion of explicitly living the life we espouse as the foundation of our newly designed program.

From the comfort of the so-called ivory tower, even a publically funded one, it is all too easy to lose a direct and meaningful connection with why we choose this profession in the first place. If a social consciousness was an underlying factor, as it was for so many of us, we need to return to that root commitment to ensure we serve as the best role models for our students. In fact, I believe that modeling the notions of activism and resistance are perhaps are best pedagogical tools to teach these ideals. Sure, syllabi and program design are important, but it is faculty who breathe life into such static documents. It seems many of us in higher education have strayed from this path of action beyond the core necessities of keeping a program up and running. We balance teaching, research, and service, but to what end?

If one were to believe the cable news networks, all university faculty are ultra-liberal spies, with the mission of recruiting generations of college students to our cause. (Zipp & Fenwick, 2006). In fact, although there are most certainly differences among disciplines, the overall trend in recent years has been a move toward the ideological center by college faculty. Regardless of one's ideological path, modeling not merely a life of the mind, but a life engaged is of paramount importance. Moving beyond the implicit messages often communicated to our students (which is perhaps why professors are often considered subversive in certain circles), I support placing those "cards of activism" face up on the table for all to see.

Academia as a profession has a rich tradition that is often misunderstood by the general public (Graff, 2003). Pure research, that which is done for its own sake, is the foundation for new knowledge and is likely a distinctive product of our humanity. We are curious, and this curiosity feeds our pursuit for understanding, sometimes without any need for a particular application (Lightman, 1996). This same characteristic likely spurs our species to create works of art, perform symphonies, and write plays. However, in a society when certain needs (education, equity, health care, etc.) are compelling and urgent, *only* pursuing knowledge for its own sake may be a luxury derived at the expense of engaging in something more critical. In academia, our system for educating graduate students, qualifying for an academic position, and gaining tenure and promotion at a university implicitly trains us to produce scholarship of a limited variety. Activism or application of our scholarly work, while not necessarily discouraged, is not explicitly encouraged. Therefore, we train ourselves to graduate from student to assistant professor and from assistant professor to tenured faculty; yet after this investment many of us may have little to offer in terms of active application of our efforts.

Even given the remarkable, diverse, and numerous contributions that universities make to society, I am profoundly disappointed with the lack of progress of educational reform given the potential of the thousands of professors like myself who engage in such work each and every day. The following quote, which I first read in a book titled *Ecological Literacy* by Orr (1992, p. 151), sums up my feelings quite succinctly:

> The vast majority of research turned out in the modern university is essentially worthless. It does not result in any measurable benefit to anything or anybody. It does not push back those omnipresent "frontiers of knowledge" so confidently evoked...it is busywork on a vast, almost incomprehensible scale. (Smith, 1990)

Although one might argue that the very nature of universities today, including the drive for national rankings, squeezed budgets, the prominence of intercollegiate sports, etc...share much of the blame for any unrealized potential, the bottom line is that faculty are the very heart of a university. We are in command of the curriculum, set our own research agendas, and mentor candidates into the profession. Any accountability must surely rest squarely on our shoulders.

Yet, certain metrics regarding the profession are enlightening regarding the very real challenges we face. The number of full-time, tenure track faculty has plummeted in recent decades as universities hire contingent, often part-time, faculty as a cost-saving measure. Presently, less than 40 percent of all faculty in higher education are in the tenure stream. AAUP membership that once topped 120,000 in the 1970s, now hovers around a third of that (Nelson & Watt, 2004). That is, there are fewer and fewer of us around who are fully invested in the longevity of our universities, especially the missions of outreach and service. The very construct of a *faculty* has eroded over time. In theory, the necessary peer review support structures exist such that risk taking and advocacy could flourish as a routine element of learning to be a professor and ultimately in accepting the responsibility of being one. Yet, we remain our own worst enemies—and our students see this each and every day.

I have advocated for an increase in tenure-line positions here at my home institution and believe the protection afforded by academic freedom is a necessity for scholars to pursue important, timely, and sometimes controversial work.

Although thought of merely as job security by those outside the academy, the earned privilege of tenure is about ensuring faculty can serve society to their greatest potential without interference from narrow special interests. The ideas of quality, advocacy, innovation, and impact should all matter to those of us immersed in academic life. As faculty, particularly as tenured faculty, we must be willing to step up and advocate for a system which rewards risk taking and the tremendous effort of advancing an agenda and seeing it all the way through, regardless of artificial metrics such as the numbers of publications in a given academic year. I am not advocating for lowering the bar in terms of faculty productivity—in contrast, I see the threshold for earning tenure and promotion to be consistent with the high ideals of true accomplishment and service. A single, seminal article will likely yield more in terms of both advancing a line of thinking and enhancing the reputation of the scholar and university than any series of marginal publications, no matter how voluminous. I am calling for a renewed vision of the professoriate beyond the prevailing model of faculty who work in insulated and conventional ways. A genuinely high bar indeed.

In *Office Hours: Activism and Change in the Academy* (2004), Nelson and Watt describe what they refer to as the tenured vampire, those established faculty who exploit the academy and squander the privileges of their position. These individuals essentially live off the system of adjunct instructors and graduate students, hoarding precious resources in terms of salary, benefits, travel, etc., and giving precious little back. They feel entitled to what they have earned, and in many ways they are, but somewhere along the way they have selectively forgotten the words uttered during the conferring of their degrees which spoke not merely of rights and privileges—but of responsibilities. Nelson and Watt (2004) argue that "universities cannot promote enlightenment values unless they exemplify them" (p. 39), and I would once again remark that this responsibility resides with the professoriate.

BUT WHERE DO WE BEGIN?

As graduate students we are taught to consider what is important to the field, or some narrow segment of it, and I offer that we might also explicitly ask what is important to society. Consider what urgent topic deserves your attention. Interestingly, many young scholars have articulated that they are not yet ready to take on such heady questions, perhaps still fine tuning their research methodologies, but more than likely they are afraid to fail by biting off more than they can chew. When risk taking is discouraged, getting to the next step professionally becomes the singular focus. "I'll take on *such and such*...once I am able to *so and so*..." is a common sentiment in the academy. But the notion of engaging in timely and urgent work in service to society need not be contemplated on such a vast scale that the logistics serve as a barrier. The environmental movement got it right when they noted one should think global and act local. I encourage the idea of starting by acting very local—perhaps at local schools.

Given my experiences in my youth, I used to think of activism as antagonistic and rebellious and something that only happened on a national stage, or at least involved national or global issues. Throughout my years as an assistant professor, I fell into the trap of waiting until I was tenured until I could take on the "big issues" in education. I recall holding my tongue at a regional meeting that advocated superficial and somewhat absurd strategies for schools to improve their scores on standardized tests. (Student chanting during lunch periods in the weeks prior to the test stands out among a series of shallow advice.) At the time, I believed this issue to be a bit out of my league, and I regret not adding my voice to those who offered reasoned and thoughtful arguments opposing such trivial recommendations. There are two lessons to be learned from this real world example; the first is for those early on in their career and the second for those more senior.

As graduate students or early career faculty, it is hard to see that our advanced preparation and commitment to research gives us clout. What power we hold through our status must not be squandered on every little injustice which may arise. But reasoned, appropriately conveyed, and substantiated arguments offer us the potential to have significant impact on issues important to us. Perhaps following the lead of others, seeking advice when appropriate, and listening as much as speaking will help guide the novice scholar through politically charged and precarious territory. On the other hand, it is the responsibility of senior faculty to not merely be out in front as an advocate on issues which resonate with them, but to serve in a leadership capacity which demands they forge a safe venue for all voices to be heard. This tremendous responsibility demands one be selfless, open-minded, and tolerant. The very protections guaranteed by the tenure system demand nothing less. For professors of education in particular, the life of the mind must be a catalyst for a life engaged.

Such a life will—I am quite certain—be the most effective means by which we can teach others of resistance, advocacy, and action. Like those galactic protagonists on *Star Trek* who exhibit the moral authority, tenacity, and clever means to fight their fights, our students will only come to understand such ideas as necessary and tangible if they see them played out in the real world. That is how we best teach such notions of resistance. Your efforts will *not* be futile.

REFERENCES

Giroux, H. A. (2003). Public pedagogy and the politics of resistance: Notes on a critical theory of educational struggle. *Educational Philosophy and Theory*, 35(1). 5–16.

Gomez, M. L. (1996). Prospective teachers' perspectives on teaching "other people's children." In K. M. Zeichner, S. L. Melnick & M. L. Gomez (Eds.), *Currents of reform in pre-service teacher education*. New York: Teachers College Press.

Graff, G. (2003). *Clueless in academe*. New Haven: Yale University Press.

Hall, E. T. (1998). The power of hidden differences In M. J. Bennett (Ed.), *Basic concepts of intercultural communication: Selected readings* (p. 53). Yarmouth, ME: Intercultural Press.

Hammer, M. R., & Bennett, M. J. (2001). *The intercultural development inventory manual*. Portland, Oregon: The Intercultural Communication Institute.

Lightman, A. (1996). Time for the stars. In *Dance for two* (pp. 107–116). New York: Pantheon Books.

Moss, D. M., Glenn, W. J., & Schwab, R. L. (Eds.). (2005). *Portrait of a profession: Teaching and teachers in the 21st century*. Westport, CT: Praeger.

Nelson, C. & Watt, S. (2004). *Office hours: Activism and change in the academy*. New York: Routledge.

Orr, D. (1992). *Ecological Literacy: Education and a transition to a postmodern world*. Albany, NY: SUNY Press.

Smith, P. (1990). *Killing the spirit: Higher education in America*. New York: Viking.

West, C. (1993). *Race matters*. Boston: Beacon Press.

Zipp, J. F. & Fenwick, R. (2006) Is the academy a liberal hegemony? *Public Opinion Quarterly*, 70(3), 304–326.

Contributors

ROBERT J. CEGLIE is an associate professor of education in the Tift College of Education at Mercer University in Macon, Georgia. His research interests are in science education, gender equity, and teacher education. He received his Ph.D. from the University of Connecticut in 2009. The title of his dissertation was *Science from the Periphery: Identity, Persistence, and Participation by Women of Color Pursuing Science Degrees*. He is currently working on the development of collaborations to promote science literacy for underrepresented groups of children.

JOHN CRAVEN is associate professor of education at Fordham University. He has a Ph.D. from the University of Iowa in science education and an M.S. in geology from the University of Memphis. He has a broad set of experiences working with youth in such settings as Covenant House, the Peace Corps as a volunteer in Tunisia, the Memphis Pink Palace Museum as a K-12 science specialist, and a high school teacher in Bridgeport, CT. His current work in science education focuses on helping new science teachers develop understandings and skills for teaching the subject through inquiry in urban schools.

JO ANN FREIBERG, consultant at the Connecticut State Department of Education, manages school climate improvement, bullying and character education. Her doctoral work at The Ohio State University was in professional and classroom based ethics. Her professional career as a classroom teacher, teacher educator and national consultant has been devoted to empowering the adults who teach and work with children to exemplify ethical and respectful behavior in order to create physically, emotionally and intellectually safe and positive learning environments. A member of the Connecticut task force on bullying, she also has the privilege of collaborating on the National School Climate Standards.

MARSHALL A. GEORGE is an associate professor of English & Literacy Education in the Graduate School of Education at Fordham University in New York City. A former teacher and department chair of English language arts in grades 7 to 12, he has spent the past fifteen years working both as a teacher educator and literacy coach in New York City Public Schools. An active member of the National Council of Teachers of English and the Conference on English Education, Marshall has written extensively about the teaching of literature and the development of adolescent literacy at the middle school level.

JASON GOULAH is assistant professor of Bilingual-Bicultural Education and director of World Language Education at DePaul University. He has taught elementary through adult English in Japan, secondary-level Japanese, ESL, and Russian in New York, and second and foreign language education at the University at Buffalo. He has also served as dean of Japanese Credit Abroad with Concordia Language Villages, Concordia College. His research interests include transformative world language learning, Makiguchi and Ikeda studies, and language, culture, identity and multiple literacies. He is recipient of the 2009 Stephen A. Freeman award from the Northeast Conference of Teachers of Foreign Languages.

TRACY HOGAN is an assistant professor of Adolescence Education at Adelphi University and an instructional coach in schools within the New York metropolitan area. She teaches courses in curriculum development in science and mathematics education and educational research. She has authored several book chapters and has published in both psychology and educational journals. Prior to earning her Ph.D. in Educational Psychology, Dr. Hogan was a middle and high school science teacher.

KATHLEEN P. KING is an award-winning author, faculty coach, keynote speaker and professor of education at Fordham University in New York City. Kathy is author of 17 books about her research regarding change in adult lives, faculty development, teaching, learning, distance learning, and technology. She is also known for her dynamic and motivational keynote speeches connected to timely topics and addressed to specific audience needs. She has received numerous professional awards including an Outstanding Publication Award from AERA in 2009 for her edited volume on distance learning.

JULIE M. KITTLESON is an assistant professor in the College of Education at the University of Georgia in Athens, Georgia. She received her Ph.D. from the University of Delaware where she studied third grade students' understandings of the nature of scientific knowledge. Her current research focuses on elementary science teacher education.

THOMAS H. LEVINE is an assistant professor in the department of Curriculum & Instruction Department at the Neag School of Education, University of Connecticut. He taught high school social studies for eight years and led professional development for social studies teachers for two years. He earned his Ph.D. in teacher education from Stanford University in 2005. He uses socio-cultural theory, including "communities of practice," to study how different types of collaboration impact in-service teachers, teacher educators, and university supervisors. He is currently developing a faculty community of practice among his colleagues to better prepare pre-service teachers to work with culturally and linguistically diverse students.

DAVID M. MOSS Is an associate professor in the Neag School of Education at the University of Connecticut, Storrs, CT. His faculty appointment is in the Department of Curriculum & Instruction, specializing in environmental education. His current research interests are in the areas of international education, environmental education, and teacher education reform. Dr. Moss has authored numerous book chapters and reviews on such diverse topics as student understandings of the nature of science, interdisciplinary education, teacher education, and forest ecosystem health monitoring. His books include *Interdisciplinary Education in an Age of Assessment* (Routledge, 2008), *Portrait of a Profession: Teachers and Teaching in the 21st Century* (Greenwood, 2005), and *Beyond the Boundaries: A Transdisciplinary Approach to Learning and Teaching* (Praeger, 2003). He earned his Ph.D. from the University of New Hampshire and completed his undergraduate work at Alfred University. He has extensive curriculum development and assessment experience on projects funded by the National Science Foundation (NSF) and the National Aeronautics and Space Administration (NASA).

MOLLY K. NESS is an assistant professor in Childhood Education at Fordham University's Graduate School of Education. Her research focuses on pre-service teacher education in literacy, reading comprehension, and reading teachers' instructional decisions. A former Teach for America corps member, she holds a doctorate in reading education from the University of Virginia. She is the author of *Lessons to Learn: Voices from the Front Lines of Teach for America* (Routledge, 2004).

DINA C. OSBORN teaches for the University of Connecticut and has taught in some of the largest school districts in the United States, including New York City public schools and Hillsborough County schools, Tampa, Florida. Working in urban settings has allowed her to view first hand the disparities and challenges faced by children and teachers in poor school districts. Her interests include critical theory and pedagogy, multicultural issues related to race, gender, and class; Christian fundamentalist curricula; and issues related to education and power.

TERRY A. OSBORN is professor and chair of the Division of Curriculum and Teaching of Fordham University and serves on the Executive Committee of the Faculty Senate. He also was a founding officer of the International Society for Language Studies. Dr. Osborn taught public school German for six years at the secondary levels. His scholarly work received the 2001 American Educational Studies Association Critics' Choice award for *Critical Reflection and the Foreign Language Classroom* and the Stephen Freeman Award for the best published article on foreign language teaching techniques. His work has appeared in *Educational Foundations, Educational Studies, Foreign Language Annals, Language Problems and Language Planning, Multicultural Education*, and *NECTFL Review*.

TIMOTHY REAGAN received his Ph.D. from the University of Illinois, Champaign-Urbana, in 1982. He has served on the faculties of Gallaudet University, the University of Connecticut, Roger Williams University, and the University of the Witwatersrand in South Africa. He is currently professor of Educational Leadership at Central Connecticut State University. His research interests are focused primarily on issues of language and culture in education, and his publications include work on foreign language education, bilingual education, TESOL, language planning and policy studies, and the linguistics of natural sign languages.

DAVID I. SMITH is associate professor of German and director of the Kuyers Institute for Christian Teaching and Learning at Calvin College in Grand Rapids, Michigan. He serves as editor of the *Journal of Education and Christian Belief*. His published work is concerned with world language pedagogy, spiritual and moral development, and the relationship between religion and education. His recent books include *Spirituality, Social Justice, and Language Learning* (edited with Terry

Osborn, Information Age Publishing, 2009) and *Learning from the Stranger: Christian Belief and Cultural Diversity* (Eerdmans, 2009).

KRISTEN HAWLEY TURNER is an assistant professor of English and Literacy Education in the Graduate School of Education at Fordham University in New York City. A former high school teacher of English and social studies, she is also a consultant for the National Writing Project and an active member of the National Council of Teachers of English. She devotes her research and writing time to issues of literacy instruction.

Index

Activist Science 219, 220, 221
Advocacy 2, 8, 10–11, 25, 192, 205, 217, 241, 245–247
African American English 56
American exceptionalism 146
American Sign Language 56
Apple, M. 44, 62, 123
Argument 3, 39, 50, 54, 55–56, 59, 73–74, 83, 85, 127, 132, 133–135, 136–139
Assessment 4, 9, 22, 28
Audience 42, 118, 133–134, 136, 150, 186–187, 189–190, 232, 234

Balanced Literacy 107–110, 112–114, 116
Becker, C. 176
Biesta 42, 44
Blogs 180, 186–188, 193, 196
Buddhism 88–90, 93, 98
Bullying 4, 159–163, 165–176
    definition of 166, 168

Cavanaugh, W. 80
Christian Right 3, 35–37, 43–44

Christian School Movement 40
Citizenship 39
Civil discussion of controversial issues 151
Collaboration 127–128, 130, 132, 139, 144, 154–155, 163, 182, 187, 190–191, 194, 231–232
Columbine High School 159, 164
Communities of practice 4, 143–144, 155
Community mapping 154
Competition 3, 9–10, 83, 84–85, 89, 91, 94–95, 99, 136, 138, 179
Conflation 43
Constructivism 181, 183–185, 195
Consumerism 68
Controversial issues 144–146, 151, 155, 205
Counter-discourse 2, 64, 73, 240
Craig, B. 62
Critical consciousness 8, 44
Critical literacy 2, 121, 147, 150
Critical pedagogy 2–3, 6, 15, 42–45, 47–49, 51, 54, 59–60, 202–203
Critical reflection 2, 8–9
Critical theory 202

Critical thinking 21, 53, 143–144, 148–149, 155, 182, 184–185, 193, 195, 198, 209, 223, 242
Curricular nullification 11–13

Debate 3, 31, 48, 57, 128, 133–139, 147, 151, 208, 218
Definitions
  descriptive/reportive 165–166
  stipulative 165–166
Democrat 40–41, 44, 53
Democratization of the media 187
Dependent origination 3, 83, 89, 94, 97, 99
Dialogue 3, 38, 44, 72, 74–76, 83, 89, 92, 95–99, 131, 152–153, 180, 184, 187–188, 191–193, 195, 197–198, 203, 205–206, 212
Differentiated Instruction 107–109, 113–114, 117, 183
Digital Media 5, 198
Digital natives 181
Discernment 67–68, 80
Discussion boards 191–192, 196
Diversity 3, 5, 12, 22, 29, 31, 36–38, 42, 44, 47, 49, 85, 88–89, 197, 227–228, 242
Dominant Paradigms 2, 13–14, 37, 42–43, 84, 86, 94, 126, 188, 192, 196, 240

Empowerment 5, 54–55, 183, 185–186, 188, 192, 194–195, 198
Engagement 75, 107, 118, 131–132, 144, 146, 149, 155, 183–185, 188, 195, 204, 211, 213
Esperanto 3, 47, 49–61

Foreign language education 3, 15, 47–49, 59–61, 85, 96
Fundamentalist 3, 35–38, 40, 42–44, 94

Giroux, H. 2, 42–43, 47, 181–185, 202–204, 240
Global Perspectives 10, 14, 55, 83–84, 87–88, 92–95, 98, 154, 180, 182, 186–187, 189–191, 193–194, 197, 201–202, 205–207, 210, 218, 247

Happiness 90–93, 95
Hegemony 10, 13, 51, 60–61
High literacy 129–130, 133, 139
Highlander Folk School 2, 10

Hillocks 107, 118, 126–130, 132–133, 135, 137–139
Hope 5, 21, 69, 71–72, 75, 77, 95, 121, 150, 169, 174, 202–203, 207, 217–219, 228, 233, 236
Human revolution 3, 83, 89, 93–94, 98
Humanistic Theory 36, 40–41, 90–92
Humanitarian competition 3, 83, 89, 91–92, 94, 99

Ideology 14, 36–38, 42–44, 84–90, 94
Imperialism 13, 48
Independent Reading 112, 114, 117, 121
Informal learning 191
Inquiry 8, 36, 49, 131–132, 135, 139, 147–151, 181, 202, 210, 213, 219, 230, 236
  critical 183–184
  science 127–129, 199, 223
  self 241
Instructional technology 4, 179–180, 195
Insults 73–75

Janton, P. 64
Journal of the American Medical Association, The (JAMA) 161

Kumaravadivelu, B. 64

Language awareness 49, 53–54
  critical 49, 53–56, 58–60
Legislation, anti-bullying 161, 174
  Connecticut 166–167, 169
  Delaware 168–169
  South Carolina 167–169
Legitimacy, linguistic 56–58, 60
LGBTQ 188–190
Liberalism 36–37, 41
Literacy 2, 4, 22–23, 86, 98, 105, 106–114, 119, 121–122, 129–133, 139, 154, 182, 195, 210, 223
  Coach 116–117
  Critical 147, 150
  Ecological 245
  Science 204, 224
Literature 14, 36, 39, 42, 48, 56–57, 89, 107, 111, 116–120, 137, 161, 181, 183–184, 216
Littleton, Colorado (see Columbine) 159

Liturgy 78
Luke, C. 64

Mandated Curriculum 120–121, 203
Meritocracy 40
Militarism 84, 87–88, 90–91, 97–98
Moss, D.M. 227–229, 237, 248
Multiple perspectives 43, 147, 152–153
National Council of Teachers of English (NCTE) 106, 122, 195, 250, 253

Negotiation of meaning 75
Neoliberalism 83–87, 95, 201
New media 5, 180, 182, 184–191, 193, 195–196
New Teacher Project, The 19
No Child Left Behind (NCLB) 3, 22–23, 83, 105–106, 121, 169, 223
    adequate yearly progress (AYP) 106, 112, 125, 169
No Child Left Behind Act of 2001 (NCLB) 121

Ortega, L. 65
Osborn, T. 15, 65, 81, 102
The Other 58, 94–95, 97, 196

Planetary consciousness 89, 98
Podcasting 180, 187–190, 196
Prayer 36, 40, 76–79
Putrescence 73, 78

Radical pedagogy 182–185
Republican 39, 41, 87
Resistance theory 3, 60
Richardson, D. 65
Rote learning 147
Rothemund, M. 72

Scheffler, I. 176
School
    "Blue Ribbon" 170
    bully-free 171
    community 4, 159, 164–165, 174–175
    culture 4, 36, 140, 160, 163–165, 171
    descriptive goals 164

    positive goals 164
    toxic 159–160, 174
    environment 168
    intervention 163, 168, 172, 196
    mission statements 155, 164
    "persistently dangerous" 169–170
    punishment in 163
    shooting(s) 159–160, 162, 164, 170–171
Science Education 5, 202–205, 215–220, 223–228, 232–234, 236, 243
Secular humanism 3, 35–36, 38–39
Secularization 35, 38, 40
Service learning 154
Silence 1, 73–75, 179
Sixteen Rules, The 51–52
Social action 4, 143–145, 147, 152–153, 155, 185
Social control 4, 143
Social studies 4, 12, 38, 86, 106, 115, 143–149, 151, 153, 155–156, 196, 208
Soka education 88, 90, 95–96, 98
Springboard . . . to Languages! Project 54
Standardized assessment/test 109, 126–127, 129, 132, 139–140
Standards 7, 11, 14, 20, 41, 47, 84, 86, 106, 109, 145, 164, 195, 197, 218, 241
Submission 3, 69, 75, 80

Talk 53, 67, 130–132, 135, 139–140, 144, 154, 189, 210, 229
Teach for America
    critique of 27–29, 31
    recruitment 19, 22, 24, 29–31
    relationship with graduate schools of education 20, 23, 30–32
    Training 18–19, 22–24, 27, 29, 31
Terrorism 85
Thinking-based writing 4, 125, 132, 135, 139
Toulmin, S. 133–134, 137
Transformative language learning 3, 83

United States Secret Service National Threat Assessment Center 161
Universala Esperanto-Asocio (Universal Esperanto Association) 51

Vandenberg, D. 66
Voice 5, 14, 25, 42, 75–77, 79, 156, 165, 180–181, 183, 185–188, 192–196, 198, 202, 208, 219, 226, 229–230, 234, 242, 247
Volapük 49

Wallace, C. 66
Web 2.0 186, 191, 193, 196, 198
White Rose 3, 67–68, 70, 72–73
Whitehead, Alfred North 166
Wikis 180, 186, 190–191, 196
Wink, J. 6, 66

Wittgenstein, L. 66
Writing instruction 107–108, 125–129, 132, 139, 243
   declarative knowledge 128–129
   environmental mode 128
   form 128–132, 139
   procedural knowledge 128–129, 139
   sequencing 136, 208
   training 18–19, 22–24, 27, 29, 31
World language education 88